The Devil & Doctor Dwight

Colin Wells

Published for the

Omohundro Institute

of Early American History

& Culture, Williamsburg,

Virginia, *by the* University

of North Carolina Press,

Chapel Hill & London

The Devil &
Doctor Dwight

SATIRE &

THEOLOGY

IN THE EARLY

AMERICAN

REPUBLIC

*The Omohundro
Institute of Early
American History
and Culture is
sponsored jointly
by the College of
William and Mary
and the Colonial
Williamsburg
Foundation. On
November 15, 1996,
the Institute adopted
the present name in
honor of a bequest
from Malvern H.
Omohundro, Jr.*

Manufactured in the United States of America

Library of Congress Cataloging-in-Publication Data
Wells, Colin, 1965–
The Devil and Doctor Dwight : satire and theology in the early
American Republic / Colin Wells.
     p. cm.
Includes index.
ISBN 0-8078-2715-0 (alk. paper)—
ISBN 0-8078-5383-6 (pbk. : alk. paper)
1. Dwight, Timothy, 1752–1817. Triumph of infidelity.   2. Christianity
and literature—United States—History—18th century.   3. Freethinkers—
United States—History—18th century.   4. Christian poetry, American—
History and criticism.   5. Verse satire, American—History and criticism.
6. Chauncy, Charles, 1705–1787—In literature.   7. Belief and doubt in
literature.   8. Rationalism in literature.   9. Theology in literature.
10. Faith in literature.   I. Title: Devil and Dr. Dwight.   II. Omohundro
Institute of Early American History & Culture.   III. Title.
PS739.T75 W45   2002
811'.2—dc21   2001054201

06   05   04   03   02   5   4   3   2   1

Design detail from *The Table's Turn'd* by James Gillray, 1797.
Courtesy, Print Collection, The Lewis Walpole Library, Yale University,
Farmington, Conn.

For John and Joyce Wells

ACKNOWLEDGMENTS

This book began as a doctoral dissertation at Rutgers University, and I thank both Rutgers and the Charlotte Newcombe Fellowship Foundation for financial assistance during the early stages of research and writing. I thank Saint Olaf College for providing the grant that allowed me time to revise the manuscript into its present form. During the course of my research, I have benefited from the assistance of librarians from the following institutions: Rutgers University, Princeton University, Yale University, the American Antiquarian Society, the University of Minnesota, Carleton College, and Saint Olaf College. I am also grateful to the editors of *Early American Literature* for permission to include portions of Chapter 1 previously published in the article, "Timothy Dwight's American *Dunciad: The Triumph of Infidelity* and the Universalist Controversy" (XXXIII [1998], 173–191).

My greatest intellectual debt is to William Dowling, who first introduced me to Dwight's poetry in his early American literature seminar and who has since been a continual source of help and advice; it is hard to imagine a more generous teacher, mentor, and friend than Bill Dowling. I am indebted also to three other Rutgers Americanists: Michael Warner and Myra Jehlen, who read my earliest drafts and provided invaluable suggestions for revision, and Richard Poirier, who, although not directly involved with this project, taught me most of what I know about reading poetry. I thank Chris Grasso for his careful reading of the entire manuscript, and Mark Allister and Rich Durocher for their feedback on significant portions of it. Conversations with friends and colleagues—John Day, Jonathan Hill, R. G. Peterson, Jack Roberts, David Shields—have been helpful at various stages of my research and writing, and I thank them. I am especially obliged to Fredrika J. Teute and Virginia Montijo at the Institute—Fredrika for helping me to recognize and develop certain implications of my argument, and Virginia for helping me to articulate that argument more clearly and eloquently. Finally, I am indebted to my wife, Martha, for her love and encouragement at every point in the writing of this book: thanks to her for supporting my intellectual excursions into the past and for giving me such a wonderful life in the present.

CONTENTS

ILLUSTRATIONS

The Devil & Doctor Dwight

Introduction

The subject of this study is an episode in American literary and religious history in which Timothy Dwight, outspoken Connecticut poet, clergyman, and educator during the Revolutionary and early republican periods, undertook to wage war against the forces of "infidelity." My argument is that an understanding of this literary campaign makes possible a reconstruction of the more momentous ideological struggles and transformations taking place in America during this period—party warfare between Federalists and Democratic-Republicans, the theological and social struggles among various groups of orthodox and dissenting Protestants, and the intellectual controversies arising from Enlightenment secularism and progressivism. Such a reconstruction, however, depends first upon an act of literary recovery, not merely of a number of lost or misunderstood works but, more important, of the ideological contexts that made the controversy surrounding infidelity so powerful in its own time, for this story has not been fully understood by modern scholars.

One reason for this misapprehension is that the specific literary work within which Dwight began his campaign against infidelity, and the key to understanding the deeper struggle around which so much of his writings center, has remained virtually unintelligible to many twentieth-century literary critics and historians. That work is *The Triumph of Infidelity*, an anonymously published satiric poem of 1788 directed most immediately at the Universalist theology of Charles Chauncy, longtime pastor of the First Church of Boston. The poem appeared in the midst of the Universalist controversy, a pamphlet war waged by opposing camps of Congregationalist clergymen over the doctrine of "the salvation of all men." Dwight's emphasis in *The Triumph of Infidelity* upon Chauncy and Universalism—what might appear at first glance simply as a heterodox form of Christianity—has left most scholars uncertain about how to treat the poem's larger claims for itself as a satiric assault against the forces of infidelity. Indeed, the increasing interest in the idea of universal salvation in the last decades of the eighteenth century has tended to be viewed as a religious or doctrinal issue, rather than as a movement containing far greater political and ideological implications within the history of the early Republic.

For readers already familiar with the larger body of Dwight's writings, including his other polemical works against Enlightenment skepticism and deism and French Revolutionary radicalism, the claim for the special importance of *The Triumph of Infidelity* will seem an unlikely one, standing in marked contrast to the way in which his literary and public careers have usually been understood. Dwight has been remembered as a commanding public figure in his home state of Connecticut, the popular minister and schoolmaster from the village of Greenfield Hill who in 1795 took over the presidency of Yale and, during the next two decades, transformed the college into a national institution. Scholars of American religious history—by far the largest group to examine Dwight's career closely—remember him as a theologian and author of *Theology; Explained and Defended, in a Series of Sermons* (1818–1819). Compiled while he served simultaneously as president and professor of divinity at Yale, this five-volume work was republished more than a dozen times in Britain and America throughout the nineteenth century. As a literary figure, he has long been known for his *Travels in New England and New York* (1821–1822), the record of nearly twenty years of excursions throughout the northeastern states; more recently, moreover, we have witnessed a rediscovery of Dwight's poetic career as the author of the biblical epic *The Conquest of Canaan* (1785) and of *Greenfield Hill* (1794), the ambitious and at times brilliant exercise in what has been described as "Connecticut Georgic."[1] Dwight the satiric poet, meanwhile, the author of *The Triumph of Infidelity*, has remained all but forgotten.

1. For studies of Timothy Dwight as an educator and outspoken public figure, see Christopher Grasso, *A Speaking Aristocracy: Transforming Public Discourse in Eighteenth-Century Connecticut* (Chapel Hill, N.C., 1999), chap. 7; and John Fitzmier, *New England's Moral Legislator: Timothy Dwight, 1752–1817* (Bloomington, Ind., 1998), chaps. 2, 4. For Dwight the theologian, see ibid., chap. 3. For a study of Dwight's poetry and a discus-

The Triumph of Infidelity

To a modern reader attempting to make even preliminary sense of *The Triumph of Infidelity*—not merely a decoding of its relevant terms or identification of its topical references but at times the more modest first-order comprehension of the words on the page—the reason for its critical neglect is not hard to find. In *The Triumph of Infidelity*, Dwight was consciously choosing to revive in the America of the late 1780s the high Augustan mode of John Dryden and Jonathan Swift and Alexander Pope, to reclaim for poetry in America the status of "language as symbolic action" that had earlier made these poets such dominant voices of political criticism in their own time. Once one has learned to locate oneself in relation to the poem's satiric idiom, and in particular to a vision of contemporary history in which local events like the Universalist controversy and specific people like Chauncy, Ethan Allen, and John Murray are enveloped always within an atmosphere of cosmic implication, *The Triumph of Infidelity* reveals itself not merely, as Lawrence Buell has argued, as Dwight's best poem but as perhaps the preeminent example of American neoclassical or Augustan satire.[2] Yet, on the way to this realization, one encounters a compressed and difficult work, written in the same dense, allusive mode that today

---

sion of *Greenfield Hill* as "Connecticut Georgic," see William C. Dowling, *Poetry and Ideology in Revolutionary Connecticut* (Athens, Ga., 1990), chap. 3.

2. Lawrence Buell, *New England Literary Culture from Revolution through Renaissance* (Cambridge, 1986), 87–88. For a discussion of how the topical nature of Augustan poetry—what often makes this poetry difficult or irrelevant for modern readers—was understood as containing universal or cosmic significance for both writers and readers in the Augustan period, see William C. Dowling, "Teaching Eighteenth-Century Poetry in the Pocockian Moment (or, Flimnap on the Tightrope, Kramnick to the Rescue)," *College English*, XLIX (1987), 523–532.

John Murray came to New England in the 1770s and preached a somewhat different version of the doctrine of universal salvation than did Chauncy. Dwight's satiric portrait of Murray is found in ll. 433–452 in the edition of *The Triumph of Infidelity* in Appendix A, below. Dwight's satire of the famous Revolutionary War general Ethan Allen would arise from his authorship of the deistic treatise *Reason, the Only Oracle of Man* (1784) and is found in ll. 387–392 of the poem.

---

makes even such acknowledged classics as Dryden's *MacFlecknoe* (1682) and Pope's *Dunciad* (1728) frustrating for modern readers.

Dwight's decision to present *The Triumph of Infidelity* as a later, American form of Augustan satire takes us to the very heart of the notion of "literary warfare," but it also poses the first major interpretive difficulty. We have always recognized the extent to which Dwight and other early republican poets such as John Trumbull and Joel Barlow imitated the formal characteristics of their earlier Augustan precursors and packed their poems with numerous specific allusions to these writers. Only recently, however, have we come to understand the deeper significance of their reassertion of an "Augustan poetic moment" in post-Revolutionary America. The first years of the early republican period were characterized by uneasiness over America's future—these are the years of Shays's Rebellion and various economic crises and interstate rivalries, which ultimately led to the calling of the Philadelphia Convention and the drafting of the Constitution. Because of this sense of crisis, as William C. Dowling has shown, American writers sought to revive the specific Augustan notion of poems as tools of ideological intervention, the same means of warding off the potential threats to the health of the Republic that Pope and Swift and John Gay had used to combat the social and political threats of their own time.[3] This notion of literature as an ideological weapon will stand in the immediate background of my own argument about Dwight, the controversy surrounding Universal salvation, and the larger issue of infidelity, which, once invoked in *The Triumph of Infidelity*, would run through the remainder of Dwight's public and literary career.

At the same time, even as readers begin to recognize the general significance of the self-conscious Augustanism of *The Triumph of Infidelity*, the sheer

---

3. Dowling, *Poetry and Ideology*, ix–xv. John Trumbull was the first of the group of poets later known as the Connecticut Wits to write satiric poetry in the Augustan mode, with *The Progress of Dulness* (1772–1773) and *M'Fingal* (1782). Joel Barlow, the youngest of the Wits, is the author of *The Conspiracy of Kings* (1792) and the epic poem *The Vision of Columbus* (1787), later revised as *The Columbiad* (1807). The two collaborated with David Humphreys, the last of the four major Wits, on *The Anarchiad* (1786–1787), which, as the title suggests, represents another extended allusion to *The Dunciad*. Humphrey's own poetry includes *A Poem on the Happiness of America* (1786) and *A Poem on Industry, Addressed to the United States of America* (1794).

number of specific allusions presents a continual challenge. The poem demands as a precondition of its intelligibility both a close familiarity with the Augustan poetic tradition and a deep comprehension of the symbolic world projected by that tradition. Here, for instance, is a passage taken from the poem's synoptic overview of the history of infidelity in eighteenth-century England. As in Pope's *Dunciad*, the narrative surrounding this passage involves a central demonic character who represents an inversion of the poem's own projected system of values; in *The Triumph of Infidelity*, befitting both Dwight's New England Puritan ancestry and the subject matter of infidelity, this character is none other than Satan, who serves as the poem's speaker for approximately half of its nearly eight hundred lines. In this passage, Satan is describing one of his most recent successes in his continuing struggle against heaven, the immense popularity of deism among the more fashionable circles of eighteenth-century English society, following the explosion of publications by John Toland, Matthew Tindal, and a host of lesser freethinkers:[4]

> As writers too, they proffer'd useful aid,
> Believ'd unseen, and reverenc'd tho' unread.
> Against their foe no proof my sons desire,
> No reasoning canvas and no sense require.
> Enough, the Bible is by wits arraign'd,
> Genteel men doubt it, smart men say it's feign'd,
> Onward my powder'd beaux and boobies throng,
> As puppies float the kennel's stream along.   (229–236)[5]

To see this passage as projecting an Augustan poetic world is to recognize that the concluding simile refers not simply to the workings of an eighteenth-century kennel—the gutter through which streets were cleared of filth by the flow of rainwater—but to the particular kennel depicted at the end of Swift's

---

4. John Toland's *Christianity Not Mysterious* (1696) was one of the earliest expositions of deism. Matthew Tindal, in *Christianity as Old as the Creation* (1730), asserted that deism constituted a purified version of essential Christian doctrines. Among the lesser freethinkers Dwight has in mind in this passage are Anthony Collins (*A Discourse of Free-Thinking* [1713]) and Thomas Chubb (*A Discourse on Miracles* [1741]).

5. Citations to the *Triumph of Infidelity* throughout will refer to the line numbers in the version printed in Appendix A and will be made parenthetically in the text.

"A Description of a City Shower": "Now from all parts the swelling kennels flow, / And bear their trophies with them as they go: / . . . Drowned puppies, stinking sprats, all drenched in mud, / Dead cats and turnip-tops come tumbling down the flood."[6] It is to recognize as well that Swift had intended this image as a withering reminder of the unflattering reality underlying precisely the same fashionable urban world to which Dwight's Satan refers above and that this irony is meant immediately to be registered by the reader of *The Triumph of Infidelity*. At the same time, that Satan is making this ironic quip is an equally important element of the implicit Augustan quality of the poem. Beyond the usual complication that occurs whenever Satan speaks—demanding, as in its ultimate source of allusion, John Milton's *Paradise Lost* (1667), a translation of everything that is said into an inverted or diabolic perspective—Satan also acknowledges in a rather good-natured way the essential folly of the "powder'd beaux" and "boobies" who blindly follow the tenets of this fashionable deism without ever reading its authors. The sense in which Satan must be read as a good-natured or comic villain, more closely resembling the goddess Dulness of *The Dunciad* than the Satan of either the Bible or *Paradise Lost*, has remained one of the most misunderstood aspects of *The Triumph of Infidelity*.

Nonetheless, a sympathetic and attentive reading of *The Triumph of Infidelity* brings to light a poem that is, in its main outlines, simple enough. With the American victory in the Revolution, the rebel archangel has left behind a corrupt and declining Europe to come to the world of "freedom, peace, and virtue" that may yet be discerned in the new American Republic. (Alluding to the ritual procession of the Roman *imperator* in a golden chariot up the Capitoline, the "triumph" of the poem's title is Satan's passage over the Atlantic and through America in his "gloomy car" drawn by dragons.) The poem contains three speakers: Satan himself, whose long and self-congratulatory account of his conquests in the name of infidelity throughout the previous eras of human history occupies the first half of the poem; a narrator representing Dwight, whose primary role is to recount the effects of Satan's influence during the time he has been at work in America and to describe the various members of the crowd who gather around the aging clergyman, Charles Chauncy; and,

6. Jonathan Swift, "A Description of a City Shower" (1709), in Swift, *The Complete Poems*, ed. Pat Rogers (New Haven, Conn., 1983), 114.

lastly, Chauncy himself, who addresses the crowd on the doctrinal points of his recently published theological treatise, *The Mystery Hid from Ages and Generations . . . ; or, The Salvation of All Men the Grand Thing Aimed at in the Scheme of God . . .* (1784).

Chauncy's central role in *The Triumph of Infidelity* will no doubt be surprising to those who remember him mainly as Jonathan Edwards's great antagonist in the earlier New England controversy occasioned by the Great Awakening, the defender of a sober and traditional Puritanism against the seemingly radical newer emphasis upon revivalism and religious affections. But Chauncy lived nearly fifty years after the Awakening, long enough to publish his own radical treatise. In it, he asserts that the great truth of Christianity, hidden from previous ages, is now revealed: the damnation promised to sinners in the Scriptures is not eternal, but will be simply a period of tribulation during which souls are purified and refined through repentance until, at last, they are welcomed into heaven. This notion of even unrepentant sinners' being promised a future of eternal happiness, regardless of their earthly crimes or vices, would make the doctrine of universal salvation immediately controversial in the years surrounding Chauncy's publication of *The Mystery Hid*. Dwight would have just this controversy in mind when he would portray Chauncy as nothing less than the great agent of infidelity in America, the central figure in Satan's plan to corrupt the still-virtuous and pious American citizens by cloaking his latest form of infidelity in scriptural interpretation.

Yet the great paradox is that Chauncy, one of New England's most prominent clergymen and the product of the same Covenant theology as Dwight, is from the beginning of *The Triumph of Infidelity* put into the intellectual and moral category of those "infidels" more commonly identified by eighteenth-century Christianity as its true enemies: skeptics like Voltaire and David Hume; materialists like Holbach and La Mettrie; deists and freethinkers like Toland, Tindal, the third earl of Shaftesbury, and Thomas Paine.[7] It is with

---

7. Voltaire (François Marie Arouet), who most fully symbolized Enlightenment infidelity for Dwight's generation, is satirized at great length in *The Triumph of Infidelity* for works such as *Candide* (1759) and *The Philosophical Dictionary* (1764) (see "Dedication" and ll. 257–306). David Hume's *The Treatise of Human Nature* (1739) is presented in ll. 237–256 as too difficult and obscure for the vulgar mind, leading Satan to look for more accessible works of infidelity. In direct contrast, Anthony Ashley Cooper, third

peculiar clairvoyance that Dwight saw Chauncy and such writers as Voltaire and Paine as on some deeper level kindred spirits. Indeed, Dwight's recognition that this New England clergyman, preaching a wholly agreeable doctrine of an all-merciful and benevolent diety, was an unwitting creature of the cold materialist universe portrayed in such works as Holbach's *System of Nature* gives *The Triumph of Infidelity* its special importance within the history of American religious and philosophical thought. This assertion also leads us outward from *The Triumph of Infidelity* and the controversy over universal salvation to the more significant ideological struggles that would occupy Dwight for the remainder of his career, struggles over French Revolutionary radicalism and Jeffersonian Republicanism and the larger discourse of the inherent virtues, capabilities, and rights of man.

Universalism, Progressive History, and the Nunc-Stans *Perspective*

Dwight recognized in Chauncy's doctrine of universal salvation the latest version of what students of intellectual history have called eighteenth-century Pelagianism. This view of human nature and human existence takes its name from Augustine's fifth-century antagonist Pelagius, who had declared the doctrine of Original Sin to be only a myth, human nature to be wholly innocent, and virtue to be attainable through a simple act of will. Pelagianism had entered eighteenth-century English moral philosophy through Shaftesbury and the Cambridge Platonists, came to dominate European Enlightenment

---

earl of Shaftesbury, is satirized as a philosophical "bumblebee" whose seminal work, *Characteristics of Men, Manners, Opinions, Times* (1711) amounts to a great deal of idle buzzing but no real truth (see ll. 201–206). Eighteenth-century materialism, which followed Julien Offray de La Mettrie's assertions in *Man a Machine* (1747) and those of Paul Henri Thiry, baron d'Holbach, in *The System of Nature* (1770) that matter and motion alone explain the workings of the universe (including the intellectual faculties of human beings), is represented in the poem by the figure Dwight calls The Infidel of Modern Breed (see ll. 565–588). In the decade following the publication of *The Triumph of Infidelity*, Dwight would argue that the radical deism of Thomas Paine's *Age of Reason* (1794) constitutes the logical conclusion of Chauncy's Universalist theology.

thought through Jean-Jacques Rousseau and others, and, through its effect on such men as Benjamin Franklin, Thomas Jefferson, and Joel Barlow, began to exert an important influence in the United States.[8] *The Triumph of Infidelity* thus emerges as much more than a satiric blast fired in a local theological controversy; even in 1788, one can see taking shape a more momentous struggle over the moral nature of the new American Republic as a whole and what this nature implied about the political course the new nation should follow.

The true momentousness of this warfare would not become wholly evident, even to Dwight, until the violent divisions of moral allegiances brought about by the French Revolution had been fully felt on the American side of the Atlantic. By this time, the mild theological reveries of Chauncy's doctrine of the salvation of all men would within the sphere of political thought be reborn as Jeffersonian democracy, the complex myth of American exceptionalism, inevitable progress, and social perfectibility that would promise to all men — or at least to all those clever or fortunate enough to live in America — a new form of salvation within history. During these years, the symbolic warfare that had begun against Chauncy and Universalism would be carried on in specifically religious terms in *Theology* and the other sermons Dwight would deliver from the Yale pulpit, such as *The Nature, and Danger, of Infidel Philosophy* (1798). It would be carried on in social and political terms in the *Travels* and in such public addresses as *The True Means of Establishing Public Happiness* (1795), and, of course, in poems from *Greenfield Hill* to his last substantial poem, "An Extract from 'The Retrospect,'" published on the eve of Jefferson's first presidential term.

Taken as a whole, the texts that constitute this period of Dwight's literary career permit a reconstruction of the ideological context within which

---

8. The Cambridge Platonists, the group of seventeenth-century rational theologians that included Benjamin Whichcote, Henry Moore (*A Brief Discourse of the Nature, Causes, Kinds, and Cure of Enthusiasm* [1656]), and Ralph Cudworth (*The True Intellectual System of the Universe* [1678]), are credited as significant precursors to eighteenth-century Pelagianism through their influence on English Latitudinarian theology, particularly its emphasis on a benign and rational Providence. More than any other figure of the French Enlightenment, Jean-Jacques Rousseau (in *Discourse upon the Origin and Foundation of the Inequality among Mankind* [1755] and *The Social Contract* [1767]) is identified with the Shaftesburian-Pelagian view of natural human innocence.

there would occur a crucial episode in early American thought. Certain theological doctrines—in particular, the Pelagian idea of natural innocence transmitted from Shaftesbury and Rousseau in Europe to Jefferson and Paine in America—would undergo a transmutation from theology and moral philosophy into political philosophy. Ultimately, in the period between Jefferson and the political ascendancy of Andrew Jackson, this Pelagian myth of natural human innocence and all that it implied about democracy and the common man would become, for many Americans, synonymous with America's national identity. The argument that the American Republic was a creation of religious thought has had a long currency, going back at least to Ernest Lee Tuveson's study of American millennialism in *Redeemer Nation*.[9] Yet what *The Triumph of Infidelity* and Dwight's own subsequent reflections on its central themes allow us to glimpse is that deeper level of ideological transmutation at which politics and religion figure largely as transient and intertranslatable vocabularies or discourses.

What Dwight's literary warfare ultimately addresses, in short, is less the change from the older Augustinian vision of human moral nature prone to weakness and error to the new Pelagianism than the more paradoxical emergence of a "theology of man" as the underlying metaphysics of Enlightenment secularization. Such a metaphysics is given ultimate expression, perhaps, in Michel Foucault's description of the "birth of man" in *The Order of Things* (but is described as well by Isaiah Berlin, John Passmore, and others). It rejects religion in the name of empirical objectivity but then reconstitutes in its place an idea of humanity within theological terms unrecognized as such. One of the fundamental preconditions for this theology of man, such theorists have asserted, is a reconceptualization of the relationship between human existence and time in which the finitude or alienation of earthly life is potentially redressed or transcended by the progressive course of history.[10]

9. Ernest Lee Tuveson, *Redeemer Nation: The Idea of America's Millennial Role* (Chicago, 1968).

10. Michel Foucault's notion of the theology of man depends on the modern conception of the human being as an "empirico-transcendental doublet," the effect of the emergence of the human sciences, biology, philology, and political economy. What distinguished the human sciences from their earlier counterparts is an understanding of

The same progressive vision can be glimpsed in all of the systems to which Dwight directs his satiric and polemical attacks, whether it be Chauncy's vision of Universalism as the great mystery of Christianity revealed (through him) to the modern age, the more explicitly secular forms of Enlightenment progressivism as envisioned by William Godwin and Condorcet, or the emerging notion of the American Republic itself as a political system capable of inspiring the collective moral improvement of its citizens. Dwight's literary warfare against infidelity is at this deepest level directed at a tendency to envision human transcendence, no longer as a state existing outside the earthly or human sphere, but as a future moment inside history itself.[11]

---

time or history as internal to being, and thus the essence of humanity as historically contingent. On the one hand, this recognition brings man face to face with the frightening truth of temporal finitude; on the other, it provides a wholly new possibility of transcendence. Man is not only the object of empirical study but also the transcendent subject who stands outside of empirical definition—"a being whose nature (that which determines it, contains it, and has traversed it from the beginning of time) is to know nature, and itself, in consequence, as a natural being." Thus, an aspect of man remains always unknowable, beyond the reach of science or human knowledge, which both confirms man's special nature in the present and allows for the possibility of future redemption at the moment this "unknowable essence" is discovered (Foucault, *The Order of Things: An Archaeology of the Human Sciences*, ed. R. D. Laing [New York, 1973], 310).

This same sense of the future perfectibility of human society is presented by John Passmore in his synopsis of the logic of eighteenth-century progressivism: "There gradually developed, then, in the eighteenth century a chain of inference which ran thus: Man had until that time been a mere child in respect of knowledge and, in consequence, of virtue; he was now at last in a position, as a result of the development of science, to determine how human nature develops and what is the best thing for human beings to do; this new knowledge could be expressed in a form in which all men would find it intelligible; once they knew what it is best to do, men would act accordingly and so would constantly improve their moral, political and physical condition" (John Passmore, *The Perfectibility of Man* [New York, 1970], 208). For an application of this idea to the study of Marx, see Isaiah Berlin, *Karl Marx: His Life and Environment* (London, 1939), chap. 3.

11. By the late 1790s, Dwight would identify as the essence of infidel philosophy the notion of human moral perfectibility, which is suggested as a theoretical possibility, at

To this vision of earthly transcendence Dwight counterposes not simply the usual insistence of Augustan satire and New England Calvinism that human moral nature is not subject to historical change, that the problem of good and evil remains in the eighteenth century what it had always been for the ancient Greeks and Romans, that what the Calvinist insistence on Original Sin is ultimately about is a weakness of the moral will that every human being knows by experience. Rather, what Dwight offers is an insistence on what J. G. A. Pocock, writing about Augustine and his influence in relation to political theory, has called to our attention as the *nunc-stans*, or eternal present.[12] This is the divine or absolute perspective from which, if one were permitted to gaze at human actions and desires, one would recognize as the central and recurring theme of human history, from the fall of Adam to Paine's *Age of Reason*, humanity's irresistible urge to worship itself in some mirror of its own devising. The theological name of this tendency, of course, is pride, and in conventional terms Dwight is simply suggesting that human pride is the hidden common denominator of a range of historical figures, events, and ideas covered under the category of infidelity. From the original moment at which Satan cast his spell over the rebel angels to the pronouncements of Voltaire or Paine or Charles Chauncy in the eighteenth century, the mind or consciousness has held up to its own gaze some flattering mirror, denying or forgetting that its origins lie beyond itself.

Importantly, Dwight reaches this conclusion not merely by way of his theological background—his reading, for instance, of his grandfather Edwards's *Great Christian Doctrine of Original Sin Defended* (1758)—but from his early immersion in the poetry of Augustan England, in Pope's ridicule of Shaftesbury and Samuel Clarke in *The Dunciad*, for instance, or in Edward Young's satiric treatment of the Latitudinarian theology of John Tillotson and the incipient Universalism of Thomas Burnet in *Love of Fame, the Universal Passion* (1725–1728).[13] Against this background, Dwight's assertion of the nunc-stans as a

---

least, in William Godwin's *Enquiry concerning Political Justice, and Its Influence on Morals and Happiness* (1793) and Antoine-Nicolas de Condorcet's *Sketch for a Historical Picture of the Progress of the Human Mind* (1795).

12. J. G. A. Pocock, *The Machiavellian Moment: Florentine Political Thought and the Atlantic Republican Tradition* (Princeton, N.J., 1975), 31–48.

13. Archbishop of Canterbury John Tillotson was reputed to believe that the period

divine corrective to the delusions of human pride will itself constitute a satiric utterance—in direct opposition to the secularizing tendencies of the new progressivism—insisting on the theological necessity of acknowledging a divinity lying always outside human consciousness. At the same time, what is even less conventional is the way in which the Dwight of *Theology*, under the name of self-examination or "conscience," identifies this nunc-stans perspective as available, at least to a limited or imperfect degree, within the time-bound sphere of moral existence. To struggle successfully against the illusory visions that originate in human pride, Dwight will suggest—and this is the struggle in aid of which both satire and theology are ultimately written—is to see oneself, if only for an instant, as one is seen by God.

Dwight will reach this conclusion in its mature or fully articulated form only in his later writings, after the French Revolution and the new gospel of progress will have led him fully to grasp the implications of the nunc-stans in his own religious and political thought. But the idea is already powerfully at work from the beginning of Dwight's early participation in the Universalist controversy, not simply in the notion of "conscience" as it is first invoked in *The Triumph of Infidelity* but in the deeper sense of "pride-in-consciousness"— the notion that human consciousness and reason are inseparable from pride— that had cleared the space for the poem's original composition. "In Pride, in reas'ning Pride, our error lies," Pope had declared in *An Essay on Man*, and it is just this sense of pride that had led Dwight, first, to see that one last utterance in the Augustan mode of Pope and Young had become suddenly pertinent to the moral and religious circumstances of the new Republic and, then, to sustain and enlarge this utterance in a variety of literary and discursive modes throughout his career.[14] The works treated in the following pages will thus

---

of punishment in hell was not eternal. In fact, Tillotson argued in *A Sermon Preach'd before the Queen at White-Hall, March the 7th, 1689/90* (1690) that there is every reason to believe hell is eternal, but, because he allowed for the opposing possibility, he was accused of undermining the doctrine. Thomas Burnet did indeed assert the finitude of hell-torment in *A Treatise concerning the State of Departed Souls, before, and at, and after, the Resurrection* (1720).

14. Alexander Pope, *An Essay on Man* (1733–1734), in John Butt, ed., *The Poems of Alexander Pope: A One-Volume Edition of the Twickenham Text with Selected Annotations* (New Haven, Conn., 1963), 509.

constitute a series of somber warnings against the self-delusions written into that gospel of progress, which, like the Satan of *The Triumph of Infidelity* flying over the Atlantic, would pass over from the Paris of Danton and Robespierre to Jeffersonian America.

The immense power of this gospel of progress will become increasingly clear in the counterattack mounted against Dwight and his ideological allies first during the period of the Universalist controversy and then during the party struggles of the 1790s and after, when Dwight's own ideas concerning America's future would be condemned in the name of a more optimistic and, in the words of its proponents, philanthropic vision. In larger terms, of course, this period will mark the beginning of that seemingly inevitable triumph of Jeffersonian Republicanism over Federalism, but it will also mark the point at which the body of assumptions governing Dwight's war against infidelity will begin to be heard more distantly and indirectly, rendered by the new progressivist logic as simply another outmoded superstition unmasked as such by an enlightened age. It is in no small part a result of this ostensible triumph that, although the story of Dwight as an early combatant against Jeffersonian Republicanism has been told numerous times, the corresponding story of Dwight as a voice of warning, within which the Jeffersonian myth appears as a powerful and dangerous ideology, has remained all but lost to American literary and cultural historiography.[15]

15. One reason this aspect of Dwight's writing has been lost or repressed may be that American literary history in general and the story of Dwight's career in particular were first written during the period in the early twentieth century dominated by progressive historians such as Vernon Louis Parrington. Parrington's view of Dwight as a "repository of the venerable status quo" and a satirist who "abusively" attacked those who put their faith in a more optimistic view of human nature would influence countless subsequent interpretations of Dwight's poetry (Parrington, ed., *Main Currents in American Thought*, 2 vols. [New York, 1954], I, 366–369). In his study of the American progressive historians, Ernst A. Breisach reveals the extent to which Parrington viewed literary history in largely the same terms as those understood by Dwight's eighteenth-century opponents. Breisach writes that, for Parrington, "American intellectual and literary history was a drama in which theologians, philosophers, and literati had acted out roles assigned to them by one of the two basic forces," generally, the spirits of progressivism and conservatism (Breisach, *American Progressive History: An Experiment in Modernization* [Chicago, 1993], 145). The influence of this perspective on American lit-

Yet this voice of protest, not simply against the Jeffersonian myth but against the more general tendency of Americans to be drawn to one or another myth of easy redemption, will survive the moment of Dwight's own literary war against infidelity to become an enduring discourse in nineteenth-century America. In religious terms, the argument of *The Triumph of Infidelity* will be revived in a steady succession of attempts, by clergymen as various as orthodox Calvinist Bennet Tyler and Unitarian Andrews Norton, to impede the movement of religious thought toward Unitarianism and transcendentalism in the early nineteenth century. In social and political terms, Dwight's insistence upon acknowledging the alienation and limitation of earthly existence will echo in Lyman Beecher's critiques of utopian communities and Elizur Wright's and William Lloyd Garrison's attacks on slavery. In literature, one of the ways in which American writers will define themselves as part of a distinct literary culture will be by waging their own satiric attacks against the continued acceptance of the Pelagian myth. To honor these traditions, as generations of students of American history and literature have done, is to recognize Timothy Dwight as one of its cultural precursors.[16]

Since a close reading and understanding of *The Triumph of Infidelity* in its literary and historical contexts is crucial to the argument of *The Devil and Doctor*

---

erary historiography, well into the twentieth century, has been remarked upon by Lawrence Buell. The story of American cultural history as told by Parrington and others, he writes, resulted in literary terms in the myth of "New England's intellectual lapse" between the Puritan era and the American Renaissance and in political terms in the tendency to view Federalism as "a futile, bigoted reaction against the tide of democratization under Jefferson and Jackson" (Buell, *New England Literary Culture*, 88).

16. Bennet Tyler, one of Dwight's students at Yale, would help found the Theological Institute at East Windsor, Connecticut (later the Hartford Theological Seminary), in 1833 in reaction to the more liberal Calvinism taught at Yale by another of Dwight's students, Nathaniel W. Taylor. After leading the attack against Calvinist doctrine in the 1810s and 1820s, Unitarian Andrews Norton would himself take the conservative position against transcendentalism in *A Discourse on the Latest Form of Infidelity* (1839). Elizur Wright would apply the religious language of sin and spiritual struggle to the slavery question in *The Sin of Slavery, and Its Remedy* (1833), which would stand as one of the enduring rhetorical tactics of William Lloyd Garrison, founder of America's most important abolitionist newspaper, the *Liberator* (Boston, 1831–1865).

Dwight, and, since no modern, annotated version of the poem exists, I have included in Appendix A to this volume a text that may permit others to undertake such a reading. I have modernized spelling and punctuation, seeing that some of the confusion in modern commentary on the poem has been the result of Dwight's decision to follow older conventions of typography, such as leaving out quotation marks setting off separate speeches. In Appendix B, I have listed all variants between the original edition of the poem and a later corrected edition as well as my editorial emendations. In my commentary on the poem in Appendix C, I have provided background information on the various historical characters and events mentioned in the poem and paraphrases for passages in which the syntax is particularly involuted or compressed; I have also done my best to identify proper names that, in the manner of Augustan satire, are given in the original text in coded or asterisked form.

In providing such glosses to *The Triumph of Infidelity,* I intend to recover for students of early America not only a lost classic of late Augustan satire but a unique example of the convergence of literature, religion, and politics at the moment the new American Republic was first being imagined. *The Triumph of Infidelity* in this sense provides us with a rare glimpse into a world in which the Universalist controversy was wholly connected to the debates being waged elsewhere over the printing of paper money, interstate rivalry, popular rebellion, and the ratification of the Constitution, and, indeed, to future conflicts (the French Revolution, the election of 1800) still undreamed of in 1788.

CHAPTER I

An American Dunciad

In the fall of 1796, at the conclusion of his first year as president of Yale College, Timothy Dwight delivered the baccalaureate sermon, "On the Duties Connected with a Professional Life." In large part, the sentiments of the sermon are conventional enough: he reminds the graduates, for example, of the responsibilities of leadership and the importance of continued study throughout their lives. Yet, midway through the sermon, Dwight begins to emphasize a lesson that might seem oddly suited to a ceremony celebrating the students' academic achievement: beware of ideas that exaggerate the virtues and capabilities of human beings. "In this age of innovation," he declares, "visionary philosophers have retailed abundantly their reveries, on political subjects, as well as others. They have discovered, that men are naturally wise and good, prone to submit to good government." Lest his students give credit to such "reveries," he advises them that, if they look more closely at human nature, they will find the opposite to be true: "*You* will find all men substantially alike, and all naturally ignorant, and wicked. You will find every man pleased, not merely to be free, but to tyrannize." Indeed, he concludes, the real threat to a free government lies with those who most enthusiastically profess such visionary ideals: "The most arrant tyranny, of which you will ever hear, is the tyranny of a mob; and the most dangerous domination, that of a Jacobin Society."[1]

To the graduates listening to this sermon, neither Dwight's withering reminder of human weakness and folly nor his special warning against Ja-

---

1. Timothy Dwight, "On the Duties Connected with a Professional Life," in Dwight, *Sermons*, 2 vols. (New Haven, Conn., 1828), I, 303.

cobinism would have been at all surprising. By now, they would have come to conceive of the events in their own lives against the backdrop of the French Revolution and the related political crises and party struggles in their own country. After a year of listening to Dwight's weekly theology lectures—delivered in fulfillment of his other position at Yale, professor of divinity—they would have recognized this sermon as Dwight's valedictory reminder of one of the central themes of his continuing campaign against the dangers of infidel philosophy. Here he directed his criticism at its latest formulation, the optimistic vision of Thomas Paine, William Godwin, and Condorcet of a future in which the evils of human society would be eradicated and an earthly utopia of reason and virtue created. Indeed, Dwight's own urgent sense that the doctrines of Enlightenment skeptics and deists had become the grounds for political activity in France and America would also inspire his baccalaureate sermon for the following year, *The Nature, and Danger, of Infidel Philosophy*, in which he would more explicitly present the problem of infidelity as a threat to the very stability of the new Republic:

> Should [infidel philosophers] succeed to the extent of their wishes, what must be the consequences? . . . How soon would law and government lose that authority and energy which are now chiefly sustained by appeals to the presence, the will, and the agency, of a Ruler all present, all powerful, and unchangeably and infinitely opposed to every iniquity? How soon would man, ceasing to reverence his God, cease to regard his neighbour?[2]

Dwight's campaign against infidelity has best been remembered for the sentiments in these sermons and lectures, in large part because they were memorialized by both Dwight's friends and his enemies for the remaining years of his life and after his death in 1817. To the generation of students and divines whom he taught during this period, such sermons represented the means by which Dwight singlehandedly vanquished infidelity at Yale. He had rescued the college from the situation in which he had found it in 1795, with the few members of the college church greatly outnumbered by those who openly professed the deist and radical republican views that had become so

2. Timothy Dwight, *The Nature, and Danger, of Infidel Philosophy Exhibited in Two Discourses, Addressed to the Candidates for the Baccalaureate, in Yale College* (1798), ibid., 366.

fashionable. When Dwight had arrived, so went the oft-repeated tale, students had been given to addressing each other by nicknames like "Voltaire" and "D'Alembert," but, by the time of his death, he had presided over several large-scale revivals of religion at the college, and the names of philosophes and infidels were once again regarded as symbols of vice and folly.[3]

To the Jeffersonian Republicans, whose own larger political vision would come to be included in Dwight's definition of infidel philosophy, on the other hand, such sermons represented the means by which Dwight used the pulpit and his position of cultural influence to control New England politics. Dwight's pronouncements appeared as part of a larger attempt by Federalist politicians and their allies among the Congregationalist clergy to oppose the cause of liberty and democracy in order to protect their own positions of power. In retrospect, these contradictory portraits amount to much the same thing: the Dwight who admonished his audiences against the dangers of infidelity is the same Dwight who embraced Federalism and worked vigorously to unmask the new party forming around Jefferson as an "American Jacobinism," a political philosophy emerging from the same violent rage against tyrants and priests that had first appeared in America in the early years of the French Revolution. This is the Dwight whom Republican newspapers and pamphlets would describe as the "Pope of Connecticut" during the height of the party wars surrounding the bitterly contested election of 1800. As one pamphleteer would declare: "At this time, Connecticut is more completely

3. The account of Yale students referring to each other as Voltaire and D'Alembert comes from Lyman Beecher, who was a student from 1793 to 1797; see Barbara M. Cross, ed., *The Autobiography of Lyman Beecher* (1864), 2 vols. (Cambridge, Mass., 1961), I, 27. For other examples, see Sereno E. Dwight, "Biographical Memoir," in Timothy Dwight, *Theology; Explained and Defended, in a Series of Sermons . . .* (1818–1819), 4th ed., 4 vols. (New Haven, Conn., 1825); Calvin Chapin, *A Sermon, Delivered, 14th January, 1817, at the Funeral of the Rev. Timothy Dwight, D.D., LL.D.* (New Haven, Conn., 1817); Benjamin Silliman, *An Address Delivered before the Association of the Alumni of Yale College, in New Haven, August 17, 1842* (New Haven, Conn., 1842). For an examination of the origins of this myth as the skewed recollections of Dwight's former students looking back on the 1790s from the perspective of the Second Great Awakening, see Edmund S. Morgan, "Ezra Stiles and Timothy Dwight," Massachusetts Historical Society, *Proceedings*, LXXII (Boston, 1963), 101–117.

FIGURE 1.

The Reverend Timothy Dwight, S.T.D. L.L.D. Engraved by J. B. Forrest,
after the 1817 portrait by John Trumbull. *Courtesy, Manuscripts and Archives,
Yale University Library, New Haven, Conn.*

under the administration of a Pope than Italy: Is more an ecclesiastical dominion. . . . A divine, a poet, eloquent, talkative, and undaunted, [Dwight] wants all the meekness, patience, vigilance, and superintendance of the people, to keep within due bounds."[4]

In such pamphlets can be glimpsed the particular nature of the threat Dwight posed to his political and ideological opponents, for instance, when the same writer quoted above contrasts Dwight with the previous president of Yale, Ezra Stiles. Although the portrait of Stiles is far from flattering—"a bigot, active, obstinate and persevering"—it pales in comparison to that of Dwight as the great menace to the cause of liberty: "Dr. Stiles chastised with the whips of sermons, and letters upon politics—But Dr. Dwight will scourge with the scorpions of Calvinism and Edwardeanism, the scorpions of polemic divinity, party politics, poetry, satirical writings, the Triumph of Infidelity, and the prejudices circulated by young men and young divines taught by him."[5] In short, Dwight is a more formidable enemy to the Republican cause because of the number of weapons at his disposal, and he is unique because of his particular skill as a satirist, which this writer recalls from a poem entitled *The Triumph of Infidelity*, published nearly a decade earlier.

In one sense, the quoted passage serves simply as a reminder that Dwight's campaign against infidel philosophy, usually associated with the sermons and addresses he delivered during the late 1790s, had actually begun in a work of verse satire from 1788. At the same time, the significance accorded *The Triumph of Infidelity* here and elsewhere in the Republican press—that is, as Dwight's principal literary weapon in a continuing ideological conflict—might come as a surprise to modern scholars, for it stands in direct contrast to the way in which the poem has since tended to be remembered.[6] Even in the decades im-

---

4. John Cosens Ogden, *An Appeal to the Candid, upon the Present State of Religion and Politics in Connecticut* (Stockbridge, Conn., 1798), 14.

5. Ibid., 11–12.

6. This was not the only time *The Triumph of Infidelity* was revived in the press as a means of attacking Dwight's politics. In 1803, a full fifteen years after the publication of the poem, Leonard Chester of the Republican newspaper the *American Mercury* published a series of articles entitled "*The Triumph of Infidelity* Resuscitated." The articles explicated passages from the poem and identified—often erroneously—its coded villains, both to expose Dwight's treatment of such figures as inappropriately harsh and

mediately following his death in 1817, when Dwight was still one of America's best-known poets, he was acclaimed primarily for *The Conquest of Canaan, Greenfield Hill,* and the "rising glory" poems of his youth, not for *The Triumph of Infidelity,* which he had published anonymously and had gone to his grave without acknowledging as his own. The poem emerges as no less of an anomaly, moreover, in the context of the political struggle within which it is invoked above. Unlike the other works in which Dwight would carry on his campaign against infidelity, *The Triumph of Infidelity* had been written in what seems to be an earlier and wholly different historical moment, years before the threat of "Jacobinism" became a constant theme for Federalists like Dwight, Noah Webster, and Fisher Ames, and when such figures as Paine and Jefferson were still held in high esteem by those who would later excoriate their names.

Yet what is perhaps most surprising about *The Triumph of Infidelity* is that Dwight's satirical "scourge" had been directed at a seemingly unrelated target, a fellow Congregationalist minister. Charles Chauncy had long served as pastor of the First Church of Boston, but in his later years he had ignited a pamphlet war over the publication of a treatise entitled *The Mystery Hid from Ages and Generations.* The mystery of the title is the doctrine of universal salvation, the agreeable belief held by a small number of Congregationalist clergymen that all people, regardless of their sins or shortcomings, will ultimately experience Christian redemption and eternal happiness. The poem had appeared, in fact, in the midst of the pamphlet war over universal salvation. This connection to the controversy has made *The Triumph of Infidelity* something of a puzzle for readers attempting to make clear sense of the poem and its specific place in American literary and cultural history. Although the poem's chief satiric targets are Chauncy and the Universalists, in the course of its nearly eight hundred lines *The Triumph of Infidelity* tells a much larger story. Indeed, the controversy over universal salvation appears as the latest chapter of a two-

---

to suggest that the Dwight of 1788 had attacked some men who later became his Federalist allies. Thus, for instance, in the first number of the series, Chester writes: "A minister of the Gospel, who ought to be an example to all men, sets at his desk in 1788, hates Yale College, hates Doctors Dana and Chauncey . . . attacks without mercy men, who had been gaining fair characters before he was born. In 1800 is a President of College, . . . is in high favor with the Clergy, and begins to rebuild the waste of characters, made by his indignant pen" (*American Mercury* [Hartford, Conn.], Jan. 27, 1803).

thousand-year history of infidelity narrated by Satan himself, and Chauncy, improbably enough at first glance, takes his place in the narrative alongside such notorious Enlightenment freethinkers as Voltaire and David Hume.

The first great puzzle surrounding *The Triumph of Infidelity*, accordingly, involves what one reader describes as the problem of "the very subject of the poem." One must reconcile its immediate satiric purpose—to intervene in a local doctrinal dispute among members of the Congregationalist clergy—with the broader category of infidelity. Such a category seems, at first, to be wholly misdirected at a professed Christian minister like Chauncy.[7] The later Republican revival of interest in "Pope" Dwight's satiric scourge against Chauncy and Universalism provides an important clue for modern readers attempting to make sense of the poem. It points toward an assumption shared by both Dwight and his ideological enemies that *The Triumph of Infidelity* belonged to a much larger and more significant contest, one that included not only the challenge to orthodox Protestantism by the countless systems of Enlightenment thought satirized as infidelity in the poem but also, importantly, the later

7. Kenneth Silverman, *Timothy Dwight* (New York, 1969), 86. Reviewing some of the earlier scholarship on *The Triumph of Infidelity*, Silverman summarizes the questions of previous critics: "Does the poem attack skeptics, or unorthodox fellow Calvinists? Did Dwight, as one critic suggests, intend to satirize Deism and materialism, but turn to heterodox Calvinists for lack of better material? Did he, as another suggests, intend simply an attack on the liberal Old Light theology and the consequences of its wide acceptance in New England?" (86–87). Silverman's own answer to the questions is that the poem is meant simply to attack "all the forces of social instability," but it fails owing to Dwight's "technical ineptitudes" (87); the comparison between Chauncy and such figures as Voltaire is meant, Silverman adds, to emphasize their contrast, to prove that "no American, certainly no New Englander, could be so poisonous as a European, much less a Frenchman" (89). For an examination of whether Dwight changed topics in the midst of composing *The Triumph of Infidelity*, see Leon Howard, *The Connecticut Wits* (Chicago, 1943), 215. For an argument that the poem was meant to satirize the liberal Old Light theology, see Jack Stillinger, "Dwight's *Triumph of Infidelity*: Text and Interpretation," *Studies in Bibliography*, XV (1962), 259–266. The most convincing solution to this problem is found in a single remark by Lawrence Buell: the true object of the poem's satire is "the fallacy of naive trust in a benign view of Providence and human nature" (Lawrence Buell, *New England Literary Culture from Revolution through Renaissance* [Cambridge, 1986], 96).

political warfare surrounding the emergence of Jeffersonian democracy and its challenge to the first Federalist administrations. Indeed, Dwight's sense of belonging to a broader cultural struggle, even in 1788, accounted in part for his decision to respond to the Universalist controversy, not in another polemical pamphlet or theological treatise, but in a satiric poem that announced itself by its very form as part of a tradition of satire going back to the beginning of the Augustan period in England.

This is the context in which the literary qualities that characterize *The Triumph of Infidelity*—verse form, syntax, tone, and, especially, the dozens of direct allusions to Alexander Pope, Jonathan Swift, John Dryden, and others— can be seen as more than simply stylistic issues; rather, they will carry the question of universal salvation beyond the bounds of narrow theological controversy. The self-conscious Augustanism of the poem (what Lawrence Buell has in mind when he calls *The Triumph of Infidelity* a Calvinist or New England *Dunciad*) communicates that more general sense of satire as a medium standing at the center of a grand struggle of historical forces. *The Dunciad* itself had demanded to be read only incidentally as Pope's ridicule of the various Grub Street dunces and more importantly as the satiric counterattack of a traditional order against the forces of a chaotic modernity. Similarly, *The Triumph of Infidelity*, announcing itself as a rewriting of *The Dunciad* for a new, American circumstance, will direct its own satiric energies, not at the doctrine of universal salvation as such, but at the ideological forces from which such a doctrine originated: the grand discourse of Enlightenment progressivism carrying post-Revolutionary American society toward a vision of innate human goodness, individual self-realization, and the perfectibility of society.[8]

8. Buell, *New England Literary Culture*, 87. The sense of struggle between opposing historical forces, larger in its implications than the controversy over Universalism, also accounts for why *The Triumph of Infidelity* is one of relatively few works by Dwight to have been republished in England, appearing in 1791 under the following imprint: *The Triumph of Infidelity: A Poem; Supposed to Be Written by Timothy Dwight, D.D. of Greenfield in Connecticut, . . . in 1788* (London: Printed for J. Mathews, No. 18, Strand). There is no evidence that Dwight was involved in this reprint; indeed, the subtitle suggests otherwise. More likely, Mathews, a Methodist lay preacher who published a variety of religious and controversial literature (including a 1776 work by George Clark entitled

The notion that Universalism has such profound implications is, in fact, borne out in the story of the Universalist controversy. This episode has often been interpreted simply as a single chapter in a series of controversies between Eastern Massachusetts Arminians and Connecticut Valley Calvinists, elsewhere fought over revivalism, Original Sin, and, eventually, the Trinity.[9] Obscured in this understanding is the degree to which Chauncy and his fellow Universalists—self-proclaimed enemies of enthusiasm and excess—realized the radical step they were taking in professing the salvation of all men. In the years prior to the controversy, the idea of universal salvation had been associated with two distinct movements: on the one hand, the radical sectarianism of itinerants such as Caleb Rich and John Murray (who had been preaching a largely different version of the doctrine in backcountry New England villages) and, on the other, certain forms of deism that had included speculations, at least, about a universal state of future happiness. Chauncy's system differed from both; unlike deism, it was argued chiefly from his interpretation of Scripture, and, unlike "backwoods Universalism," it did not deny the existence of hell. Rather, it asserted only that punishment in hell is not eternal, that those who die in sin will be punished for a finite period before they, too, ascend to heaven. Despite these distinctions, Chauncy knew that universal salvation in any form had serious implications, not merely for Christianity but for one's very conception of human earthly existence. As suggested in the title of his treatise, *The Mystery Hid from Ages and Generations*, Chauncy sensed that he had discovered a hidden scriptural truth meant only to be revealed in the modern age, and which would literally set human beings free even within their mortal lives.

The Triumph of Truth, Exemplified in the Fall of the Antitrinitarian Dagon), saw Dwight's poem as participating in a transatlantic struggle against infidelity.

9. In his classic study of the origins of American Unitarianism, Conrad Wright exemplifies this view of universal salvation as an extension of the theological challenge to Calvinism by Arminians, who had from the 1750s emphasized the benevolence of God and greater human agency in the process of salvation. After outlining earlier controversies over Original Sin, freedom of the will, and justification by faith, he writes, "The salvation of all men, then, was the conclusion to which the Arminian concept of divine benevolence unmistakably pointed" (Wright, *The Beginnings of Unitarianism in America* [Boston, 1955], 185).

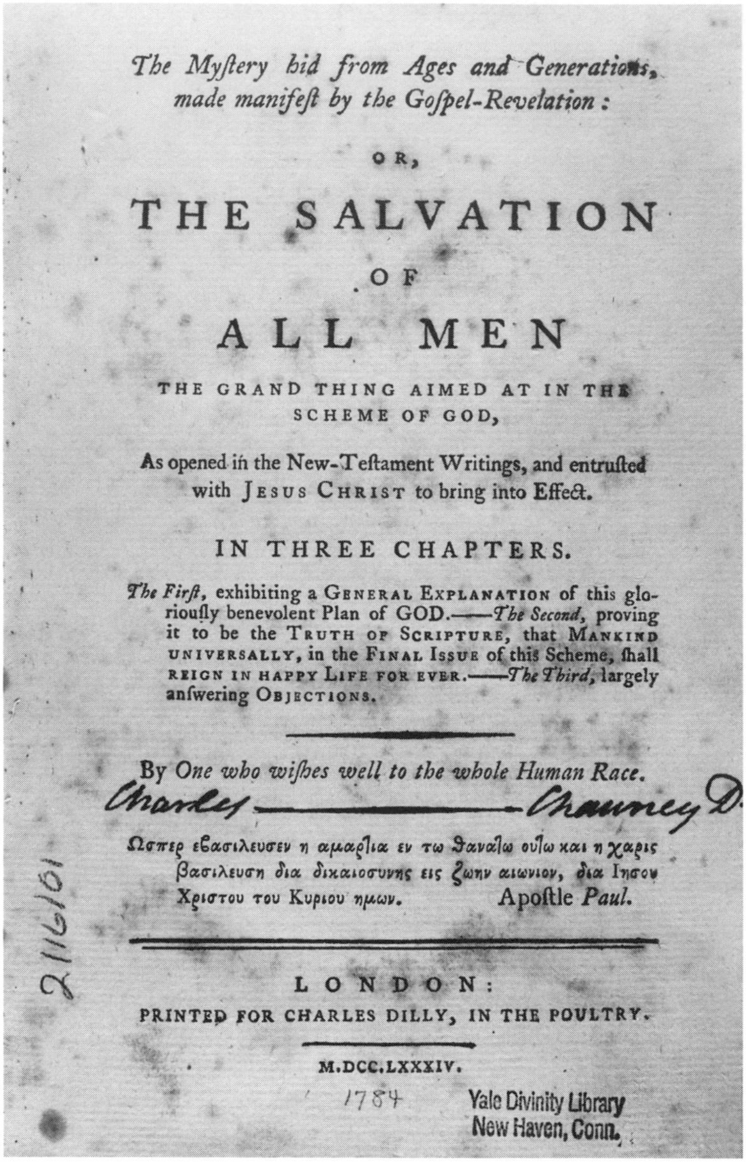

The *Myſtery hid from Ages and Generations,*
made manifeſt by the Goſpel-Revelation :

OR,

THE SALVATION

OF

ALL MEN

THE GRAND THING AIMED AT IN THE
SCHEME OF GOD,

As opened in the New-Teſtament Writings, and entruſted
with JESUS CHRIST to bring into Effect.

IN THREE CHAPTERS.

The Firſt, exhibiting a GENERAL EXPLANATION of this glo-
riouſly benevolent Plan of GOD.——*The Second,* proving
it to be the TRUTH OF SCRIPTURE, that MANKIND
UNIVERSALLY, in the FINAL ISSUE of this Scheme, ſhall
REIGN IN HAPPY LIFE FOR EVER.——*The Third,* largely
anſwering OBJECTIONS.

By One who wiſhes well to the whole Human Race.

Charles ———————— *Chauncy D.*

Ωσπερ εβασιλευσεν η αμαρ]ια εν τω θανα]ω ου]ω και η χαρις
βασιλευση δια δικαιοσυνης εις ζωην αιωνιον, δια Ιησου
Χριστου του Κυριου ημων.   Apoſtle *Paul.*

LONDON:
PRINTED FOR CHARLES DILLY, IN THE POULTRY.

M.DCC.LXXXIV.

1784

FIGURE 2.
Charles Chauncy, *The Mystery Hid from Ages and Generations,*
Made Manifest by the Gospel-Revelation; or, The Salvation of All Men the Grand
Thing Aimed at in the Scheme of God . . . (London, 1784), title page.
Courtesy, Yale Divinity Library, New Haven, Conn.

At the time Chauncy made this discovery, however, he was equally certain that this was a truth the public was not yet ready to have revealed. That is why, although he had completed the manuscript that would become *The Mystery Hid* as early as the 1750s, he had chosen to keep it a secret from even some of his closest colleagues for nearly thirty years. During this period, he would show the manuscript—largely a series of detailed scriptural translations and proofs—to a select circle of clergymen whom he felt would be open to the doctrine. It became, as one of Chauncy's confidantes Jeremy Belknap termed it, a "secret among learned men." Chauncy even devised a code name, "the pudding," to be used in letters and conversations among members of his inner circle of Universalists, allowing one to inquire about another's sentiments by asking, "Doth he relish the pudding?"[10]

As his own letters make clear, Chauncy was willing to wait until after his death for "the pudding" to be made public. He even describes the treatise in a letter to Ezra Stiles—without confessing its subject to his more orthodox colleague—as a work "written with too much freedom to admit of a publication in this country" and adds, "I am not yet determined whether to permit its being then printed, or to order its being committed to the flames." Yet, by the end of the Revolutionary War, some of Chauncy's more daring younger colleagues—John Clarke, John Eliot, Jeremy Belknap—began to push for publishing "the pudding." Chauncy agreed, but not to the publication of the 350-page manuscript; rather, he allowed Clarke, his fellow minister at First Church, to compose a short pamphlet laying out the major points of the doctrine, with a preface by Chauncy himself. This pamphlet appeared anonymously in 1782 under the title *Salvation for All Men, Illustrated and Vindicated as a Scripture Doctrine*.[11]

10. *Belknap Papers*, MHS, *Collections*, 5th Ser., II (Boston, 1877), 171, 6th Ser., IV (1891), 207.

11. [John Clarke], *Salvation for All Men, Illustrated and Vindicated as a Scripture Doctrine* (Boston, 1782); "A Sketch of Eminent Men in New-England; in a Letter from the Rev. Dr. Chauncy to Dr. Stiles," MHS, *Colls.*, 1st Ser., X (1809), 163. So serious was Chauncy about protecting the secret of his manuscript that he never told his closest colleague and fellow Arminian, Jonathan Mayhew, of its existence; later, Jeremy Belknap, one of the members of Chauncy's inner circle, found it necessary to defend himself to John Eliot against the charge that he had let the secret out too soon, and to too many

The controversy began almost immediately, when *Salvation for All Men* was answered by the orthodox clergyman Joseph Eckley; this response was in turn answered by another anonymous pamphlet written by Chauncy, and thus began a sometimes bitter exchange that would last for the next several years. The main points of disagreement in the pamphlets centered on the proper translations of several verses found primarily in St. Paul's Epistles (specifically, whether the Greek word αιωνιος, used to describe the duration of torment in hell, should be translated as "forever" or merely "a very long, but finite, period"). Even as an increasing number of orthodox clergy continued to be drawn into the debate with the anonymous Universalist pamphleteers, they failed to realize that the dynamic of the controversy had already conceded a considerable victory to the Universalist position: merely by participating in this purely scriptural debate, Eckley and his colleagues were acknowledging at least a degree of plausibility in the dissenting argument. For his part, Chauncy was becoming convinced that the pamphlets had given the public "a mere castrated version of the whole" of his argument and arranged for *The Mystery Hid* to be published in its entirety in 1784.[12] Yet this treatise, devoted

---

people: "When I am fond of *pudding* myself I am willing to help my neighbors to a slice of it" (*Belknap Papers*, MHS, *Colls.*, 6th Ser., IV [1891], 603). For a fuller account of the secret of the pudding, see Wright, *The Beginnings of Unitarianism*, 187–193; Edward Griffin, *Old Brick: Charles Chauncy of Boston, 1705-1787* (Minneapolis, Minn., 1980), 168–177; Charles H. Lippy, *Seasonable Revolutionary: The Mind of Charles Chauncy* (Chicago, 1981), 108–112.

12. *Belknap Papers*, MHS, *Colls.*, 6th Ser., IV (1891), 233. Samuel Mather responded quickly with a point-by-point critique of John Clarke's scriptural interpretations in *All Men Will Not Be Saved Forever; or, An Attempt to Prove, That This Is a Scriptural Doctrine* (Boston, 1782) and was, in turn, answered by Clarke in *A Letter to Doctor Mather; Occasioned by His Disingenuous Reflexions upon a Certain Pamphlet, Entitled, Salvation for All Men* (Boston, 1782). Joseph Eckley then attempted a different argument in the pamphlet *Divine Glory, Brought to View, in the Condemnation of the Ungodly; or, The Doctrine of Future Punishment, Illustrated and Vindicated, as Rational and True* (Boston, 1782), to which Chauncy responded with a witty use of Eckley's own title, *Divine Glory Brought to View in the Final Salvation of All Men* (Boston, 1783). Other pamphlets published during this controversy include William Gordon, *The Doctrine of Final Universal Salvation Examined and Shown to Be Unscriptural: In Answer to a Pamphlet Entitled: Salvation for All Men* (Boston, 1783); Nathaniel Emmons, *A Discourse, concerning the Process of the General*

---

almost entirely to close textual exegesis, only increased the possibility that the Universalist controversy would be regarded as an arcane theological exercise, having little to do with essential doctrines of Christianity.

After the publication of *The Mystery Hid*, the controversy entered a period of stalemate, with no major theological works published on either side until *The Triumph of Infidelity* in 1788. The date of the poem raises the question of why Dwight might have waited until the pamphlet war had cooled down to publish his own response to Chauncy and Universalism. He had long been open about his opposition to the doctrine, and, indeed, one of the members of Chauncy's circle had described him as early as 1783 as one who "thunders out his anathemas against all who stir the pudding." Yet, only by the late 1780s— after Shays's Rebellion, the threat of interstate war, and the debate over the Constitution had raised with heightened urgency the relationship between individual moral action and the future of the new Republic—would Dwight come to understand the significance of the doctrine outside the bounds of the theological debate. In this later context, then, the appearance of the poem would reassert the historical importance of Universalism, which Chauncy and his colleagues had themselves always sensed but which had been left out of the earlier pamphlet war.[13]

Judgment (Providence, R.I., 1783); [Samuel Hopkins], *An Inquiry concerning the Future State of Those Who Die in Their Sins* . . . (Newport, R.I., 1783). By this time, Chauncy made arrangements for the publication of *The Mystery Hid*. Chauncy's work was later answered in another lengthy treatise by Jonathan Edwards [the younger], *The Salvation of All Men Strictly Examined* (New Haven, Conn., 1790).

John Clarke, in particular, recognized the dynamic in which simply to engage the orthodox camp in the debate lent plausibility to the doctrine. Thus, for instance, in response to Samuel Mather's biting remarks about the advocates of universal salvation, he writes: "I took for granted . . . that you know, others might differ from you without being knaves or fools. . . . The advocates for Universal Salvation wish for nothing more than a fair discussion of the subject" (Clarke, *A Letter to Doctor Mather*, 1, 8).

13. *Belknap Papers*, MHS, *Colls.*, 6th Ser., IV (1891), 249. One explanation for Dwight's waiting until 1788 to publish the poem is that only after the death of Chauncy in 1787 did he feel comfortable satirizing him as Satan's chief means of spreading infidelity in America. Yet one clue to Dwight's growing sense that the social and political implications of Universalism demanded satiric response is found in the 1787 appear-

This sense of urgency is announced by the form of the poem, written in the high Augustan strain that had originated in the social and political satire of Pope and Swift and Gay in the 1720s and 1730s and that had more recently been employed by fellow Connecticut Wits John Trumbull, David Humphreys, and Joel Barlow in *The Anarchiad* (1786–1787) to combat the more pressing political and economic threats facing the new Republic. At the same time, Dwight's decision to respond with satire to a theological controversy placed *The Triumph of Infidelity* into a particular tradition within Augustanism, that of turning to satire at moments of perceived religious crisis. This tradition had given to eighteenth-century poetry the figure of the clergyman-satirist, of which Swift is only the most famous example. Others include such poets as John Brown and Edward Young, who announces in the opening lines of *Love of Fame, the Universal Passion* his own turn to satire in response to a similar crisis among his fellow Anglican ministers: "Instructive satire, true to Virtue's cause. . . . / When churchmen scripture for the classics quit, / Polite apostates from God's grace to wit."[14]

Within his own career as a writer, moreover, Dwight had witnessed first-hand the strategy of using satire to draw public attention away from the minute doctrinal details of a theological controversy and toward its moral and social issues. As early as 1770, when he and his former Yale classmate John Trumbull had been working together on a series of essays entitled "The Correspondent," published in a local New Haven newspaper, Trumbull had written an extended satire against the "speculative metaphysics" underlying the New Divinity theology of Samuel Hopkins and Joseph Bellamy. This piece would

---

ance of William Pitt Smith's *Universalist.* After paying tribute to the recently deceased Chauncy, Smith goes on to predict a future in which the revelation of salvation for all effects a full-scale transformation of Christianity into something more nearly resembling an enlightened utopia. All vestiges of earlier Christian superstition and all intolerance of heterodox beliefs will be eradicated; deists and skeptics, recognizing Christianity as once again consistent with the light of reason, will return to the faith, creating a true brotherhood of man that will, in turn, effect a worldwide social transformation. For more on Smith, see Chapter 2, below.

14. Edward Young, *Love of Fame, the Universal Passion* (1728), in John Doran, ed., *The Complete Works, Poetry and Prose, of the Rev. Edward Young . . .* , rev. ed., 2 vols. (London, 1854), I, 347–348.

later become the basis for Trumbull's subsequent attack, in *The Progress of Dulness,* against clergymen whose penchant for controversial divinity served only to alienate their parishioners from their own sense of religious duty.[15] This earlier satiric intervention by one of his fellow Connecticut Wits would inform Dwight's turn from parish pastor and popular author of patriotic and scriptural poetry to the anonymous satirist of *The Triumph of Infidelity.*

The decision to publish *The Triumph of Infidelity* anonymously provides another crucial clue to the poem's claims for its significance and the signifi-

15. In *The Progress of Dulness, Part First* . . . (New Haven, Conn., 1772), which describes the education and eventual ordination of "Tom Brainless," Trumbull digresses into a long discussion of the New Divinity as prone not simply to excessive speculation and needless controversy but to the more serious sin of philosophical pride:

Vain man, to madness still a prey,
Thy space a point, thy life a day,
A feeble worm, that aim'st to stride
In all the foppery of pride!
The glimmering lamp of reason's ray
Was giv'n to guide thy darksome way.
Why wilt thou spread thine insect-wings,
And strive to reach sublimer things?
Thy doubts confess, thy blindness own,
Nor vex thy thoughts with scenes unknown.

. . . .

For metaphysics rightly shown
But teach how little can be known:
Though quibbles still maintain their station,
Conjecture serves for demonstration,
Armies of pens drawn forth to fight,
And [Bellamy] and [Hopkins] write.

Edwin T. Bowden, ed., *The Satiric Poems of John Trumbull* (Austin, Tex., 1962), 36–37. See "A New System of Divinity," "The Correspondent," *Connecticut Journal and New-Haven Post-Boy,* Mar. 23, Apr. 6, 27, June 1, 1770. For Dwight's involvement in "The Correspondent" column and his authorship of at least one of the essays, see Victor E. Gimmestad, *John Trumbull* (New York, 1974), 41. For the implications of this episode on Dwight's relationship with the New Divinity, see Chapter 2, below.

cance of the Universalist controversy. Although Dwight had been quite open concerning his opposition to Universalism, he also recognized that an anonymous satiric poem would have the effect of exploding the limits of purely scriptural debate. Augustan satire had always communicated, through the ideology of form (in which purely formal or generic characteristics reveal some deeper ideological significance), a notion of poetry, not as personal composition, but as the symbolic utterance of an impersonal or anonymous public discourse. Dwight's poem, in this sense, would constitute a response to the entire atmosphere of secrecy surrounding "the pudding" and Chauncy's anonymous campaign of pamphlet writing. It would confront Universalism as it was already publicly understood, as an impersonal discourse of enlightened theology, heralding the certainty of future happiness and freedom from earthly alienation.[16]

The same attempt to draw attention away from the specific details of Dwight's authorship or the immediate circumstances surrounding the poem's appearance and to emphasize instead a more universal significance is found on the title page: *The Triumph of Infidelity* was almost certainly published in Hartford or New Haven, Connecticut, but the only bibliographic information provided reads, "Printed in the World / M,DCC,LXXXVIII." Indeed, a corresponding point is made in the dedication, which is addressed, not to the central character, Chauncy, but to Voltaire, the very archetype of the threat of

16. *Belknap Papers*, MHS, *Colls.*, 6th Ser., IV (1891), 249. The term "ideology of form" is from Fredric Jameson, and he, in turn, derives the term from Louis Hjelmslev's notion of "the content of form" (Jameson, *The Political Unconscious: Narrative as a Socially Symbolic Act* [Ithaca, N.Y., 1981] 99; Hjelmslev, *Prolegomena to a Theory of Language*, trans. Francis J. Whitfield, rev. ed. [Madison, Wis., 1961], chap. 13). For the argument that anonymity communicates the idea of literary texts as part of an impersonal struggle of historical forces, see Gregory B. Stone, *The Death of the Troubadour: The Late Medieval Resistance to the Renaissance* (Philadelphia, 1994), which deals with the resistance to the Renaissance notion of individual authorship in late medieval troubadour songs. Stone argues that such songs relied upon an authorial self that was "always already absorbed by and dissolved in a collective anonymity," and thus applicable to all of society (3). Similarly, the appearance of anonymous literary works in the eighteenth century would reassert the notion of a collective voice, particularly in response to what is perceived as an impersonal or anonymous historical movement.

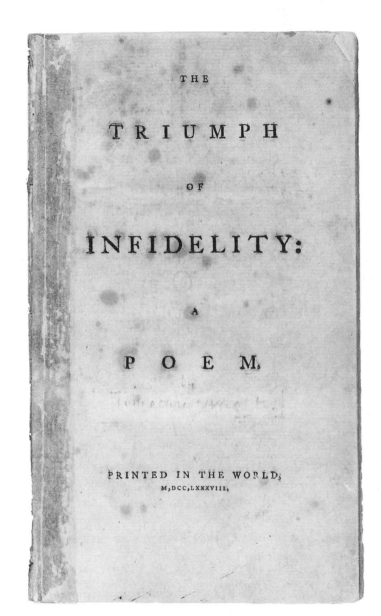

THE

TRIUMPH

OF

INFIDELITY:

A

POEM.

PRINTED IN THE WORLD;
M,DCC,LXXXVIII.

FIGURE 3.

Timothy Dwight, *The Triumph of Infidelity: A Poem* (1788), title page. *Courtesy, Beinecke Rare Book and Manuscript Library, Yale University, New Haven, Conn.*

irreligion for Calvinists and Arminians alike. Here Dwight explains that the recent appearance of Universalism is more than simply the latest means by which the purveyors of infidelity have sought to attack Christianity; rather, it constitutes a crucial strategic advancement even from Voltaire's time. The deism and skepticism of the earlier eighteenth century had announced themselves as irreligion by their outright rejection of Scripture, but the newer and more subtle strategy of advancing the cause of infidelity is to disguise it as a form of scriptural interpretation itself:

To Mons. de VOLTAIRE.

SIR,

. . . To whom could such an effort as the following be dedicated, with more propriety, than to you. The subject it celebrates is the most pointed attack upon your old enemies; an attack more happily devised, at least, than any of yours; as yours were more advantageously concerted than the efforts of any of your predecessors. Reasoning is an unhappy engine to be employed against Christianity; as, like elephants in ancient war, it usually, in this case, turns upon those who employ it. Ridicule is a more convenient weapon, as you have successfully evinced; but ingenious misinterpretation is a still more sure and effectual annoyance; for the sword and javelin, however keen, may be dreaded and shunned, while the secret and deadly dirk is plunged to the heart of unsuspecting friendship, unhappily trusting the smooth-faced assassin. (Appendix A)

This image of a continuing war between the forces of infidelity and the defenders of the faith is played out in comic detail throughout Satan's narration in *The Triumph of Infidelity*. Satan tells the story of the various successes and failures in his ongoing scheme to promote infidelity from the time of Christ to the end of the eighteenth century. He explains, for example, that, in response to God's great victory during the Protestant Reformation, his own strategy had been to employ the specious rationalism of English deists like John Toland and Matthew Tindal to disprove scriptural truth—an attempt that ultimately failed against the superior reasoning of such Christian apologists as John Locke and Isaac Newton.[17] His next weapon had been the ridicule

17. Eighteenth-century defenders of Christianity would remember John Locke as having demonstrated the consistency between Christian doctrine and reason in *The*

and irony of Voltaire and the Encyclopedists, a tactic that converted scores of Europeans but failed to appeal to the more serious-minded and pious Americans. Thus, when Satan arrives in America at the conclusion of the Revolutionary War, he realizes that he needs to devise a more insidious plan; he must undermine Christianity from within: "To wound the eternal cause with deepest harms, / A cheated gospel proves the surest arms: / Those arms, no hand can, like a preacher's wield; / False friends may stab, when foes must fly the field" (429–432).

In specific terms, what allows Dwight to treat Chauncy's theology as a form of infidelity in the poem is not simply its rejection of the orthodox belief in eternal punishment, although a major orthodox critique during the Universalist controversy was that unrepentant sinners would no longer fear God's retribution for their actions. Chauncy had already preempted this charge by emphasizing that his version of Universalism, unlike that of John Murray, for instance, did not deny the existence of hell but maintained only that the punishment of sinners was not eternal; he also made a point of adding that those who would abuse God's beneficence by continuing their lives of sin would indeed suffer hell's torments — "God only knows how *long*, or to what an *awful degree*."[18] In *The Triumph of Infidelity*, however, the crucial issue has less to do with the threat of infernal punishment than with what the doctrine implies about the nature of human existence itself. To assert that punishment in hell leads eventually to eternal happiness in heaven is to believe, first and foremost, that a period of trial and moral education is enough to repair the sinful nature of any human being. Similarly, to argue that human beings can be universally certain of their redemption is in a crucial sense to grant them in their present lives the freedom from alienation that other forms of Christianity had always reserved for a future state that is necessarily outside the human or earthly sphere.

The opposing categories of "truth" and "infidelity" thus emerge in *The Triumph of Infidelity*, not as a function of any nominal adherence to or rejection of

---

Reasonableness of Christianity as Delivered in the Scriptures (1695). Isaac Newton, they would similarly point out, was not only a physicist and mathematician but an amateur theologian and author of the posthumously published *Observations upon the Prophesies of Daniel, and the Apocalypse of St. John* (1733).

18. Charles Chauncy, introduction, in [Clarke], *Salvation for All Men*, iii.

Christ and his teachings, but according to a more fundamental set of assumptions about human nature and the meaning of human existence. Dwight's ostensible defense of orthodoxy in the poem is actually a defense of what students of eighteenth-century literature and moral philosophy call the "Augustinian" conception of human existence. This notion posits earthly life as a state of profound alienation from the sphere of the divine, characterized in moral terms by a permanent tendency toward weakness and error. In direct contrast, infidelity nearly always refers to one or another version of what has been called "eighteenth-century Pelagianism," the moral belief in natural human virtue that takes its name from Augustine's own rival Pelagius. His denial of the effects of Original Sin had been revived in the eighteenth century by the third earl of Shaftesbury, Francis Hutcheson, and a host of English Latitudinarian divines preaching doctrines of benign Providence and human benevolence.[19]

The great advantage of these categories is that they keep in view the theological element of the Universalist controversy—that an implicit or explicit denial of Original Sin will amount, for Dwight, to a consequent denial of the moral truth that made Christ's redemption of man necessary. They also reveal the underlying Augustan critique in *The Triumph of Infidelity:* Universalism constitutes only one of countless ways in which human beings, throughout history, have deluded themselves about their own virtues and capabilities. The great error of modern Pelagianism as defined in *The Triumph of Infidelity* will have less to do, accordingly, with a rejection of the traditional Calvinist insistence on the doctrine of Original Sin than with a denial of what Dwight will understand as an empirical truth about the world: despite what human civilizations have been able to achieve, the world has remained a constant scene of war and crime and injustice. "History," he will state in one of his Yale divinity sermons, is "a satire upon our race, scarcely less severe than any of those, pro-

19. For an application of Augustinianism and Pelagianism to the controversy surrounding the Great Awakening, particularly the Pelagian assumptions in Charles Chauncy's response to this movement, see Norman Fiering, *Moral Philosophy at Seventeenth-Century Harvard* (Chapel Hill, N.C., 1981), chap. 3. For a detailed discussion of Dwight's Augustinianism, see William C. Dowling, *Poetry and Ideology in Revolutionary Connecticut* (Athens, Ga., 1990), chap. 3.

fessedly, written under this name."[20] In contrast, the confident Pelagian assertions implicit in universal salvation as well as the more common Enlightenment promise that humanity will soon overcome the conditions responsible for the crimes and injustices of the past will always constitute, for Dwight, simply different forms of the same basic delusion.

Satan defines infidelity in this way throughout *The Triumph of Infidelity*, describing his ceaseless efforts to draw "the webs of sophism" over "truth's fair form" (134) by creating entire structures of belief, from Roman paganism to modern skepticism, that deceive ordinary people about the true conditions of their existence. More precisely, the success of such delusive systems is the result of their appeal to a profound human tendency toward self-deception, the part of the human will that wants to believe the best about oneself and to submit to an easier and more flattering moral or cosmological vision. As Satan declares, "Whate'er sustains, or flatters sinning man; / Whate'er can conscience of her thorns disarm, / Or calm, at death's approach, the dread alarm" (370–372). The threat of this particular conception of infidelity is thus imagined less as the sort of rife lawlessness that is often conjured up by the word "depravity" than as the more subtle threat of moral complacency, the temptation of every individual to rationalize one self-interested act at a time until, finally, the society as a whole is crippled by corruption.

At the same time, readers of eighteenth-century English poetry will recognize this as the great threat to civic virtue, understood everywhere in Augustan satire, and, in this context, in turn, we can fully understand what it means to read *The Triumph of Infidelity* as an American *Dunciad*. This title implies more than the notion of a poem that imitates or alludes to *The Dunciad;* rather, it assumes as a necessary precondition for the poem's intelligibility that the symbolic world projected by Augustan satiric verse—the moral and social environment in Dryden and Swift and, especially, the later Pope of *The Dunciad* and the *Imitations of Horace*—has not disappeared with the conclusion of the Augustan period in England or the end of British colonial rule in America. This world lives on precisely because the fundamental threat of a society drawn unwittingly toward its own corruption by self-interest and moral complacency is understood to be a permanent aspect of human nature. Indeed, a collective

20. Dwight, *Theology*, I, 440.

denial or repression of this threat is implied in *The Dunciad* by the notion of dulness—itself always a moral as a well as an intellectual category. This same sense of moral dulness will give special meaning to the category of infidelity in *The Triumph of Infidelity* as a tendency of human beings to dull their vision of the meaning of their existence.

What is also implicit in *The Dunciad* is the idea that complacency or dulness has risen to the level of an autonomous historical force—something akin to the modern conception of ideology. Dwight makes the same point in *The Triumph of Infidelity* by emphasizing infidelity as a ubiquitous force capable of lulling into moral slumber even the most diligent believers. This idea is most obvious in the lengthy description of the crowd of rogues who gather to hear Chauncy proclaim his doctrine, each representing a local American version of Pope's "sons of Dulness." It is also why Dwight chooses to include in the poem the story of Chauncy's delayed publication of *The Mystery Hid* after thirty years of secrecy. As Satan recounts, Chauncy had always been a faithful servant of God, and his delving into universal salvation was to a great degree a momentary lapse in his theological judgment. Indeed, the only reason Chauncy can now be persuaded to publish the manuscript, Satan declares, is that, being nearly eighty years of age, the venerable clergyman has reached his dotage:

> Twice fifteen suns are past, since C*******'s mind,
> Thro' doctrines deep, from common sense refin'd,
> I led, a nice, mysterious work to frame,
> With love of system, and with lust of fame.
>
> . . . .
>
> Now palsied age has dimm'd his mental sight,
> I'll rouse the sage his master's laws to fight,
> The injuries, long he render'd, to repair,
> And wipe from Heaven's fair book his faith and prayer.   (413–428)

This same *Dunciad* world, dominated by pride and self-delusion, extends also to the characterization of Satan as he recalls his continuing "war" against heaven since the time of Christ. By means of such pride, Dwight's Satan serves as an extended allusion to John Milton's Satan in *Paradise Lost*, endowed with the same diabolic perspective that allows him willfully to exaggerate his own power as a rival "god," while rationalizing his setbacks as merely the temporary victories of "yon haughty sky" (34). Indeed, characteristic of the Satan

of *The Triumph of Infidelity* is the projection of his own demonic motives onto
Christ himself, interpreting, for instance, the fall of the Roman Empire at the
hands of the Germanic tribes as Christ's counteroffensive against Satan's corruption of the early Roman church:

> Surpriz'd, enrag'd, to see his wiles outdone,
> His power all vanquish'd, and his kingdom gone,
> From the stern North, he hail'd my darling host,
> A whelming ocean, spread to every coast;
> My Goths, my Huns, the cultur'd world o'er-ran,
> And darkness buried all the pride of man.   (57–62)

At the same time, however, Dwight's Satan retains none of the high seriousness of his counterpart in *Paradise Lost*, precisely because this allusion is
indirect or "once-removed"—an allusion to Milton's Satan *through* an allusion
to Pope's own demonic character, the goddess Dulness of *The Dunciad*. Just
as Pope's own frequent allusions to Milton in *The Dunciad* had been meant
to emphasize the comic distance between the two works, this distance is assumed throughout *The Triumph of Infidelity*. Satan is rendered as a comic or
diminished demon who acts and speaks at times more like Dulness herself,
praising his favorite infidels and celebrating the absurdity of their systems in
the same manner as Pope's goddess dotes on Colley Cibber for his superior
dulness. Satan thus has an ironic side, and he has a sentimental side, seen, for
instance, when he recalls Henry St. John, first Viscount Bolingbroke, as one
of his particular favorites, a figure so "fir'd" with thoughts of fame and glory
that he even reminded Satan of himself. In particular, that Bolingbroke's reputation among Christians had been damaged in the late eighteenth century by
the posthumous publication of his deistic or skeptical writings leads Satan to
conclude sadly: "In views, in pride, in fate, conjoin'd with me, / Even Satan's
self shall drop a tear for thee" (215–216).[21]

21. There is also a jocular side to Satan's character, which emerges, for instance,
when he recalls that, in Origen's early version of the doctrine of universal salvation,
Satan, too, is expected finally to go to heaven. Here he responds ironically by reciting
to himself an incantation along the lines of "open sesame": "On cap, huzza! and thro'
the door go I!" (424).
    That Dwight chose to include Bolingbroke in his list of infidels may seem surpris-

At any such moment, the comic irony of Satan's assertions of godlike gran-
deur is meant to be registered, but nowhere is this made clearer than in
the final lines of the poem, as he watches the throng of dunces cheering for
Chauncy's promise of universal salvation. Just as in *Paradise Lost,* the great
narrative irony of *The Triumph of Infidelity* is that, at his moment of apparent
victory, Satan's triumph is suddenly cut short:

> From a dim cloud, the spirit eyed the scene,
> Now proud with triumph, and now vex'd with spleen,
> Mark'd all the throng, beheld them all his own,
> And to his cause NO FRIEND OF VIRTUE won:
> Surpriz'd, enrag'd, he wing'd his sooty flight;
> And hid beneath the pall of endless night.   (773–778)

If the "endless night" of the final line recalls the "universal darkness" at the
end of *The Dunciad,* the crucial difference here is that, unlike Pope's goddess,
Satan is foiled at his moment of apparent victory. The cause of Satan's rage
is that, upon seeing the crowd of sinners and infidels, he realizes that not a
single soul among them had ever been one of the *true* friends of virtue. The

---

ing for at least two reasons. First, Dwight's own writing, including *The Triumph of Infidelity,* draws on the same discourse of virtue, luxury, and corruption employed by
Bolingbroke in his fierce opposition to Sir Robert Walpole in *The Craftsman* (1726–1736)
and elsewhere. Second, Dwight's critique of Chauncy's rationalist theology draws on
passages from *An Essay on Man* and book 4 of *The Dunciad* that reveal Bolingbroke's
influence on Alexander Pope's theological and philosophical thought (see Chapter 2,
below). However, after the posthumous publication of *The Works of the Late Right Honorable Henry St. John, Lord Viscount Bolingbroke* (1754), Bolingbroke's reputation was
so greatly altered that many in Dwight's generation would remember him first and
foremost as an uncompromising critic of revealed religion. Thus, for instance, Bolingbroke is included in similar lists of infidel philosophers in works by Chauncy's friends
Jonathan Mayhew and Simon Howard. Mayhew warns against "a Collins, a Woolston
and a Tindal; . . . a Shaftesbury, a Morgan, a Chub and Bolingbroke" (*Christian Sobriety: Being Eight Sermons on Titus II.5* [Boston, 1763], 326); similarly, Howard antici-
pates Dwight's opposition of Christian philosophers such as Newton and Locke with
Voltaire, Hume, Shaftesbury, Tindal, Collins, Morgan, and Bolingbroke (*Christians No
Cause to Be Ashamed of Their Religion* [Boston, 1779], 26–33).

---

number of sinners Satan recognizes as his own is the same number as there would have been had he never employed Universalism or any other form of infidelity to tempt humankind. Satan is enraged, in short, because he has suddenly realized that, for all his efforts, he has never really been an agent in the historical process; the war he has been waging against God has all along been merely a figment of his deluded imagination. The irony of the poem's title is thus fully understood. Referring to the celebratory procession of a Roman *imperator*, Satan's "triumph" through the American countryside becomes a scene of humiliation, just as it had been in the case of every *imperator* who, according to ritual, had been accompanied in his chariot by a slave whose function was to repeat the phrase, "Remember that you are mortal."[22]

At a deeper level, the ironic distance separating Satan's delusional perspective from the narrative truth of the poem serves as an emblem for the distance between any such limited vision of reality and the perspective posited in Christian historiography as God's view of human existence. This conception of reality, standing as a divine corrective in *The Triumph of Infidelity* behind not only Satan's narrative of history but all of the various systems of infidelity, demonstrates most clearly the extent to which the poem's own historiography is grounded in an Augustinian understanding of the world. At the heart of Augustine's conception of human earthly alienation lay the fundamental distinction between two opposing temporal realities, corresponding in Augustine's own more familiar language to the *civitas terrena* and the *civitas Dei*. On the one hand, human beings perceive only a partial reality from inside the *saeculum*, or secular history; on the other, God alone is witness to a divine or absolute

---

22. Most readers of *The Triumph of Infidelity* have commented on the final lines by concluding, with Robert Arner, that the poem is "flawed by a perplexing conclusion" (Arner, "The Connecticut Wits," *American Literature, 1764-1789*, ed. Everett Emerson [Madison, Wis., 1977], 243). Silverman cites these lines as an example of the poem's "technical ineptitudes" (Silverman, *Timothy Dwight*, 86-87). Stillinger attempts to make sense of the paradox, arguing that these lines show Satan "vex'd with spleen" because he realizes that his victory over the soul of man has been a pushover, for there has been "no friend of virtue" among the entire human race; yet it is clear that the "throng" of sinners at the end of the poem does not refer to all people, but only those whom Satan witnesses celebrating Chauncy's doctrine (Stillinger, "Dwight's *Triumph of Infidelity*," *Studies in Bibliography*, XV [1962], 265-266).

reality from a perspective known as the *nunc-stans*, or eternal present. The point of such a distinction, from Augustine's time forward, was to insist upon the limitations of human understanding whenever one peered out from a moment inside history and attempted to make sense of the cosmos in anything resembling divine or eternal terms.[23]

Dwight's emphasis upon this distinction places him in an Augustan-poetic epistemological tradition that includes, for instance, Pope's *Essay on Man* (1733–1734); at the same time, it separates him from many of his Calvinist forbears and contemporaries. This older Augustinian historiography had long since been displaced as the predominant Protestant conception of history. By the seventeenth century, radical Protestants, in particular, had come to view the saeculum in millennial terms—seeing their own local religious struggles as imperative to the larger story of Christ's return—thus emphasizing a greater cosmic or absolute significance for secular history than had ever been allowed within a strict Augustinian position. Although Dwight would never disavow the older Puritan tendency to interpret historical events according to a millennial eschatology, his own reminders of this Augustinian historiography have the simultaneous effect of exposing the vanity of investing too great an importance in mere human events and attainments. The distance between the nunc-stans and the saeculum thus serves as a means of understanding the role of God within the cyclical theory of history assumed in classical republicanism. In this story of the rise and fall of empires, described everywhere in eighteenth-century political theory, even the greatest achievements of civilization ultimately collapse under the weight of their own corruption, from ancient Greece to Rome to modern Europe.

By the time Dwight began to compose *The Triumph of Infidelity*, his commitment to a vision of the world that acknowledges the illusory tendency of a misguided millennialism had distanced him from his earlier poetry, particularly *America; or, A Poem on the Settlement of the British Colonies* and the popular hymn "Columbia," written while he was a chaplain in the Continental army. The theme of these poems, the millennial hope of America's rising glory—borne of a profound sense of uncertainty over whether the American Revolution would succeed—would be immediately discarded at the moment

23. J. G. A. Pocock, *The Machiavellian Moment: Florentine Political Thought and the Atlantic Republican Tradition* (Princeton, N.J., 1975), 31–48.

victory was secured. This change is clearly evident in *A Sermon, Preached at Northampton,* delivered on the occasion of the British surrender at Yorktown. Without even pausing to celebrate America's newly secured independence, Dwight places the victory inside a narrative of modern history that emphasizes the reasons the Revolution was necessary in the first place. Britain, he asserts, had long been on a steady course toward moral corruption that had begun in the seventeenth century with the introduction of the Hobbesian, and later Mandevillian, assertion that true virtue is a mere myth and self-interest "the only possible spring, from whence the actions of intelligent beings can proceed." This moral system, he adds, had not only been articulated by a few idle philosophers; it had been practiced in the early eighteenth century by the members of the British Parliament, proving "the famous political dogma, of Sir Robert Walpole—that every man has his price—or in terms more explicit, that every man living, however just, however excellent, if his personal interest be suitably addressed, will, like Ahab, *sell himself to work wickedness.*"[24]

The story Dwight tells here, particularly his invocation of the name of Sir Robert Walpole, has become familiar to students of eighteenth-century British and American history. It constitutes the narrative of history told from the perspective of Country ideology, the synthesis of classical republican and Florentine political thought recovered by Bernard Bailyn, Gordon Wood, and others as the moral discourse of American independence. This discourse was shared by opposition politicians and Augustan poets who had fought to unmask Walpole and his "Robinocracy" as agents of social and political collapse. It was also the language employed a few generations later by American patriots who had come to envision the court of George III in largely the same terms, and who united behind the conviction that the colonies' only hope would be to cut themselves off from the corrupt British empire before its inevitable downfall.[25]

24. Timothy Dwight, *A Sermon, Preached at Northampton . . . Occasioned by the Capture of the British Army, under the Command of Earl Cornwallis* (Hartford, Conn., 1781), 14, 17.

25. Bernard Bailyn, *The Ideological Origins of the American Revolution* (Cambridge, Mass., 1967), chaps. 2, 3; Gordon S. Wood, *The Creation of the American Republic, 1776–1787* (Chapel Hill, N.C., 1969), chaps. 1, 2. See also, for example, Lance Banning, *The Jeffersonian Persuasion: Evolution of a Party Ideology* (Ithaca, N.Y., 1978), chap. 2; Ban-

Against this backdrop, the crucial point of *A Sermon, Preached at Northampton* and Dwight's subsequent writings from the 1780s, then, is that the real war for the preservation of a virtuous Republic—within which the Revolutionary War had constituted only one part—was far from over. Yet, as the decade continued and Dwight witnessed the financial and legal crises that brought states to the brink of military conflict over paper money and public debt and claims to western territories (as well as the foreclosures that led to Shays's Rebellion so close to his birthplace in Northampton), he became increasingly fearful that this larger struggle might be lost within only a few years of achieving independence. Dwight thus came to locate in the concept of the nunc-stans a specific moral purpose, to cause people to reflect upon such crises, not merely as weaknesses of policy—the need to discard the Articles of Confederation in favor of a stronger federal government, for instance—but as the result of moral complacency and self-interest that had taken hold in America after the war.

Dwight gets at this perspective in particular in a short newspaper article entitled "An Essay on the Judgment of History concerning America," published a year before *The Triumph of Infidelity*, in 1787. Imagining the history of the American Republic written decades in the future, Dwight describes the success of the Revolution as the direct result of "a spirit of union and virtuous exertion." He adds, however, that, within only a few years of winning independence, this spirit had given way to the selfish tendencies caused by "those freaks of human nature which are very common, though unaccountable." And, as he raises the issue of the fearful uncertainty of the future of the Republic, his underlying point is that only by imagining the events of the present from a distant perspective can one clearly comprehend the reality, and the probable result, of such a loss of moral fortitude:

> The danger over and past, and the little selfish passions, with all their baleful influence, rushed in upon them at once. . . . From hence arose amongst themselves (for they had no foreign controul) disunited councils and opposing measures, ingratitude to their benefactors, injustice, cruelty and op-

ning, "Jefferson Ideology Revisited: Liberal and Classical Ideas in the New American Republic," *William and Mary Quarterly*, 3d Ser., XLIII (1986), 3–19; Nathan O. Hatch, *The Sacred Cause of Liberty: Republican Thought and the Millennium in Revolutionary New England* (New Haven, Conn., 1977), chap. 2.

pression, contempt of government and laws human and divine, disaffections, distrust and jealousy, with a numberless train of follies and vices, and, at length the flames of a civil war were kindled and ——— What follows let future historians record. What they record depends on ourselves.[26]

Despite this image of impending civil war, the essay nevertheless holds out hope that, by looking past the limitations of present and selfish interests, Americans might stave off the early collapse of their own Republic. The same sense of hope arising from a recognition of "follies and vices," importantly, would stand behind the more general reassertion of an Augustan satiric moment in American poetry during the middle and late 1780s. More specifically, it is precisely the Augustan-poetic emphasis upon what William C. Dowling calls "poetry as ideological unmasking"—the capacity of poems to expose the false systems of value propelling a society unwittingly downward—that inspired the shared sense among Dwight and the other poets collectively known as the Connecticut Wits that they represented the direct heirs to the literary Augustans. This ideological function of poetry is evident, for example, in *The Anarchiad,* the anonymous collaboration of Dwight's fellow Wits John Trumbull, David Humphreys, and Joel Barlow. As the title suggests, this poem self-consciously employs the same satiric weapons used by Pope and others against Walpole's government to unmask the weaknesses of the Confederation government in similar terms, as chiefly the effects of greed and narrow self-interest: "Of bankrupt faith, annihilated laws— / Of selfish systems, jealous, local schemes."[27]

Dwight makes the same point in the middle of *The Triumph of Infidelity* in an extended section in which he takes over the narration to describe in satiric detail the various "moral dunces" who gather to hear Chauncy proclaim that "Hell is no more, or no more to be fear'd" (654). This section, which com-

26. Timothy Dwight, "An Essay on the Judgment of History concerning America," *New-Haven Gazette, and the Connecticut Magazine,* Apr. 12, 1787.

27. David Humphreys et al., *The Anarchiad: A New England Poem* (1786–1787), ed. Luther G. Riggs (Gainesville, Fla., 1967), 58. For more on the way in which American satire of the 1780s provided a moral interpretation of political and economic crises, see Kenneth Silverman, *A Cultural History of the American Revolution: Painting, Music, Literature, and the Theatre in the Colonies and the United States from the Treaty of Paris to the Inauguration of George Washington, 1763–1789* (New York, 1976), 504–519.

prises a virtual catalog of rogues and the vices they embrace, serves also as a crucial reminder that, beneath the comparatively innocuous folly of Satan and his failed scheme to win the souls of Americans, lies a more serious social and political threat. Among this throng of villains are a number of characters whose particular vices could directly jeopardize the future of the Republic: a corrupt member of Congress who calls himself "the Devil's Man of Ross" (alluding to Pope's own great symbol of virtue in the *Epistle to Allen Lord Bathurst* [1733]), whose office serves merely to support a life of profligacy at the expense of his constituents (486); a paid perjurer who, upon realizing that all is forgiven, "sold his friend, and country, for a song" (756); a wealthy creditor who sees no reason to stop abusing the deflated value of federal stock certificates, even if it means impoverishing the wives and children of soldiers killed during the Revolution: "'In vain,' he cried, 'their woes let orphans tell; / In vain let widows weep; there is no hell'" (499–500).

The political function of such passages in *The Triumph of Infidelity* is thus to rouse the public from a tendency to be drawn to those illusory visions of self-satisfaction and moral ease that, beyond encouraging merely private sins or vices, actually constitute a public crisis. At the same time, this belief is simultaneously informed by the general conclusion that the earlier Augustan satirists had been unsuccessful in their attempt to stem the tide of corruption in Britain. This conclusion, moreover, is reached not merely by way of the countless American pamphlets assailing the "Luxury" and "Corruption" of British society but from the earlier eighteenth-century English works on which such pamphlets had drawn. In the case of Dwight and other Connecticut poets such as Trumbull and Humphreys, it had been reached by way of their own extensive reading of Augustan and post-Augustan verse as undergraduates. This reading collectively provided a narrative within which satire — invoked as a necessary moral corrective for a society grown immune to the moral influences of institutions such as religion — had become wholly ineffectual. Pope, for instance, tells this story in his later works, such as the *Epilogue to the Satires*, his symbolic farewell to the *Imitations of Horace* in which he declares satire to have become a futile moral gesture. Although he had always presented satire as the last hope for a society in which the ordinary institutions for regulating morality had failed — "Safe from the Bar, the Pulpit, and the Throne, / Yet touch'd and sham'd by *Ridicule* alone" — he had also foreseen a new moral logic emerging, one in which vice and apathy were synonymous with social refinement, and in which "Not to be corrupted is the Shame."[28]

The conclusion to this story would not be written until Dwight's own time, in the body of poetry Dowling has called "elegiac Augustanism," which includes such well-known works as Oliver Goldsmith's *Deserted Village* (1770) and *The Task* by William Cowper. In the latter, for instance, published only three years before *The Triumph of Infidelity*, Dwight's generation would find confirmation of their own sense of the extent of British corruption, recognizing Cowper's lament not merely for the general moral decline of his society but for the even more disheartening conclusion that satire could no longer intervene: "Yet what can satire, whether grave or gay? / . . . What vice has it subdued? whose heart reclaim'd / By riguour, or whom laughed into reform? / Alas! Leviathan is not so tamed." Against the background of this narrative, in turn, the new United States occupies an earlier position in the same historical process. On the one hand, by gaining their independence the American colonies had protected their own comparative virtue and, with it, an environment in which satire could still bring about moral reform; on the other, by remaining subject to the inexorable forces of history, they would continue to be threatened by this same tendency toward corruption.[29]

---

28. Alexander Pope, *Epilogue to the Satires* (1738), in John Butt, ed., *The Poems of Alexander Pope: A One-Volume Edition of the Twickenham Text with Selected Annotations* (New Haven, Conn., 1963), 694, 702. Pope's explanation of his "farewell to satire" is given in the following footnote at the end of *Epilogue to the Satires*: "This was the last poem of the kind printed by our author, with a resolution to publish no more; but to enter thus, in the most plain and solemn manner he could, a sort of PROTEST against that insuperable corruption and depravity of manners, which he had been so unhappy as to live to see. Could he have hoped to have amended any, he had continued those attacks; but bad men were grown so shameless and so powerful, that Ridicule was become as unsafe as it was ineffectual" (703).

29. William Cowper, *The Task* (1785), in John D. Baird and Charles Ryskamp, eds., *The Poems of William Cowper*, 3 vols. (Oxford, 1980), II, 147. Dwight's sense of the failure of satire, in fact, is taken directly from his reading of *The Task*, as he makes clear in a footnote in *Greenfield Hill* (1794), which he was also writing during the period he published *The Triumph of Infidelity*. Dwight uses Cowper to support his own poem's contrast of a Europe that has all but collapsed under its own corruption and an America

In postwar New England, this tendency toward corruption would be given concrete form in the idea of "fashion," a category that, like "luxury," articulated the growing concern among Americans that, even after liberation from British political control, a more subtle form of subjection remained in the lingering devotion to the manners and fashions of European society. This concern is seen everywhere in public discourse during these years, from the scorn directed at the simple American farmer who affects the dress and manners of the European elite, parading around his rural village in the styles of fops and dancing masters, to the more general rhetoric championing American homespun over foreign textiles as simultaneously symbolic of moral and economic independence.[30] Dwight addresses this specific concern over European fashion at several moments in *The Triumph of Infidelity*, but he also makes a crucial point of extending the idea of fashion beyond the sphere of dress and manners, such that infidelity is presented as a particularly corrupting form of European fashion. Indeed, in Satan's gleeful narration, he personifies Fashion as a version of the goddess Dulness, the "all-subduing" power who has led even some of the most learned in Europe continually to alter their beliefs in an ever fluctuating atmosphere of philosophical speculation: "From courts to cottages, her sovereign sway, / With force resistless, bade the world obey. / She molded faith, and science, with a nod; / Now there was not, and now there was, a God" (139–142).

Even as *The Triumph of Infidelity* acknowledges the failure of deism, skepticism, and other fashionable doctrines of the European Enlightenment to take hold in America, fashion remains a constant danger in the important sense

---

in which public virtue might still be preserved: "*The Task*, one of the most sensible and valuable performances, in the English language, is alone a sufficient justification of no small part of what is here declared" (William J. McTaggart and William K. Bottorff, eds., *The Major Poems of Timothy Dwight, 1752–1817, with a Dissertation on the History, Eloquence, and Poetry of the Bible* [Gainesville, Fla., 1969], 528).

30. The problem of fashion was identified with more immediate economic problems during the hard-money crisis of the mid-1780s, leading to the proposal of sumptuary laws in Connecticut and the formation of "Ladies' Oeconomical Associations," which emphasized the practical and moral benefits of forswearing foreign textiles for American homespun; see, for example, *New-Haven Gazette, and the Connecticut Magazine*, Oct. 12, Nov. 16, 1786.

that it sustains the moral logic of cosmopolitanism—which, as had already been emphasized in a number of English Augustan satires, is capable of transforming Christianity. Dwight makes this point explicitly in the portrait of the particular clergyman whom Dwight calls the Smooth Divine, which is not only the longest and most detailed portrait of all the moral dunces in the poem but one that would be extracted and republished in a number of literary anthologies.[31] The Smooth Divine is so accustomed to preaching to wealthy and self-consciously sophisticated parishioners that, to ensure his own place in polite society, he no longer preaches any unpopular moral or religious truths. Instead, he spends his time visiting and gossiping and in his sermons avoids even the most basic Christian doctrines for fear of upsetting his congregation:

> There smil'd the Smooth Divine, unus'd to wound
> The sinner's heart, with hell's alarming sound.
> No terrors on his gentle tongue attend;
> No grating truths the nicest ear offend.
> That strange new-birth, that methodistic grace,
> Nor in his heart, nor sermons, found a place.
> Plato's fine tales he clumsily retold,
> Trite, fireside, moral seesaws, dull as old;
> His Christ, and Bible, plac'd at good remove,
> Guilt hell-deserving, and forgiving love.   (533–542)

31. The Smooth Divine passage was reprinted in the twentieth century in Frederick C. Prescott and John H. Nelson, eds., *Prose and Poetry of the Revolution; the Establishment of the Nation, 1765–1789* (1925; reprint, Port Washington, N.Y., 1969); Norman Foerster, ed., *American Poetry and Prose* (Boston, 1947); and Jay B. Hubbell, ed., *American Life in Literature*, rev. ed., 2 vols. (New York, 1949). Stillinger suggests that these reprints as well as the title entry "The Smooth Divine" (1788), in Chester Noyes Greenough and Joseph Milton French, *A Bibliography of the Theophrastan Character in English with Several Portrait Characters* (Cambridge, Mass., 1947), may indicate the existence of an earlier reprint of the extract in an eighteenth- or nineteenth-century periodical (Stillinger, "Dwight's *Triumph of Infidelity*," *Studies in Bibliography*, XV [1962], 260). A larger passage that includes the portrait of the Smooth Divine as well as other figures was excerpted under the title "The Gathering," in Jane Donahue Eberwien, ed., *Early American Poetry: Selections from Bradstreet, Taylor, Dwight, Freneau, and Bryant* (Madison, Wis., 1978).

As with a number of the figures satirized, the Smooth Divine passage has tended to be read as Dwight's own local attack against a particular New England clergyman whom he opposed on doctrinal grounds. Yet Dwight is never more the self-conscious heir to English Augustanism than here, and the Smooth Divine is a version of precisely the type of clergyman that poets like Pope and Edward Young had satirized decades before. To be sure, this divine is a Latitudinarian not unlike the group of Arminians to which Chauncy himself had always belonged, whose theology had long since discarded its Calvinist emphasis upon free grace ("That strange new-birth") in favor of "Plato's fine tales," the liberal Protestantism of Archbishop Tillotson, Samuel Clarke, and the earlier Cambridge Platonists. But he also represents what had been identified in Augustan poetry as the religion of the wealthiest and most cosmopolitan Britons who had shunned the older language of grace as a way to distance themselves from the "methodistic" Christianity of the lower orders.

More particularly, the religion of the Smooth Divine is the religion practiced by the worshipers described in Pope's *Epistle to Burlington*. These worshipers attend services in the chapel at Timon's mansion, itself an emblem of luxury and extravagance that inspires, not religious reflection, but "all the Pride of Pray'r" as well as the comforting notion that their own version of Christianity is wholly harmonious with their more obvious devotion to lives of physical and moral ease: "To rest, the Cushion and soft Dean invite, / Who never mentions Hell to ears polite." [32] For Pope, such self-flattery represents the particular sin of the wealthy, whose sense of self-importance has made them unwilling to hear anything that challenges the belief in their own moral and spiritual propriety. Thus, when Dwight revives this argument in reference to the Smooth Divine, he raises the greater irony that, in the wake of independence—when most Americans believe they have remained untainted by European corruption—those whose primary role is to speak out on issues of morality, in exchange for a parasitic enjoyment of their standard of living, merely flatter those who have been most corrupted by fashion: "He bow'd, talk'd politics, learn'd manners mild; / Most meekly questioned, and most smoothly smil'd; / At rich men's jests laugh'd loud; their stories prais'd, / Their wives' new patterns gaz'd, and gaz'd, and gaz'd" (553–556).

32. Alexander Pope, *Epistle to Richard Boyle, Earl of Burlington* (1731), in Butt, ed., *Poems*, 593.

At the same time, the satire of the Smooth Divine draws upon a similar passage from Edward Young's *Love of Fame*, and this allusion makes a crucial additional point within the larger argument of *The Triumph of Infidelity*. Like Pope, Young had satirized the religion of the wealthy, charging that church services had become little more than an extension of their busy social life, where well-dressed ladies go to shine on the one day dances are not held. Young's satire is taken one step further, however, suggesting that this new form of religion has surpassed mere hypocrisy. The doctrine that the upper classes are most unwilling to hear—that Christian redemption requires a profound change of heart brought on by God's grace and accompanied by intense spiritual labor—is not merely avoided but radically redefined. What Young argues, in short, is that the logical conclusion of the religion of the very rich is a form of Universalism:

> Atheists are few; most nymphs a Godhead own,
> And nothing but His attributes dethrone.
>
> . . . .
>
> Shall pleasures of a short duration chain
> A *lady's* soul in everlasting pain?
> Will the great Author us poor worms destroy
> For now and then a *sip* of transient joy?
> No; He's for ever in a smiling mood;
> He's like themselves; or how could He be good? [33]

In specific terms, this is Universalism as it had emerged in Young's time in the doctrinal views attributed to Tillotson and Thomas Burnet—the assertion that God's infinite benevolence precludes the possibility of eternal damnation. In a crucial sense, however, it is an expression of the more general

33. Young, *Love of Fame*, in Doran, ed. *Complete Works*, I, 400. The connection between this speech and the sentiments of Dwight's Smooth Divine might in fact have been suggested to Dwight by an erroneous citation in Joseph Warton's *Essay on the Genius and Writings of Pope*, 4th ed., 2 vols. (London, 1782) (Dwight had likely read the *Essay* by the time he wrote *The Triumph of Infidelity*, because it is mentioned in a footnote in *Greenfield Hill*). When Warton quotes this passage, he attributes it, not to Young's fashionable belle, but to "a certain smooth, and supple, and inoffensive Divine" (I, 257).

tendency of the upper classes to reject a belief in any God who could ever punish *themselves*. Such pride, Young had suggested, issues from the curious way in which the trappings of luxury are transformed into something meaningful even in cosmic or theological terms. Dwight's additional point in *The Triumph of Infidelity* is that, if this pride issues first from the wealthy, it eventually trickles down to those who aspire to a similar state of self-importance. Thus, when he presents this same logic in an American context, it is in the character of "Demas," a version of the familiar figure from English Augustan poetry who becomes corrupted by a grand tour of Europe—in particular, the mindless youths from book 4 of *The Dunciad* who "saunter'd Europe round, / And gather'd ev'ry Vice on Christian ground."[34] Once virtuous and modest, Demas is "borne beyond the Atlantic ferry" to witness firsthand the luxuries of European society—mansions and coaches, "great men" and "Great ladies" (609–612)—and, from this exposure, he reaches the identical conclusion of Young's genteel lady:

> Chameleon like, he lost his former hue,
> And, mid such great men, grew a great man too;
> Enter'd the round of silly, vain parade;
> His hair he powder'd, and his bow he made.
> "Shall powder'd heads," he cried, "be sent to hell?
> Shall men in vain in such fine houses dwell?"   (615–620)

Such allusions mark the means by which the literary, theological, and political contexts of *The Triumph of Infidelity* ultimately converge into a single symbolic context for understanding the significance of the Universalist controversy. The satires of Pope and Young, drawing on the language of luxury as it had been used to understand the creation and uses of wealth in the emerging capitalist marketplace, had provided Dwight and others in post-Revolutionary America with an immediate critique of the aspirations of certain wealthy Americans to imitate the intellectual as well as the material fashions of Europe. Insofar as such fashions included religious beliefs, moreover, the same satiric sources would allow for an interpretation of Universalism not simply as an example of the ways in which Americans were turning away from the values of virtue and moderation that had in large part inspired the

---

34. Pope, *The Dunciad* (1728), in Butt, ed., *Poems*, 782.

Revolution but as a modern embodiment of the vanity and self-flattery that had brought about the general corruption of eighteenth-century Britain. In the light of Young's *Love of Fame*, Chauncy's publication of *The Mystery Hid* thus appears as a manifestation of the religion of the idle rich, an inability to imagine a God who could punish *themselves*, raised to the level of systematic theology.

This point, too, is made by way of direct allusion at the moment in *The Triumph of Infidelity* when Chauncy appeals to the theological sources of his own proof of universal salvation, explaining that "First Origen, then Tillotson, then I / Learn'd their profoundest cunning to descry, / And shew'd this truth, tho' nicely cover'd o'er, / That hell's broad path leads round to heaven's door" (667–670). The explanation of theological sources here corresponds most immediately to the actual Chauncy, who, in the preface to the shorter pamphlet *Salvation for All Men,* deflects the notion that Universalism is a novelty by mentioning Origen specifically as an ancient source of the doctrine. At the same time, however, Chauncy is also betraying a more recent cultural source of Universalism, for he echoes almost directly the language of Young's lady. "Dear Tillotson!" she proclaims, "be sure, the best of men; / Nor thought he more, than thought great Origen."[35]

If this passage from Young's *Love of Fame* would allow Dwight to glimpse Universalism as a general moral or social threat going back to Augustan England, Cowper's use of the same passage in *The Task* would provide Dwight with a means of locating Chauncy's theology within the larger Enlightenment movement that included deism, skepticism, and the other systems satirized in the poem as infidelity. Cowper had quoted the speech by Young's wealthy lady in a footnote to a much more somber passage in *The Task* where he attempts to describe the mental process by which one ultimately comes to profess deism. Such a process, he explains, is characterized by a painful recognition of the vanity of earthly life and followed by a desperate attempt to avoid this truth. Even one with the best moral intentions is dragged by human nature downward "in the fathomless abyss / Of folly, plunging in pursuit of death." Motivated merely by a desire for peace, this person turns first to Christianity but finds the struggle for moral and spiritual reform impeded by too many instances of failure. Finally, "Reason now / Takes part with Appetite, and pleads

35. Young, *Love of Fame,* in Doran, ed., *Complete Works,* I, 400.

---

the cause, / Perversely, which of late she so condemn'd," leading the desperate soul to follow, in earnest, the same moral logic as Young had presented in
satiric terms, rationalizing moral weakness as something actually ordained by
God:

> Hath God indeed giv'n appetites to man,
> And stored the earth so plenteously with means
> To gratify the hunger of his wish,
> And doth he reprobate and will he damn
> The use of his own bounty? making first
> So frail a kind, and then enacting laws
> So strict, that less than perfect must despair?
> Falsehood! which whoso but suspects of truth,
> Dishonours God, and makes a slave of man.[36]

This same logic is presented in comedic or satiric terms in *The Triumph of
Infidelity* where, in an extended passage near the end of the poem, Chauncy
addresses the crowd gathered around him and presents his proof of universal
salvation. No longer deluded into believing the truth of his doctrine, Chauncy
now accepts his favored place in Satan's chariot, and, most closely resembling Pope's "loyal" dunces, he acknowledges that, despite his own elaborate
method of scriptural interpretation, the only necessary proof of the doctrine
is a method of reasoning in which cosmological truth is determined merely
by its appeal to human desire. Thus, he declares that the "ruling principle" of
his own theology is "The love of sweet security in sin: / Beneath whose power
all pleasing falsehoods, blind / And steal, with soft conviction, on the mind"
(686–688). In doing so, Chauncy simultaneously affirms his own devotion to
Dulness, personifying this ruling principle as an embodiment of Pope's goddess and recalling specifically the beginning of *The Dunciad*, book 4, in which
Dulness mounts her throne while beneath her Science and Logic and Morality
are bound in chains:

> . . . she mounts th' Eternal Throne,
> And makes the universe around her own,
> Decides the rights of Godhead with her nod,

36. Cowper, *The Task*, in Baird and Ryskamp, eds., *Poems*, II, 226–227.

And wields for Him dominion's mighty rod.
Whate'er He ought, or ought not, she descries,
Beholds all infinite relations rise,
Th' immense of time and space surveys serene,
And tells whate'er the Bible ought to mean;
Whate'er she wishes, sees Him bound to do,
Else is His hand unjust, His word untrue.   (691–700)

This is Universalism less as a specific theological doctrine than as a means
by which doctrines are determined, the same attempt to comprehend the
cosmos from the perspective of mere human reason that Pope had deemed
"Man's pride and dulness" in *An Essay on Man*. Yet the particular image of
human pride as a force so powerful that it pulls God from his throne and
assumes the rod of his dominion is behind Dwight's own larger conception
of infidelity, both in *The Triumph of Infidelity* and in his later writings, as a
virtual displacement of an omniscient God with a false deity of human self-
worship. In such cases as Universalism or even deism, this notion of infidelity-
as-idolatry is not immediately evident, because "God" or "Christ" is still the
ostensible object of devotion. Dwight will maintain, however, that such objects exist only as empty symbols of authority in a radically secular vision in
which the assurance of human happiness is the ultimate teleology and the
desire for moral comfort the ultimate truth. Thus, we recognize in this passage the last important allusion to Young's *Love of Fame*, serving as Dwight's
reminder that modern infidelity is merely a variation on the same delusion
recognized decades earlier in the Latitudinarians' discomfort with anything
resembling Godly retribution toward sinners: "Devoutly, thus, Jehovah they
depose, / The pure, the just! and set up, in his stead, / A deity that's perfectly
well-bred."[37]

The essence of what Dwight will call infidelity thus emerges, not as the act
of dispensing with God or religion, but as worshiping in the place of God some
mirror of the human will. Dwight will continue to insist upon this ideological tendency in his later writings even as the Universalist controversy begins
to give way to other, more pressing, religious and political concerns. If the

37. Pope, *Essay on Man*, in Butt, ed., *Poems*, 506; Young, *Love of Fame*, in Doran, ed.,
Complete Works, I, 400.

allusions to *The Dunciad* and *Love of Fame* suggest that Chauncy's system is too transparent a fulfillment of human desire to be taken seriously as a legitimate threat to religion, the underlying point even in *The Triumph of Infidelity* is that its satire is engaged only incidentally with Chauncy and Universalism and more crucially with the Pelagian assumptions on which Chauncy's system depends. To the extent that these assumptions constitute the real subject of the poem, its argument could thus be applied to any of the visions of certain human transcendence that had since appeared in such guises as Enlightenment rationalism or progressivism. The same proof of universal redemption illustrated in one context by scriptural interpretation might elsewhere be offered by way of an idealized vision of nature or reason or man, as in the deism of Paine or in any of the later eighteenth-century manifestations of Shaftesburian benevolism or a universal moral sense. Similarly, the salvation promised by Universalism in religious terms might also be imagined as a future of moral or social perfectibility within history, as in the secular progressivism of Godwin and Condorcet.

Such utopian visions as these, arising in America at the height of the French Revolutionary enthusiasm, will represent for Dwight the "salvation of all men" transposed into somewhat different terms. Yet, when Dwight asserts that Chauncy and such later Universalists as William Pitt Smith and Hosea Ballou are at the deepest level kindred spirits with radical deists and atheists like Paine and Condorcet, he is also addressing the extent to which a similar utopian vision had always been implicit in Universalism. Universalism promised not merely that all men would be saved but that this very revelation would commence a period of moral progress and perfectibility within the sphere of secular time. As implied in the title of *The Mystery Hid from Ages and Generations,* universal salvation constitutes the revelation of the last great Christian mystery, and the ultimate effect of its revelation will be nothing less than the collective recognition by human beings that Providence, distorted for centuries by myths of human alienation and depravity, is indeed rational and beneficent and that sin and vice are wholly inconsistent with human happiness. Thus would Universalism promise salvation, not merely in a future state beyond the grave but at a future moment inside history itself.

This teleology of purely secular redemption will characterize the disparate systems of infidel philosophy against which Dwight will continue to wage ideological warfare. Importantly, the status of this teleology as infidelity will depend on the way it is understood implicitly to collapse the distinction between the secular or timebound sphere of human existence and the divine or nunc-stans reality lying outside its limits. At the same time, precisely because such visions retain an image of human transcendence even in their most secular forms, Dwight will continue to conceive of infidel philosophy as, in its own way, essentially religious. Dwight will thus increasingly draw upon the Enlightenment strategy of unmasking superstition as a means of combatting various manifestations of Enlightenment thought itself. Such systems, he will assert, constitute none other than misguided versions of religious thought in which the object of devotion is man, reconceived in religious terms.

Dwight's use of this strategy, too, originates in *The Triumph of Infidelity* in the satire of the figure Dwight simply calls the Infidel of Modern Breed. Although this man is open and unabashed about his infidelity — "Alike no Deist, and no Christian, he; / But from all principle, all virtue, free" (567-568) — he is nevertheless presented as a religious believer. In specific terms, the belief system of the Infidel of Modern Breed will most closely approximate the materialism of Holbach and La Mettrie and their conception of a bare material universe without a creator, in which "soul" is merely an empty name for the elaborate workings of the material body, *l'homme machine.* At the same time, this material self, Dwight suggests — "That work more nice than Rittenhouse can plan" (583) — constitutes an object of religious devotion in itself. This modern form of infidelity is understood as, paradoxically, a revival of the ancient veneration of material embodiments of divinity, a substitution of the physical self for "Dagon," the Old Testament god of the Philistines. The modern infidel understands himself as "Made, not to know, or love, the all-beauteous mind; / Or wing thro' heaven his path to bliss refin'd: / But his dear self, choice Dagon! to adore" (575-577).

The satire of the Infidel of Modern Breed constitutes Dwight's early glimpse of the hidden theological element that is recognizable today as one of the great paradoxes of eighteenth-century materialism. The otherwise bare atomic universe of Holbach's *System of Nature* is still governed by a quasi-religious ideal of natural providence, and La Mettrie's notion of l'homme machine implies a utopian future in which such human machines and the societies they make up could be perfected by scientific and intellectual advancement. Dwight's own response to this theology, beginning in *The Triumph of Infidelity* and carried on in *Theology; Explained and Defended, in a Series of Sermons, Travels in New*

England and New York, and *The Nature, and Danger, of Infidel Philosophy*, will be unmistakably and witheringly Augustan, a constant reminder that what is being deified in the materialist theology of man is the very antithesis of divinity, a brute creature whose ultimate end, as Dwight puts it, is to become the final resting place for other brute creatures: "Man, that illustrious brute of noblest shape, / A swine unbristled, and untail'd ape: / To couple, eat, and die—his glorious doom— / The oyster's church-yard, and the capon's tomb" (585–588).

Such a devotion to man as the transcendent center of a world of mere matter was indeed a long way from Chauncy's agreeable belief in a benevolent God who grants universal salvation. This distance, too, is acknowledged in *The Triumph of Infidelity*, which allows for the possibility that this implicit progress of infidelity might be prevented or forestalled. Even at the end of the poem, when Chauncy finishes his speech and is answered by "a shout, from all the throng" (735)—a moment at which "Conscience . . . ceas'd her stings to rear, / And joy excessive whelm'd each rising fear" (737–738)—there is also a reminder that even those drawn to Chauncy's illusory promises of future happiness are simultaneously pulled by an opposing moral force. The celebration is soon halted by the ever persistent power of the conscience to cause even this throng of rogues to reflect a moment, to cut through the veils of self-delusion and force "the soul to doubt the luscious lie" (744). This moment of doubt is also fleeting, however, and the crowd is once again charmed by "sophistic wishes" (745) into a renewed sense of moral dulness—but not before the point has been made that will sustain Dwight's continued campaign against infidelity: even as human beings are naturally drawn to such flattering systems, they retain a capacity to peer into their hearts and clearly comprehend, if only momentarily, the moral truths otherwise obscured by the dulness of human pride.

In turn, the Dwight of the *Theology* will present in positive terms the same notion of conscience as the key to his own system of spiritual and moral growth. Precisely by attending to the stings of conscience in the course of spiritual self-examination, Dwight will argue, does one prepare to receive grace. The struggles against the tendency to reach easy or flattering conclusions leads ultimately to a recognition of the reality of one's own moral condition, to a glimpse of oneself from the perspective of the nunc-stans. Dwight will thus be carrying on in his system of theology the implicit moral purpose of satire, to inspire those often painful moments of moral clarity that bring about a profound change of heart. His insistence upon the need to preserve this satiric element of theology will lie at the heart of his continued defense of orthodox Protestantism against those systems that, like Chauncy's, would present a more "pleasing" vision of God and man as the alternative to the dread and despair of Calvinism.

The same satiric element, importantly, stands behind Dwight's political critique of the wave of radical republicanism carrying America toward the politics of Paine's *Rights of Man* (1791–1792), Barlow's *Conspiracy of Kings* (1792), and the declarations of the French National Convention. In the enthusiasm over the American and French Revolutions as singularly regenerative events, bringing about a social and political environment within which a vision of global perfectibility suddenly appears a reasonable possibility, Dwight would recognize a version of the same promise of universal transcendence now in the guise of political philosophy. Yet, even as Dwight would continue to attack such promises in the name of a political perspective grounded in the Augustinian view, a large-scale conversion to the opposing myth of eighteenth-century Pelagianism was already under way.

CHAPTER 2

The Salvation of All Men

Shortly before his death in 1787, the eighty-one-year-old Charles Chauncy sat for what he no doubt knew would be his final portrait. In it, he holds a copy of *The Mystery Hid from Ages and Generations*, announcing to posterity that, however hesitant he had once been about making his belief in universal salvation publicly known, he had finally come to accept his role as the leader of the Universalist camp within the Congregational Church. This decision may perhaps surprise those who remember Chauncy mainly for such earlier works as *Seasonable Thoughts on the State of Religion in New-England*, when, as Jonathan Edwards's principal antagonist in the revivalist controversy occasioned by the Great Awakening, he announced himself as an outspoken enemy of "enthusiasm" and the sober voice of what he called "the Good Old Way." Yet to examine his last three published works is to understand precisely what the portrait of Chauncy seems to symbolize, that Universalism represented the combination of the theological system he had been working out since the 1750s.[1] The challenge for the older Chauncy was thus to present universal salvation as still consistent with the New England theological tradition he had always represented. To do this would mean to distinguish his own version of the doctrine both from the Universalism associated with itinerant preachers, such as John Murray and Caleb Rich, and from the idea of a universal future state as theorized by many deists.

---

1. Charles Chauncy, *Seasonable Thoughts on the State of Religion in New-England, a Treatise in Five Parts* (Boston, 1743), 337. For a study of the symbolic value of Chauncy's portraits, see Norman B. Gibbs and Lee W. Gibbs, "Charles Chauncy: A Theology in Two Portraits," *Harvard Theological Review*, LXXXIII (1990), 259–270.

Immediately after publishing *The Mystery Hid*, Chauncy revived two other works that he had written thirty years earlier and left to lie dormant, *The Benevolence of the Deity* and *Five Dissertations on the Scripture Account of the Fall*. The three treatises together form a comprehensive theology that begins with a demonstration of the harmonious coexistence of moral evil with a wholly benevolent God, moves to a representation of human beings as imperfect but singularly important within God's plan, and concludes with the great proof of God's mercy and beneficence, the certainty of salvation for all men. Evident in each of these works is Chauncy's belief that his theology provides the last and best solution to the problem lying at the heart of all of the controversies that had divided the Congregationalist clergy since the 1740s: the gloomy shadow cast by Calvinism over the religious lives of ordinary men and women, taught to believe that there is a small number of saints who themselves have little to do with being favored by God's grace and a vast majority who will suffer eternally through no fault of their own. By the end of the 1750s, Chauncy was convinced that this bleak picture had not only led divines like himself to the Arminianism of British theologians such as Samuel Clarke and John Taylor; but, because resigning oneself to such a vision was understood as one of the foundations of the self-described Consistent Calvinism of Edwards's successors, Samuel Hopkins and Joseph Bellamy, it had also led more moderate Calvinists to protest publicly against this "New Divinity."[2]

2. Charles Chauncy, *The Benevolence of the Deity, Fairly and Impartially Considered* (Boston, 1784); Chauncy, *Five Dissertations on the Scripture Account of the Fall; and Its Consequences* (London, 1785).

In *A Demonstration of the Being and Attributes of God* (1704–1705), British rationalist philosopher and theologian Samuel Clarke argued that human reason can comprehend God's attributes in something resembling absolute terms. This allowed later British Latitudinarians such as John Taylor of Norwich (*The Scripture-Doctrine of Original Sin Proposed to Free and Candid Examination* [1740]) to assert that certain interpretations of traditional doctrines were inconsistent with the divine attribute of benevolence. Taylor's work inspired similar critiques of the Calvinist notion of Original Sin, such as Samuel Webster's *Winter Evening's Conversation upon the Doctrine of Original Sin* (1757). The publication of this work, in turn, led to a counterattack against Arminianism by Jonathan Edwards's theological heir and leader of the New Divinity, Samuel Hopkins. By the late 1760s, Hopkins's strict Calvinist understanding of Original Sin (as presented

FIGURE 4.

Charles Chauncy. Oil on canvas, by an unidentified artist, undated.

Courtesy, Massachusetts Historical Society, Boston

The belief that Calvinism had become as troubling for its apologists as for its opponents would lead Chauncy to declare early in *The Mystery Hid* that, to preserve the true essence of the New England theological tradition, certain long-held tenets would have to be given up: "And it is high time they should be renounced, and others embraced in their room, that are *more honorable* to the Father of mercies, *and comfortable* to the creatures whom his hands have formed." At the same time, Chauncy would claim that his renunciation of these older doctrines was part of a system meant merely to return Covenant theology to its true course. He purported to oppose only the more recent tendency of the New Divinity to go so far in the direction of divine sovereignty and human dependence as to declare that the damnation of millions is actually desirable and that neither prayer nor faith nor outward goodness can ever influence God's mercy. Thus, for instance, in *Five Dissertations on the Fall* Chauncy gestures toward a moderate Calvinism, accepting the scriptural account of the fall of Adam; at the same time, he suggests that the fall simply means human beings are imperfect, prone to those excesses of the passions resulting so often in sin. Chauncy could thus accept the doctrine of Original Sin while asserting that the all-rational deity, far from merely condemning his creatures for their inherent imperfections, has endowed them with the capacity to overcome such passions by an act of will. This stance would then become, in *The Mystery Hid*, a justification of universal salvation: "Since sin and death entered into the world, and have reigned over all men, without any wilful fault of theirs, but purely by the disobedience of one man . . . it seemed agreeable to the infinite wisdom and grace of God that this damage should be repaired."[3]

---

in *Sin, thro' Divine Interposition an Advantage to the Universe* [1759]) and free grace (in *The True State and Character of the Unregenerate* [1769]) would draw criticism not only from Arminians like Chauncy but moderate Calvinists such as Jedidiah Mills (*An Inquiry concerning the State of the Unregenerate under the Gospel* [1767]) and William Hart (*Brief Remarks on a Number of False Propositions, and Dangerous Errors, Which Are Spreading in the Country* [1769]), thus beginning the splintering of the New England clergy into three distinct camps: Arminians, Old or moderate Calvinists, and Edwardseans or New Divinity men.

3. Charles Chauncy, *The Mystery Hid from Ages and Generations, Made Manifest by the*

In the same way, the basic argument of *The Benevolence of the Deity*, which maintains that there is no contradiction between God's infinite goodness and the existence of natural and moral evil, would have been typical for an Arminian or a Calvinist alike. In his application of this concept of benevolence, however, Chauncy moves beyond the conventional Arminian protest of the Calvinist view of God, which arbitrarily condemns the greater part of the human race to eternal punishment. Although he begins *The Benevolence of the Deity* with the common Arminian view of life as a trial, with each individual making moral choices that will affect his or her future state, he concludes, in *The Mystery Hid*, with the assertion that all of humankind will ultimately succeed in this trial. That earthly life is finite should not, he suggests, put an end to an otherwise fruitful process.[4] The virtuous, then, go directly to heaven, and sinners to hell, but hell is a temporary state in which the soul undergoes a new series of trials that will last as long as it takes to reform even the most unrepentant of sinners until, finally, they too will proceed to heaven with the rest of the saints.

By always insisting on this point—that Universalism must acknowledge at least a temporary period of punishment in hell—Chauncy could claim his admittedly unorthodox theology was grounded in the orthodox Protestant tradition, denying neither the scriptural references to hell nor the justice of God's punishment of sinners. More specifically, this tenet would provide the crucial distinction between his theology and other versions of Universalism, such as that professed by John Murray. Murray had come to America from London in 1770 after being dismissed by the Methodist Church for espousing his Universalist doctrines. Like most others preaching universal salvation in New England at the time, Murray was associated with backcountry enthusiasm. Unlike these others, however, he had settled permanently in Gloucester

----

Gospel-Revelation; or, The Salvation of All Men the Grand Thing Aimed at in the Scheme of God . . . (1784), ed. Edwin Gaustad (New York, 1969), 14, 30.

4. Chauncy does not, in *The Benevolence of the Deity*, go so far as to assert or even mention universal salvation, but he does appeal to many of the same arguments that he uses in his Universalist tracts to deny the doctrine of eternal punishment. For instance, he argues that, if God's punishment is to be called just, it must necessarily be instructive to the sinner, thus implicitly rejecting the possibility that eternal punishment can be consistent with a benevolent deity (237–246).

and in 1779 became pastor of America's first Universalist Church. Murray was under continual attack by members of the established clergy. Rumors about Murray's past abounded, that he had served time in prison and that he had begun his career as a weaver and took up preaching simply as a more lucrative way to earn a living. His close proximity to Boston, moreover, made him a source of particular apprehension for Chauncy's circle of learned Universalists. During their debate over whether to make public the secret of "the pudding," their primary fear, as suggested in a letter by John Eliot, for example, was that it may "give offence to many serious, good Xtians, and cause them to think that we were giving up the sentiments generally supposed to be agreable to Scripture for the sake of gratifying the humours of Murray and others of a loose way of thinking."[5]

Murray's Universalist doctrine differed from Chauncy's in its premise, popularized in Britain by James Relly, that there exists a metaphysical union between Christ and all of humanity, making Christ's death the immediate and total retribution for sin. Suffering vicariously through Christ, human beings deserve, and can expect, no further suffering in hell. This difference would allow Chauncy to respond to Murray in precisely the terms used by others against his own doctrine, to argue that outright denial of hell remains a constant temptation to sin and vice. Thus, in the preface to *Salvation for All Men*, he warns against both Murray and his doctrine, referring to him as a "stranger, who has, of himself, assumed the character of a *preacher*" and whose teaching "looks very like an encouragement to *Libertinism*, and falls in with the scheme of too many in this degenerate age, who, under pretence of *promoting religion, undermine it at the very root*."[6]

At the other extreme, Chauncy would also make sure to distinguish his system from a version of the doctrine that was not really Universalism at all but a quasi-universalist belief assumed within certain forms of deism: after death, all human beings ascend to a higher state of purely spiritual existence. Although deists had never been unified around a particular view of the future state of the soul, their conception of the soul as an eternal entity that must

5. *Belknap Papers*, Massachusetts Historical Society, *Collections*, 6th Ser., IV (Boston, 1891), 202.

6. Charles Chauncy, introduction, in [John Clarke], *Salvation for All Men, Illustrated and Vindicated as a Scripture Doctrine* (Boston, 1782), ii–iii.

necessarily proceed to some other state after the death of the body could be compared to universal salvation. As in the case of Murray, Chauncy responds to this similarity before his opponents have the chance to do so. He states in the conclusion to *The Mystery Hid* that the deists' reliance upon reason alone for their idea of universal future happiness is troubling because it diminishes the role of God in human redemption. Deism may indeed reveal the rational nature of the doctrine, he writes, "but it cannot, upon solid grounds, *assure us of a blessed immortality. . . .* nothing can be said, upon the principles of *mere reason*, that will represent the blessed God in so amiable and endearing a light."[7]

The publication of Chauncy's three final treatises in 1784 and 1785 revealed a logic within which universal salvation followed largely from doctrines to which many Congregationalists already assented; it also provided a crucial contrast between his own theological reasoning and the assumptions underlying itinerant Universalism and deism. As in the earlier pamphlet war, however, Chauncy's system remained exposed to precisely these comparisons, and Dwight would take full advantage of them in *The Triumph of Infidelity*. At the same time, the immediate satiric force of comparing Chauncy's doctrine to such systems would arise from a different context: the perception of various threats to the political and economic stability of the Republic during the uneasy period between Shays's rebellion and the ratification of the Constitution. Thus, Satan, at the moment in *The Triumph of Infidelity* when he is conceiving his plan to uncover the forgotten manuscript of *The Mystery Hid*, will recall his own most recent attempts to further the cause of infidelity by employing two American figures who already represented these threats: Murray, who had come to symbolize throughout New England something of a rogue preacher, and Ethan Allen, the Vermont general and Revolutionary leader who was also the representative voice of a nascent American deism and who had recently published the treatise *Reason, the Only Oracle of Man* (1784).

In the case of Murray, the explicit connection is made when Satan remembers him as an ill-fated version of Chauncy himself, whose own Universalist doctrines might have better served Satan's cause had the transparency of his self-serving motives not undermined his success. Thus, pondering the notion

7. Chauncy, *The Mystery Hid*, 359–360.

that infidelity might be more effective if it is disseminated by "false friends" of religion, Satan declares:

> This M***** proves, in whom my utmost skill
> Peer'd out no means of mischief, but the will.
> He, in hard days, when ribbons gave no bread,
> And Spitalfield's brave sons from Tyburn fled,
> Scampering from bailiffs, wisely dropp'd the shuttle,
> To preach down truth, and common sense to throttle.   (433-438)

Satan here retells the popular, though largely apocryphal, story of Murray as a former weaver in London's Spitalfield community who, in the midst of financial hardship ("when ribbons gave no bread"), narrowly escaped his possible fate at the Tyburn gallows and thus gave up his trade ("dropp'd the shuttle") because he realized that preaching universal salvation would assure him a more comfortable living. The passage thus serves to associate Chauncy not only with Murray's theology but with his reputation as one of several imposter ministers and quack doctors perceived during the 1780s as a threat to social order—the notorious imposter and counterfeiter Stephen Burroughs as he had already appeared in print and popular legend, for instance, or the peddlers of miracle cures as described in Lemuel Hopkins's 1785 poem "Epitaph on a Patient Killed by a Cancer Quack."[8] The threat posed by Murray in this

---

8. Contrary to the popular legends of John Murray (1741–1815), he had not begun his career as a weaver, nor did he have a criminal past. He did, however, work for a short time as an inspector at a textile factory, and he served time in a London debtor's prison after the death of his wife. Murray met John Wesley during the 1750s when his father joined the Methodists, and Murray himself held a position of leadership in the Methodist Church in London until he was expelled for professing Universalism. For his own account of these events, see Murray, *The Life of the Reverend John Murray . . . Written by Himself* (Boston, 1833). For an example of some of the apocryphal stories of Murray's life, see Ezra Stiles, *The Literary Diary of Ezra Stiles D.D., LL.D., President of Yale College*, ed. Franklin Bowditch Dexter (New York, 1901), I, 289-291.

The earliest newspaper article on Stephen Burroughs (author of the *Memoirs of Stephen Burroughs* [1798]) appeared in the *Hampshire Herald* (Springfield, Mass.), Aug. 30, 1785, while Burroughs was in jail in Springfield for attempting to pass counterfeit

---

sense is one of social chaos, a world in which public identity is no longer an indicator of true worth and in which even theological truth is determined by market forces; in exchange for the promise of universal redemption, even a rogue like Murray can gain a following of believers willing to support him financially. This point is further emphasized by the references to Tyburn and Spitalfield, recalling the landscape of works such as *The Beggar's Opera* (1728) by John Gay and the rogues and confidence men who populated that world. The effect is thus symbolically to bring Chauncy and his own promise of universal salvation down to this level: as Satan wryly suggests, the only difference between the two is that, whereas Chauncy's superior ability and spotless reputation will more effectively serve his ends, the unfortunate Murray lacked in "means" what he possessed in "will."

A similar point is made in reference to Allen's *Reason, the Only Oracle of Man,* which Satan—referring to the book as "The great Clodhopping Oracle of man" (388)—laments as a somewhat feeble attempt by a Vermont rustic to draw New Englanders toward a radical critique of the superstition and error of revealed religion. At the same time, Allen's special significance in *The Triumph of Infidelity* arises from his exemplifying precisely the tendency toward deistic Universalism from which Chauncy had attempted to distance his own work. In addition to a comprehensive system of natural religion, Allen's treatise also included an argument for universal salvation, which Dwight and others believed to be rooted in the same desire to excuse his own and his followers' self-interested motives. As Dwight would later explain in his *Travels,* "Allen was surrounded by a herd of [followers], both parties being equally pleased: he, to be listened to as their oracle; and they, to learn that a virtuous character was no better than a vicious one, and that God would punish vice neither here, nor hereafter."[9]

money. The article accuses him of impersonating a minister and stealing a watch and a suit of clothes belonging to another clergyman. Hopkins's poem first appeared in the *Connecticut Courant* (Hartford), Nov. 7, 1785, and was later reprinted in Elihu Hubbard Smith, ed., *American Poems, Selected and Original* (1793), ed. William K. Bottorff (Gainesville, Fla., 1966), 137–140.

9. Timothy Dwight, *Travels in New England and New York* (1821–1822), ed. Barbara Miller Solomon, with the assistance of Patricia M. King, 4 vols. (Cambridge, Mass., 1969), II, 283.

Yet, if placing Chauncy in Allen's company is meant, as with Murray, to satirize the venerable divine by way of association with someone who "In Satan's cause . . . bustled, bruised, and swore" (390), it is more importantly meant to remind the audience of *The Triumph of Infidelity* of the political threat represented by just such an association. No less than that of Daniel Shays, Allen's name had become synonymous in the 1780s with the threat of lawlessness, first and foremost because of his leadership in the Vermont rebellion against New York authority but also because of his role in the land dispute between Connecticut settlers and the government of Pennsylvania over the Wyoming Valley territory. Two years before the publication of *The Triumph of Infidelity*, he had gone to the territory and offered to lead a rebellion there as he had done in Vermont, causing many to see him as the embodiment of the threat of popular violence during the period of the Articles of Confederation. Moreover, as Lemuel Hopkins had suggested in an earlier satiric poem, "On General Ethan Allen," the ease with which Allen could support such violent measures went hand in hand with his deistic beliefs:

Behold inspired from Vermont dens,
The seer of Antichrist descends,
To feed new mobs with Hell-born manna
In Gentile lands of Susquehanna;

. . . .

One hand is clench'd to batter noses,
While t'other scrawls 'gainst Paul and Moses." [10]

Beyond the association between infidelity and a disregard for any authority except that based on brute power, the connection between Chauncy's Universalism and Allen's deism in *The Triumph of Infidelity* arises from a specific

10. Lemuel Hopkins, "On General Ethan Allen" (1786), in Smith, ed., *American Poems*, ed. Bottorff, 142. After returning to Vermont following the Revolution, Allen led a sort of coup d'etat in 1779, in which the Green Mountain Boys took the New York territorial officials captive and set up an unofficial Vermont government. At the time Dwight was composing *The Triumph of Infidelity*, Vermont was under the control of this government. For more on Allen and the movement for Vermont separatism, see Michael A. Belleslies, *Revolutionary Outlaws: Ethan Allen and the Struggle for Independence on the Early American Frontier* (Charlottesville, Va., 1993), chaps. 3, 6.

ideological similarity, their shared faith that modern thought would liberate human beings from superstition and false consciousness. This faith is evident, for example, in the confidence that both Chauncy and Allen place in the superiority of their respective methods, which, despite their incompatibility —the one being a method of scriptural interpretation, the other an outright rejection of scriptural validity—is suggested in the titles of both works as the belief that they had successfully wrested the truth from earlier systems of error. For a self-proclaimed freethinker like Allen, such a position was entirely conventional, though he makes a point of explaining that his own system is nothing more than a collection of thoughts he had recorded as a younger man that seemed to him "most consonant to reason." He adheres not even to the views of other deists, for "I know not strictly speaking, whether I am one or not, for I have never read their writings . . . but have written freely without any conscious knowledge or prejudice for, or against any man, sectary or party whatever."[11]

What is perhaps less conventional is that Chauncy, too, presents his method of scriptural interpretation as entirely original within American theology, the result, as he puts it in the preface to *The Mystery Hid*, of "being willing, in opposition to previous sentiments and strong biasses, to follow the light wherever it should lead." This light came gradually, he explains, only after a diligent study of the Greek Testament, following British Arminian John Taylor's technique of comparing all the usages of specific Greek words and phrases, particularly those of the Epistles, to determine the sense in which they were originally meant. This method, which he had begun using in the 1750s, had first convinced him that he had discovered something unseen in previous interpretations of the Bible, as he had asserted enthusiastically in a letter to his cousin, Nathaniel Chauncy, in 1754: "I wish I could have an opportunity to converse with you, or to let you see what I have written upon Paul's Epistles. I think I could let you into an entirely new set of thoughts, which it is surprising has escaped the notice of so many. . . . The commonly received opinions are quite remote from the truth." And, as he illustrates in hundreds of pages of specific proofs in *The Mystery Hid*, the great truth that has for so

11. Ethan Allen, *Reason, the Only Oracle of Man* (Bennington, Vt., 1784), preface [i, iii].

long escaped the notice of previous scriptural interpreters is that we can be assured of universal salvation.[12]

Chauncy's claim that his method leads to a conclusion that is nothing less than earth-shattering in its implications would call forth his satiric counterpart in *The Triumph of Infidelity* as a bewildered dotard, blinded by ambition into believing he had discovered, at a remote moment in the history of Christianity, that the New Testament had been fundamentally misread for nearly two thousand years. The poem ridicules this method as merely a belabored argument over the translation of certain Greek words that can be manipulated to produce any desired conclusion—"See *kai*'s and *epi*'s build the glorious scheme! / And *gar*'s and *pro*'s unfold their proof supreme!" (671–672). The crucial point concerns the conclusion itself, which, if true, would constitute the very truth that would liberate modern man from the profound sense of alienation that had characterized human existence in all previous ages. To be sure, this ambition underlies a great deal of Enlightenment thought, but in Chauncy's case there is the particular difficulty of his discovering this truth in the Bible. That is, Toland, Tindal, or Allen could simply reject revelation as mere myth or superstition, but Chauncy has to explain why God would have waited eighteen centuries to reveal such an essential doctrine:

12. Chauncy, *The Mystery Hid*, x. Following this claim to a sort of theological free-thinking, Chauncy assures his readers that his work has been influenced only by John Taylor's method, and not his particular conclusions: one approaches the truth, he explains, by using the work of one's precursors "as *helps* . . . founding our *faith*, not on what *they say*, but on what we are enabled by their assistance to be satisfied is the *word and will of God*" (xiv). See also Charles Chauncy to Nathaniel Chauncy, in William Chauncey Fowler, "President Charles Chauncy, His Ancestors and Descendants," *New England Historical and Genealogical Register*, X (1856), 335. Chauncy's proof of universal salvation depends on this method of comparing certain key words and phrases used in the Bible to describe the punishment of sinners with other scriptural usages of this language. In specific terms, he argues that the Greek word αιωνιος, used by Paul and others to describe the period of infernal torment, had long been assumed to mean "forever" or "eternity" but that, in most other places in the Bible, it signifies merely a long, but finite, period of time.

'Tis all a specious irony, design'd
A harmless trifling with the human kind:
Or, not to charge the sacred books with lies,
A wile most needful of the ingenious skies,
On this bad earth their kingdom to maintain,
And curb the rebel, man: but all in vain.   (661–666)

Beyond asserting that Chauncy's conclusions are wrong, this critique articulates the sense of Universalism as an ideology of modernity, one so subtle in its deceptive power that it appears in the guise of a liberation from all previous ideologies. For, despite Chauncy's gestures toward an orthodox position, as in his critique of Murray's system as the product of a "degenerate age," the implications of his system suggest that the modern age is the singularly *regenerate* moment in religious history, the point at which the mystery concerning the future of humankind has finally been revealed. This is the moment, moreover, at which human redemption can be understood as taking place, not at a point outside of human history—the sphere of the divine, the *nunc-stans*—but inside the *saeculum,* or human secular history. Indeed, Chauncy's treatise purports to reveal the singular truth that will literally set humanity free inside the limits of history; at the moment men and women are finally convinced of God's infinite benevolence as made manifest in universal salvation, he suggests, there will commence a new era of human moral progress, a revolution that no previous religious truth had ever inspired.

This logic stands in the immediate background of Chauncy's and John Clarke's disclaimer in *Salvation for All Men* that the large-scale acceptance of the doctrine of universal salvation will lead people, not toward moral complacency and vice, as their opponents had maintained, but to a renewed commitment to virtue. Sinners continue to live unrepentantly even as they are warned of eternal damnation, the authors explain, because they are unable to make clear sense of their universe: "The conceptions they *naturally* form of the ALL MERCIFUL BEING are a counter-balance to their fear of *never-ending misery.*" To the direct contrary, the notion of a temporary period of punishment corresponding to each individual's particular sinfulness is analogous to the earthly system of punishment that is generally accepted as reasonable. More important, the design of Universalism is intended to reform as well as punish and is thus wholly harmonious with the truth of God as a beneficent parent. As a result, say Chauncy and Clarke, the general recognition of this truth will "strike the mind with *full force*, and operate to a much better purpose, restraining men more *effectually* from their *wicked courses*."[13]

The discovery that will strike the mind with such force as to guarantee the moral regeneration of millions is not simply that the universe is ruled according to reason and benign justice but that each individual's life is guided by an inevitable moral progress. Chauncy calls this principle the "capacity of rising in glory," an aspect of human rational nature that allows people to "employ and improve their original faculties, from one degree of attainment to another; and hereupon, from one degree of happiness to another, without end." Importantly, the same principle of moral and spiritual improvement is shared by all of the otherwise distinct versions of universal salvation, even those that avoid referring to moral improvement after death as "hell." John Murray, for example, whose entire theology is based on the idea that Christ's death has paid the price for the sins of all human beings, and, thus, that there is no such thing as hell, nevertheless denies that salvation is therefore immediate. "He who dies in Unbelief," he explains, "lays down in sorrow, and will *rise to the resurrection of damnation*, or, more properly, *condemnation*"; but, after a period of reflection on past sins and the experience of guilt, "it is from these poor unhappy Beings, that the *Lord God will wipe away all tears*." By the same token, Ethan Allen, who rejects the Christian conceptions of heaven and hell altogether, acknowledges that the future state is characterized by a moral and rational development similar to that of earthly life: whatever punishment might exist in that state "will *finally* terminate in the BEST GOOD OF THE PUNISHED . . . and be productive of *the restoration and felicity of all finite rational nature*."[14]

The common Universalist vision of human moral progress is underwritten by the eighteenth-century conception of the soul known as intellectualism, the idea that moral advancement depends upon intellectual growth, with each individual becoming attracted to virtue and reverence for God as a result of recognizing certain rational truths about the world. In this view, the mind or soul is divided into two separate faculties, the will, which determines human

13. [Clarke], *Salvation for All Men*, 25.

14. Chauncy, *Five Dissertations*, 33; John Murray, *Some Hints Relative to the Forming of a Christian Church* (Boston, 1791), 34, 36; Allen, *Reason, the Only Oracle*, 119.

action, and the intellect, which allows the will to decide what is the most reasonable course. The virtue of this division, accordingly, is that it allows vice or sin to be understood largely as an error in judgment. If a particular act proves later to be an immoral one, the will did not desire to sin, but the intellect failed to recognize the true good. This assumption was at the heart of the Arminian argument throughout most of the religious controversies that had divided the New England clergy in the latter half of the eighteenth century. Thus, for instance, in the dispute over the freedom of the will, Chauncy's Arminian colleagues had argued, not that the will was wholly free, but that human beings were free to improve themselves morally by educating their rational faculties, gradually recognizing the nature of virtue in a consistent manner.[15]

The theological controversies of eighteenth-century New England thus constituted at the abstract or ideological level the great clash between the older Augustinian conception of human nature and an emerging Pelagianism reintroduced at the beginning of the century by Shaftesbury and absorbed into American thought through its influence on Francis Hutcheson, Joseph Butler, and various other English Latitudinarian divines. The specific prem-

15. On the ideological background of the theological controversies of eighteenth-century New England, see Norman Fiering, *Moral Philosophy at Seventeenth-Century Harvard* (Chapel Hill, N.C., 1981), 138–144. Chauncy's commitment to the intellectualist conception of the soul had led him, throughout his career, to explain moral transgressions as the effects of a disorder of the rational faculties. During the Great Awakening, for example, he had accounted for the excesses of the religious affections of the New Lights by arguing that their passions simply had conquered both the will and the rational faculties that guide the will: "There is the Religion of the *Understanding* and *Judgment*, and *Will*, as well as of the *Affections;* and if little Account is made of the *former*, while great stress is laid upon the *latter*, it can't be but people should run into Disorders" (Chauncy, *Seasonable Thoughts*, 422). Four decades later, in *The Mystery Hid*, he would similarly suggest that only such a deficiency of the understanding would lead someone to conclude that universal salvation implies that all people are free to sin at will: "This folly will rather deserve the name of *downright madness*, if it be remembered, that they *must cease from being wicked, before they can possibly be fixed in final happiness*. . . . Those men must act in contradiction to *all prudence*, and in defiance of *common sense*" (343–344).

ise of intellectualism that illustrates its relationship to Shaftesburian Pelagianism is that human beings naturally possess the desire to follow a moral
course of action even if they are at times mistaken about what that course
might be. At the same time, this connection has been difficult to recognize
because Chauncy and the Boston Arminians were most directly influenced,
not by Shaftesbury, but by Samuel Clarke, the founder of the intellectualist school of moral philosophy in Britain. Clarke's system is based upon the
notion that moral truths are revealed in nature to the mind's rational faculties.
These truths guide the moral actions of all but those whose reason is imperfect, or those who are under the influence of an excess of affections. Shaftesbury's theory of moral sense, on the other hand, had emphasized the very passions and affections that Chauncy had so strongly opposed during the Great
Awakening. Despite this difference, something very much like Shaftesbury's
theory of moral sense emerges in the intellectualist assumption that reason
can determine moral action only if there also exists a strong natural attraction
to virtue.

More specifically, the intellectualist argument draws upon one of Shaftesbury's central points in *An Inquiry concerning Virtue or Merit:* vice is in large
part simply a misguided or misapplied sense of virtue. No reasonable person,
Shaftesbury had argued, fails to realize that certain actions are applauded by,
and others offensive to, one's fellow human beings: "Of this even the wicked-
est creature living must have a sense." This point became the basis, in turn,
of Shaftesbury's famous statement that a criminal, from a sense of community with his fellows, will more likely suffer death than betray their trust, for
even this most vicious character carries within him a principle of virtue, "however he may misapply it." The crucial implication of this assertion within the
intellectualist tradition generally—hinted at by Shaftesbury when he says that
one's natural sense of right and wrong can only be perverted by a "contrary
habit and custom"—is that, if the moral sense is somehow misguided, it can
also be restored through proper education.[16]

16. Fiering, *Moral Philosophy*, 295–302; Anthony Ashley Cooper, third earl of Shaftesbury, *An Inquiry concerning Virtue or Merit* (1699), in Shaftesbury, *Characteristics of Men,
Manners, Opinions, Times* (1711), ed. Lawrence E. Klein, Cambridge Texts in the History
of Philosophy (Cambridge, 1999), 177, 178, 179.

This belief accounts for the enormous attraction of American liberal Protestants like Chauncy, Jonathan Mayhew, and Ebenezer Gay to the various systems of natural theology, such as Samuel Clarke's *Demonstration of the Being and Attributes of God* (1705) or his disciple William Wollaston's *Religion of Nature Delineated* (1722). Such works argue not simply that religious truths are revealed in nature but that all moral obligations can be discovered through a method of reasoning that is available to virtually everyone. The principal argument of Wollaston's treatise, for instance, is that the concepts of good and evil, virtue and vice, can be derived simply from an understanding of truth and falsehood, allowing every moral action to be tested according to its consistency with rational truth. One recognizes murder as a sin because it denies the natural truth of God's creation of life, theft because it repudiates the natural rectitude of private property, and adultery because it disclaims the natural fitness of marriage. Thus, from the Pelagian-intellectualist view, natural theology serves as the intellectual basis for what Chauncy calls the universal capacity of rising in glory.

For orthodox divines like Dwight, for whom Wollaston's identification of truth and virtue was equally influential in its own way, the potential benefits of natural religion would always be limited by the Augustinian understanding of human nature, on which Calvinist theology as well as civic humanist or classical republican moral theory ultimately depended. From this perspective, human beings possessed the capacity to comprehend good and evil, but this very ability only underscored the seriousness of the problem; they were not naturally inclined to follow even the dictates of reason against the more powerful tendency toward self-interest. At the same time, however, this opposition of virtue and self-interest is what the Pelagian-intellectualist tradition had long since sought to nullify by means of their own compelling distinction between a true and false sense of human self-interest. As Shaftesbury had shown in *Sensus Communis, an Essay on the Freedom of Wit and Humour in a Letter to a Friend,* the idea of a natural inclination toward virtue is not simply a denial of the competing Hobbesian or Mandevillian view of human beings as ruled by self-love; it is an argument over the true meaning of self-interest. Because true self-interest is tied always to personal happiness, and personal happiness to the happiness of one's society at large, self-interest is not synonymous with selfishness but with virtue. "It is the height of wisdom, no doubt, to be rightly selfish," Shaftesbury observes, "but a wretched life is no wise man's wish. . . . And a life without natural affection, friendship or sociableness would be found a wretched one, were it to be tried."[17]

This truth—which, for Shaftesbury, is understood both by the merchant whose honesty rewards him with affluence and the rogue who finds himself more miserable for his viciousness—would provide Chauncy, more than a half-century later, with a powerful moral defense of the doctrine of universal salvation. In *Salvation for All Men*, the notion of moral education assumed in the intellectualist view of the soul is described as chiefly the act of convincing ordinary people of their real self-interest: "It is objected yet further, that [Universalism] will greatly tend to encourage wicked men, in their vicious courses, to be told that the *future torments* will have an *end*, which must be the case, if *All are finally saved*. To this it is answered, that *moral depravity* is absolutely inconsistent with *rational happiness*."[18] At the same time, however, the very obviousness of this truth raised the potential problem of accounting for the extent of moral evil in an otherwise rational world, of explaining why human beings have long persisted in behavior that is directly contradictory to their own true interests. The answer to this problem would again be found by drawing upon a well-known point of Shaftesburian moral theory and would give Chauncy and other Universalists their most effective counterargument against the charge that the doctrine of universal salvation tended ultimately toward moral complacency or corruption.

17. Shaftesbury, *Sensus Communis, an Essay on the Freedom of Wit and Humour in a Letter to a Friend* (1709), in Shaftesbury, *Characteristics*, ed. Klein, 56. Although Dwight would follow Wollaston's argument, stating that *"virtue is nothing but voluntary obedience to truth; and Sin nothing but voluntary obedience to falsehood,"* he would remain skeptical of the effect of mere natural religion on the moral lives of ordinary people (Timothy Dwight, *Theology; Explained and Defended, in a Series of Sermons . . .* [1818–1819], 4th ed., 4 vols. [New Haven, Conn., 1825], I, 100). After explaining his system of natural religion, for instance, he asserts that, however useful it may be for human beings to recognize the principles of morality in nature, such principles are destined to fail. Even if we fully understand which is the virtuous course of action, our will is incapable of consistently following it: "The real and only reason, why we perform not this obedience, is, that we do not possess such a disposition. . . . Our natural powers are plainly sufficient: our inclination only is defective" (III, 21).

18. [Clarke], *Salvation for All Men*, 23.

The principle point of Shaftesbury's *An Inquiry concerning Virtue or Merit* is that all forms of religion cannot equally be said to inspire virtue. In fact, the history of religion has shown that too often the opposite has been true. Thus, he distinguishes between systems that seek to regulate conduct merely through rewards and punishments and those that inspire virtue by example: religion might restrain its believers by emphasizing God's sheer power, but it inspires true virtue only by illustrating his "excellency and worth." By the same token, a set of religious beliefs can also exacerbate the spread of immorality if it represents the world in such a way that defies one's rational or moral sense. The result will be none other than a collective sense of cosmological despair in which otherwise reasonable people, having been taught that Providence is arbitrary or nonexistent, that goodness is neither justly rewarded nor evil justly punished, are led to pursue vice as a sort of desperate rebellion against the very meaninglessness of it all. "Nothing indeed can be more melancholy than the thought of living in a distracted universe, from whence many ills may be suspected and where there is nothing good or lovely which presents itself, nothing which can satisfy in contemplation or raise any passion besides that of contempt, hatred or dislike. Such an opinion as this may by degrees embitter the temper and not only make the love of virtue to be less felt but help to impair and ruin the very principle of virtue."[19]

The Pelagian vision of a world of natural virtue and harmony thus will always imply a corresponding argument about the power of this vision to liberate human beings from a false sense of alienation and despair caused by other, misguided cosmological views. No other aspect of Shaftesburian moral theory more clearly illustrates its enormous influence on eighteenth-century thought; by the end of the century, when Shaftesbury's special importance within this tradition would be for a time forgotten, this assumption would be shared by countless Christians and deists and Enlightenment progressivists alike. Its prevalence is explained in large part by the extent to which Pelagianism as such would remain theologically neutral—a discovery of a truth about the nature of human existence rather than God or Christ or the Scriptures. The various figures drawn together in *The Triumph of Infidelity* under the category of "infidelity," then, despite their obvious theological differences, speak an identical language of freedom from the paralyzing myth of the Augustinian

19. Shaftesbury, *Inquiry*, in Shaftesbury, *Characteristics*, ed. Klein, 183, 189.

view of the world. Thus, for instance, the moral project of Ethan Allen's *Reason, the Only Oracle*, to ennoble the human mind and "be the means of cultivating concord, and mutual love in society," is presented as the result of an intellectual enlightenment similar to that found later in Paine's *Age of Reason*, an unmasking of all forms of religious superstition. This ennobling of the mind will be advanced only by first breaking the fetters of the aspects of orthodox Protestantism that emphasize human moral and spiritual alienation:

> In these parts of America, they are most generally taught, that they are born into the world in a state of enmity to God and moral good, . . . that the way to Heaven and future blessedness is out of their power to pursue, . . . that human nature, which they call "the old man," must be destroyed, perverted, or changed by them, and by them new modeled, before it can be admitted into the Heavenly kingdom. Such a plan of superstition, as far as it obtains credit in the world, subjects mankind to sacerdotal empire.[20]

Conversely, what is for Allen a liberation from believing in the necessity of religious conversion is presented by John Murray as the very moment of his own conversion experience, on which his spiritual autobiography is centered. Murray describes the state of his soul prior to his encountering Universalism as one of profound terror, which his father and other members of his Congregation interpreted as a sign of his holiness: "I was not ten years old when I began to suffer; the discovery of my sufferings gave my fond father much pleasure; he cherished hope of me when he found me suffering from my fears, and much indeed was I tortured by the . . . terrifying apprehensions of what I had to expect from the God who created me." Later, when he recounts his eventual acceptance of the doctrine of universal salvation, he describes his renewal of moral and religious commitment as a sudden moment when he realized that his earlier fears had been unfounded, that God's beneficence and Christ's sacrifice guarantee his ultimate happiness: "The Bible was indeed a new book to me; the veil was taken from my heart, and the word of my God became right precious to my soul."[21]

This same sense of liberation from despair is found in Chauncy's radical assertion in *The Mystery Hid* that certain long-held Protestant doctrines must be

---

20. Allen, *Reason, the Only Oracle*, 456, 467–468.
21. Murray, *Life*, 15, 110.

given up in favor of others that are more comfortable to God's creatures. Similarly, the notion of Universalism as an infinitely more optimistic system would also provide Chauncy with a powerful countercharge: what had long passed as revealed truth for so many of his fellow New Englanders is nothing other than an embodiment of what Shaftesbury had called a "distracted universe," a vision of the world that is not only mistaken but dangerous, serving ultimately to impair the principle of virtue. When this charge—which Shaftesbury had directed chiefly against atheism and the Hobbesian theory of self-interest— is leveled against the theology of Chauncy's fellow Congregationalists, however, something altogether more damaging emerges: a curious sense in which the egocentric world of Thomas Hobbes and the fallen world of Augustinian Christianity are characterized by an identical sense of alienation and meaninglessness.

Chauncy makes this assertion most directly, not in his Universalist tracts, but in the less-controversial work, *The Benevolence of the Deity*, his own contribution to the tradition of natural theology that had begun with Samuel Clarke's *Demonstration of the Being and Attributes of God*. The great unspoken point of *The Benevolence of the Deity* as a logical demonstration, of course, is that it scarcely needed to be made, being the shared first assumption of all forms of Christian theology. Indeed, the only direct or explicit opposition that Chauncy assumes at the outset of the work is a brand of skepticism and atheism that was virtually nonexistent in America at the time, the view symbolized by the later Voltaire, for whom the extent of human suffering revealed only the bitter reality of a world devoid of Providence. Yet the real reason for Chauncy's publication of *The Benevolence of the Deity* is soon made evident. He means to counter a very different error, that of professed Christians who ascribe to the idea of God's infinite benevolence but who conceive it in a way that is "equally malignant with a total denial of it." And, without explicitly naming this group, he makes clear that he has in mind the very Calvinists who were at that moment objecting to his anonymous treatise on universal salvation: "A more shocking idea can scarce be given of the *Deity*, than that which represents him as *arbitrarily dooming the greater part of the race of men to eternal misery*. Was he wholly destitute of goodness, yea, positively *malevolent* in his nature, a worse representation could not be well made of him."[22]

22. Chauncy, *Benevolence of the Deity*, viii.

In the context of the endless charges and countercharges that Calvinists and Arminians had leveled against each other in the decades leading up to the Universalist controversy, this attack upon orthodox Protestantism was as powerful as anything that could be mounted by the Enlightenment skeptics themselves. What had united the opposing sides in all of the earlier New England controversies had been their equally strong language against the threat of European infidelity. Consequently, Dwight's own catalog of infidels in *The Triumph of Infidelity* had been anticipated by several liberal Protestants, including Chauncy's friend and fellow Arminian Jonathan Mayhew, who had warned against the "imaginary triumphs of vanity in a Collins, a Woolston and a Tindal; in a Shaftsbury and a Morgan, a Chub and a Bolinbroke."[23] The force of Chauncy's attack in *The Benevolence of the Deity*, then, comes from the sense in which the Calvinists' idea of God is built upon the very assumption that is presupposed in the atheist argument. The only real difference between the two views, Chauncy suggests, is that the atheists are reasonable enough to reject such an arbitrary deity, whereas the New Divinity men continue to glorify this image of malevolence.

Neither is Chauncy simply turning the charge of infidelity back upon those who would similarly attack his own system. No less than Dwight did he believe their generation to be living through a period of religious crisis in which men and women were retreating in alarming numbers from Christianity and embracing one or another form of infidelity as a vain justification of their discontent. But the blame for this apostasy, he also believed, belonged less to the apostates themselves than to those who had taken Christianity so far in the direction of certain Calvinist tenets that otherwise good people had rejected all of Christianity as equally irrational or superstitious. Thus, when he distinguishes his own proof of universal salvation from that of deistic Universalism in *The Mystery Hid*, he accompanies his critique of deism with an even stronger critique of the theology of many of his fellow Congregationalists: "It is, I am verily persuaded, very much owing to the *false light* in which *revelation* has been placed, and by its very good friends too, that so many have been led to *reject* it. And, in truth, if the *sense* of revelation *really* was, what it has too generally been represented to be, even by Christians themselves, I see not

23. Jonathan Mayhew, *Christian Sobriety: Being Eight Sermons on Titus II.5* (Boston, 1763), 326.

that blame could justly be reflected on them."[24] The true means of combating infidels, he then concludes, is simply to remove their grounds for reasonable disbelief by incorporating into Christianity the deists' own critique of theological systems that subscribe to the Augustinian view of human nature.

Bringing Pelagianism into Christian theology would clear space for Chauncy's next radical assertion: the liberation from cosmological despair implicit in the belief in universal salvation is itself a crucial embodiment of Christian virtue. What would increasingly be held up against orthodox fears of moral backsliding would be a new variation of Shaftesbury's argument concerning the moral effects of imagining a benevolent and harmonious universe. If such an optimistic doctrine as Universalism naturally inspires good moral conduct, those most attracted to the doctrine must possess a certain disposition toward universal human happiness that calls to mind the Christian virtue of loving thy neighbor. This connection is found in Chauncy's choice of pseudonyms for *The Mystery Hid*—"one who wishes well to the whole human race"—and had also been articulated everywhere in the early correspondences among those privy to the secret of Chauncy's Universalist writings. Even those who expressed their doubts about Chauncy's scriptural proofs could not deny their moral attraction to the idea. "There is something in the supposition that will strike a benevolent heart very agreably," writes one member of Chauncy's circle. "And I doubt not but that good men may be very favourably disposed towards it."[25]

In the midst of the Universalist controversy, when *Salvation for All Men* was being attacked by a barrage of pamphlets, Chauncy would discover a formidable counterattack by drawing out just these moral implications. In the same way that the act of believing in universal salvation implied a particularly Christian disposition, the opposing act of defending the idea of eternal punishment or of the Augustinian moral vision generally implied precisely the opposite. He would use this argument, for instance, in response to a pamphlet by Joseph Eckley that attempted to explain in positive terms the theological and rational necessity of eternal punishment. Chauncy replies simply by contrasting his own hopes for universal human happiness with the somewhat cool response of Eckley and his allies to the prospect of so many of their fellow men

24. Chauncy, *The Mystery Hid*, 361.
25. *Belknap Papers*, MHS, *Colls.*, 6th Ser., IV (1891), 173.

suffering unending torment: "From these few hints it must be evident to all, the Gods we respectively serve are very unlike each other; and that our prospects beyond the grave do as widely differ. . . . *You* expect to look down from heaven upon numbers of wretched objects, confined in the pit of hell, and blaspheming their creator forever. *I* hope to see the prison-doors opened; and to hear those tongues, which are now profaning the name of God, chanting his praise." [26]

Within the pamphlet war itself, Chauncy's identification of Universalism with the spirit of Christian benevolence would neutralize his opponents' moral argument, forcing Eckley, in a later edition of his pamphlet, to distance himself from some of the more inflexible tenets of New Divinity orthodoxy. [27] At the same time, however, the attractiveness of Chauncy's argument—of any argument that locates an inherent moral value in professing more comfortable doctrines—would both explain and lend urgency to Dwight's initial decision to wage satiric warfare against Chauncy in *The Triumph of Infidelity*. What was most troubling to Dwight about Universalism and the Pelagian system of metaphysics on which it stood was precisely that it was a comfortable vision, infinitely more appealing than anything proposed by orthodox Congregationalism. Indeed, it is clear throughout *The Triumph of Infidelity* that Dwight imag-

---

26. [Charles Chauncy], *Divine Glory Brought to View in the Final Salvation of All Men* (Boston, 1783), 4. For Joseph Eckley's argument for the necessity of eternal punishment, see *Divine Glory, Brought to View, in the Condemnation of the Ungodly; or, The Doctrine of Future Punishment, Illustrated and Vindicated, as Rational and True* (Boston, 1782), 33–47.

27. In the appendix to *Divine Glory, Brought to View*, Eckley attempts to address Chauncy's moral critique of his system, asserting that, because the overall scheme of Providence—including the existence of sin and the eternal damnation of sinners—must be understood as ultimately good, one can rejoice in this scheme without rejoicing in the damnation of others: "That sin should be over-ruled for this *good*, is indeed a proper matter of joy. But it is the *good* only, which is the supposed object of joy, and this is a virtuous feeling. Sin is an evil in its own nature. To rejoice in it as such, is absolutely to reject and oppose the *good* or *grace*, which, not by men or angels, but by the power and wisdom of God, to whom alone the work belongs, it is rendered a means of illustrating" ("Appendix: In Answer to a Later Letter, Entitled, Divine Glory Brought to View, in the Final Salvation of All Men," 6).

ines his audience as, to a certain degree, already attracted to the harmonious vision of Shaftesburian moral theory. Thus, the overwhelming emphasis of the poem's satire is given to unmasking as self-delusion doctrines that are described variously as "sweet sophistry" and "pleasing falsehoods," of which universal salvation is only the most obvious example.

In general terms, the point of emphasizing the illusory nature of such a comfortable vision as Universalism is, first, that it engages this vision at the level of epistemology. Behind Dwight's parody of Universalist theology as a reinvention of God as a doting parent, bound by the wishes of his creatures— "Else is His hand unjust, His word untrue" (700)—lies the crucial point of contention over simply what human beings could say about God or Providence. From the perspective of the eighteenth-century Latitudinarianism on which Chauncy draws, a great deal could be said about both. As Samuel Clarke had first asserted, God reveals the moral truths of nature to human beings in absolute terms, granting them the capability not only to demonstrate that God is benevolent but to understand the essence of benevolence itself. The more controversial implication of this idea, however, taken almost verbatim from Clarke in Chauncy's *Benevolence of the Deity*, is that the ability to comprehend benevolence also allows human beings to rule out certain doctrines as logically inconsistent with God's nature: "There is, beyond all doubt, a certain *fitness* and *unfitness* of conduct, in order to the production of good, antecedently to, and independently of, all will whatsoever, not excepting even the will of *God* himself."[28]

Dwight's response, once again, will be rooted in Augustine's earlier insistence upon the fundamental gap separating the divine perspective of the nuncstans from that of human consciousness, struggling to understand the nature of things from inside the limits of secular history. As Dwight would remind his Yale undergraduates in the divinity lectures later compiled into *Theology; Explained and Defended, in a Series of Sermons,* only a mind ruled by pride would presume to comprehend the universe in such absolute terms: "When man undertakes to determine what is proper, or improper, for his Maker to do in the government of the world; he ought to remember, that, *As the heavens are high above the earth, so are his ways above our ways, and his thoughts above our thoughts.*" In one sense, this was the standard answer of New England Cove-

28. Chauncy, *Benevolence of the Deity*, 34.

nant theology; but the significance of this critique within Dwight's theological system depends upon our also recalling that Dwight would have seen this point made with more frequency and urgency in the poetry of Pope, Young, and Cowper than in the theological treatises of Edwards or Samuel Hopkins. Indeed, by the 1760s, most Congregationalists had come to concede the preeminence of human reason, such that Hopkins's own controversial writings are characterized by an attempt to answer the Arminians according to their own rationalist assumptions. In direct contrast, the Pope of *An Essay on Man*, for instance, offered a direct critique of the fallacy of glorifying reason:

> In Pride, in reas'ning Pride, our error lies;
> All quit their sphere, and rush into the skies.
> Pride still is aiming at the blest abodes,
> Men would be Angels, Angels would be Gods.
>
> . . . .
>
> And who but wishes to invert the laws
> Of ORDER, sins against th' Eternal Cause.[29]

Yet the more immediate source on which Dwight's critique of Chauncy's epistemology draws, not surprisingly, is an extended passage from *The Dunciad*, book 4, that might be described retrospectively as Pope's own triumph of infidelity. Announcing her wish for philosophical systems that teach men "to wonder at their Maker, not to serve," the goddess Dulness is answered by

29. Dwight, *Theology*, IV, 463; Alexander Pope, *An Essay on Man* (1733–1734), in John Butt, ed., *The Poems of Alexander Pope: A One-Volume Edition of the Twickenham Text with Selected Annotations* (New Haven, Conn., 1963), 509. As Joseph A. Conforti points out, despite the "hyper-Calvinist emphasis on the sovereignty of God" by Hopkins and Joseph Bellamy, the New Divinity men tended not to extend this emphasis to the question of epistemology and conclude, with Pope or Dwight, for instance, that human beings are simply not equipped to judge God in this manner. Rather, they tacitly agreed with the liberal protestants that God's ways could be comprehended and justified according to human understanding and attempted—"with considerable intellectual difficulty at times," as Conforti puts it—to reconcile this conception of divine sovereignty with what they argued was the true definition of benevolence (Conforti, *Samuel Hopkins and the New Divinity Movement: Calvinism, the Congregational Ministry, and Reform in New England between the Great Awakenings* [Grand Rapids, Mich., 1981], 163).

the Gloomy Clerk who then speaks for all of the various forms of delusion in theology and moral philosophy. As the pun on "Clerk" suggests, this figure is a direct caricature of Samuel Clarke, and his method of demonstrating the being and attributes of God is presented as the first step toward what Pope describes as "theological" dulness:

> Let others creep by timid steps, and slow,
> On plain Experience lay foundations low,
> By common sense to common knowledge bred,
> And last, to Nature's Cause thro' Nature led.
> All-seeing in thy mists, we want no guide,
> Mother of Arrogance, and Source of Pride!
> We nobly take the high Priori Road,
> And reason downward, till we doubt of God.[30]

The initial problem associated with Clarke's a priori demonstration is that, if the human conception of benevolence is taken as absolute, the God who oversees the actual world of natural disasters and moral failures can never live up to the image of his own benevolence, leading some such reasoners to "doubt of God." The deeper problem, pursued throughout the remainder of the Gloomy Clerk's speech, involves the possibility that Clarke's reasoning will become a model for a variety of disparate systems in which human reason is assumed to constitute the only true certainty. Within such systems, God exists either as an empty symbol of the harmonious and beneficent works of nature—here the direct reference will be made to Shaftesbury—or as an anthropomorphic being whose raison d'être is simply to provide happiness in human terms. In either case, "the Progress of Dulness," as Pope calls it, begins with the gradual obfuscation of God and ends with his virtual displacement by man, or, more specifically, the self: "Or, at one bound o'er-leaping all his laws, / Make God Man's Image, Man the final Cause, / Find Virtue local, all Relation scorn, / See all in *Self*, and but for self be born."[31]

---

30. Pope, *The Dunciad* (1728), in Butt, ed., *Poems*, 789.

31. Ibid., 790. The reference to Shaftesbury comes later in this same passage, when the Gloomy Clerk suggests that one way to obscure the view of the true God is to "that bright Image to our fancy draw, / Which Theocles in raptur'd vision saw" (791). Here the speaker is referring to the Shaftesbury of *The Moralists, a Philosophical Rhapsody*,

First reading *The Dunciad* during his undergraduate days at Yale, Dwight discovered in this passage the theological perspective that would later allow him to recognize Chauncy as Clarke's direct theological heir. What is crucial here, however, is not simply that Pope's satire of Clarke could be used in the same terms against Chauncy but that Pope's critique takes as its own fundamental principle the Augustinian insistence upon distinguishing between the nunc-stans and the saeculum. The underlying assumption of the conception of dulness as an intellectual descent into illusory systems of belief is that such systems arise from an unwillingness to acknowledge the limitations of human earthly existence. As the Gloomy Clerk's speech suggests, the progress of dulness is the process by which an already imperfect reason, under constant pressure from the part of the will that is controlled by pride, attempts to imagine the self as a transcendent center around which the universe as a whole revolves. The move Dwight will then make is to translate this notion of dulness into the explicitly religious language of infidelity and sin, the most obvious example being the personification of the "ruling principle" of Chauncy's theology, "The love of sweet security in sin" (685–686), as a version of the goddess Dulness: "No good more luscious than their truth she knows, / And hence their evidence will ne'er oppose" (689–690).

The Triumph of Infidelity also makes explicit the theological point implicit in *The Dunciad* and other Augustan satires in another way: it restores to the

---

Being a Recital of Certain Conversations on Natural and Moral Subjects (1709), in which the author's spokesman, Theocles, addresses nature explicitly as God: "O glorious nature! Supremely fair and sovereignly good! All-loving and all-lovely, all-divine! . . . Wise substitute of Providence! Empowered creatress! Or thou empowering deity, supreme creator! Thee I invoke and thee alone adore" (Shaftesbury, *Characteristics*, ed. Klein, 298). Pope quotes this passage in a footnote, but renders it in verse to emphasize this quality of a "raptur'd vision."

Dwight alludes directly to this enraptured image of Shaftesbury—as one who pays a kind of religious devotion to nature, but who is really venerating the self—in the passage in *The Triumph of Infidelity* where Satan remembers him as one of his favorite infidels: "In vain my Shaftesbury, to his master true, / Dread humble bee! o'er burrs and thistles flew; / Encupp'd, and ravish'd with the fussful noise, / To praise the wondrous flowers, he rais'd his voice. / Of nature, beauty, dream'd and humm'd amain, / And sung himself, and buzz'd at truth, in vain" (201–206).

---

center of the general Augustinian view of earthly alienation the religious myth of Original Sin and the fall of man. This is no doubt why Dwight chose Satan to be the poem's principal speaker, recounting all of modern history as a scene of perpetual temptation to various flattering cosmological systems. The point is not so much to insist upon the essential Christian orthodoxy of the Augustinian view, however, as to emphasize its permanence. The tendency toward pride and moral blindness, lamented throughout history by a host of Christians and non-Christians alike, has its roots in the origins of human existence. Infidelity thus emerges at once as a denial of the Augustinian moral reality and a form of the very temptation that brought this reality into being, as is evident at the moment in the poem when Satan contemplates his plan for the publication of Chauncy's Universalist tracts. Satan suggests that this latest form of infidelity is as old as the archetypal temptation:

> But what new onset shall I now begin,
> To plunge the New World in the gulph of sin?
> With sweet declension, down perdition's steep,
> How, in one host, her cheated millions sweep?
> I hail the glorious project, first, and best,
> That ever Satan's bright invention blest;
> That on this world my kingdom first began,
> And lost my rival paradise, and man.   (405–412)

The specific connections between the temptation of Adam and Eve and the modern temptation of Universalism are illustrated in a footnote to this passage referring to the third chapter of Genesis, in which Satan promises Eve that she will not die by eating the fruit of the tree of knowledge; rather, she will "become like a god." All of the symbols are connected to Chauncy: the promise of eternal life, the diminishment of the distance between divine and human, and the particular sense in which the sign of this transcendence is human knowledge (bringing to mind Chauncy's use of Clarke's assertion that human beings are capable of understanding the workings of the universe in a manner congruent to that of God).[32] And, just as the original temptation

32. Dwight reiterates this point in *Theology* in a sermon discussing the temptation that led to the fall. Of the promise to Eve that "ye shall not surely die," he writes: "Thousands and millions of times has this story been told; and repeated through every age,

had been the cause of the fall of Adam, Dwight will argue, to yield to any modern form of this same illusion of human transcendence will produce a similar result, a paradoxical fall into mere brute existence, represented elsewhere in *The Triumph of Infidelity* by the figure embodying the logical conclusion of all other infidel philosophies, the Infidel of Modern Breed. Nowhere is the Augustinian warning of the dangers of denying the distance between human and divine more clearly illustrated than in this character's creed, a glorification of man and of "his dear self" that is revealed, ironically, as the antithesis of divinity: "that illustrious brute of noblest shape, / A swine unbristled, and untail'd ape" (585–586).

In turn, the negative strategy of satiric unmasking, taken from Augustan poetry and reinvested with explicit theological significance in *The Triumph of Infidelity,* will thus become the basis for Dwight's positive system of practical religion in *Theology.* If the monitory point of *The Triumph of Infidelity* is that any attempt to project an image of transcendence onto mere secular existence will lead human beings paradoxically downward, the instructional point of *Theology* is that the opposite is also true, that only by recognizing the often painful reality of their own moral condition can they ever hope to be redeemed from this reality. This point, moreover, will constitute Dwight's particular but largely unremarked contribution to the New England theological tradition, an equally paradoxical explanation of Christian redemption: men and women are redeemed, he will explain, as a result of their own inward struggle against the very tendency of the will that causes them to believe they are deserving of regeneration.

In bringing this inner struggle to the forefront of religious life, Dwight was drawing upon an older emphasis in New England Calvinism. Self-examination as one of the "means of grace" had been especially important in the sermons of his distant Connecticut ancestor, Thomas Hooker. The crucial aspect of Hooker's theology had been an insistence upon meditation as a source of moral or religious truth, a way of revealing what he had called "the true sight of sin" within the human heart. This same emphasis would become, in the midst of the zeal and enthusiasm of the Great Awakening, a means of checking one's tendency to rely upon religious affections. Even Edwards, who would

---

from the apostasy to the present hour. Thousands and millions, also, of foolish and unhappy wretches, listen to the tale, because it is loved" (I, 418).

never give up his hope that the conversions he had witnessed were truly the work of God, would acknowledge, in a strain of skepticism running through all his writings, that the heart is always prone to self-deception. Dwight's debt to this tradition can thus be traced in his own treatment of self-examination as a kind of self-directed skeptical method. This method is given ultimate expression in the sermon entitled "The Folly of Trusting Our Own Hearts," where he warns against believing that humans are morally or spiritually deserving of regeneration. On the contrary, he asserts, "Reason demands, the Scriptures demand, their own eternal interests loudly demand, that they should search both their hearts, and their lives, with unceasing diligence, deep solicitude, and entire impartiality; . . . that they should bring their character for trial."[33]

Within the context of Dwight's more general Augustinian moral vision, self-skepticism constitutes, once again, the standard assertion of the primacy

33. Timothy Dwight, "The Folly of Trusting Our Own Hearts," in Dwight, *Sermons*, 2 vols. (New Haven, Conn., 1828), II, 57–58. Norman Pettit, in his study of the British and American Puritan tradition of self-examination as a preparative to receiving grace, writes that Hooker, more than any other New England divine, emphasizes the necessity of an arduous process of self-doubt: "He deliberately fostered an attitude of doubt so that no man could claim to be regenerate without close self-examination" (Pettit, *The Heart Prepared: Grace and Conversion in Puritan Spiritual Life* [New Haven, Conn., 1966], 101). Jonathan Edwards's skeptical treatment of the tendency to believe in one's own regenerate state is most evident in *Religious Affections*. Even as the ostensible purpose of this work is to defend the existence of affections that are truly inspired by God and to catalog the "distinguishing signs" of affections of grace, the thrust of his argument is that such signs are neither immediate nor easily recognizable: "Our wisdom and discerning, with regard to the hearts of men, is not to be trusted. We can see but a little way into the nature of the soul, and the depths of man's heart. The ways are so many whereby persons' affections may be moved without any supernatural influence" (Edwards, *Religious Affections* [1746], ed. John E. Smith, The Works of Jonathan Edwards, II [New Haven, Conn., 1959], 460). Such quotations lead Richard Bell to characterize Edwards as a skeptical thinker; it is necessary, however, to distinguish this more limited sense of skepticism, both in Edwards and Dwight, from the more common meaning of the term (Bell, "On Trusting One's Own Heart: Scepticism in Jonathan Edwards and Soren Kierkegaard," *History of European Ideas*, XII [1990], 105–116).

of the nunc-stans perspective in relation to that of the saeculum, a moral reminder that God sees clearly what the human will struggles to repress. In his explanation of spiritual regeneration in *Theology*, however, Dwight will posit a relationship between self-examination and the nunc-stans that is at once more original and more complex: the possibility that human beings, by clearing away the veils of self-delusion, can glimpse the truth of their own moral conditions — can see themselves, if only for an instant, as they are seen by God. The faculty that makes this insight possible is the conscience, and in Dwight's system it will represent nothing less than God's greatest gift to humanity, more important than reason itself. The power of the conscience, as had first been illustrated in *The Triumph of Infidelity*, lies in its capacity to work in opposition to the will, to pierce the heart with painful reminders of guilt, even for those who continue to seek out ways of remaining secure in lives of moral ease. Thus, even the wretch who is able to ignore such reminders most of the time experiences in his most private moments the fearful truth of his moral condition:

> In the deep midnight of his guilty mind,
> Where not one solitary virtue shin'd,
> Hardly, at times, his struggling conscience wrought
> A few, strange intervals of lucid thought,
> Holding her clear and dreadful mirror nigher,
> Where villain glow'd, in characters of fire.[34] (593–598)

The conscience as it is personified here, the ghostly figure in whose mirror even the most hardened sinner recognizes his true villainy, is not the conception of conscience as it was already being rewritten in the tradition of Locke's defense of religious toleration. The latter, understood as something all people possess as individuals, allowing them to discern for themselves the light of

---

34. Dwight will draw upon this same image of the conscience in *Theology:* "Wherever falsehood is loved, and uttered, conscience pierces the soul with stings of agony; and holds up to the culprit a dreadful mirror, by which his deformity and guilt are forced upon his view. The terrible likeness he is compelled to own. At the sight of this awful image he trembles; falters; and reluctantly, but irresistibly, sinks beneath the proper level of his nature" (III, 482–483).

God's truth, stands in direct opposition to the faculty that allows human beings to glimpse, however imperfectly or momentarily, a truth that transcends subjectivity or private judgment. Rather, as the image of the "dreadful mirror" suggests, Dwight understands the conscience in the terms used elsewhere in Augustan poetry to depict the particular capacity of satire to expose moral self-delusion, as in these lines from *An Essay on Satire* by the clergyman-satirist John Brown:

> In this clear mirror with delight we view
> Each image justly fine, and boldly true;
> Here vice, dragg'd forth by truth's supreme decree,
> Beholds and hates her own deformity;
> While self-seen virtue in the faithful line
> With modest joys surveys her form divine.[35]

For satirists like Brown, the capacity to lay bare otherwise unacknowledged vices stands at the center of the moral function of satire, which, as he puts it elsewhere in the poem, is comparable to the surgeon's knife: "Though painful is her art / . . . she only strikes to heal." One of the ways in which satire heals, he argues, is by forcing readers to confront their own moral failings, however painful. Against this background, in turn, we recognize the necessary satiric function implicit in Dwight's notion of the conscience as a window to the nunc-stans perspective. As in the case of satire, such momentary glimpses of an objective or timeless reality that are revealed during self-examination lead only toward what Dwight calls "the conviction of sin," a state that extends "beyond the common views of the mind concerning its sins" and involves a "serious, solemn, and heartfelt sense of their reality, guilt, and danger." One comprehends this reality, he explains, only in stages, from the recognition of one's guilt to that of the justice of God's condemnation and the helplessness of human beings to save themselves from this condition: "He sees himself perfectly helpless; and if left to himself, utterly ruined. In the anguish of his mind, produced by this view of his situation, he casts himself at the footstool of Divine Mercy, as a mere suppliant." This final stage corresponds to the precise moment of regeneration, for, when the sinner fully experiences this awe-

35. John Brown, *An Essay on Satire* (1745), in Robert Anderson, ed., *A Complete Edition of the Poets of Great Britain,* 13 vols. (London, 1792–1795), X, 881.

some reality, it is so painful to the heart that God bestows his grace as an act of mercy.[36]

If the importance of uncovering such difficult moral truths constitutes Dwight's answer to the pleasing falsehoods offered by Chauncy and others, the extent to which self-examination is presented as a necessary precondition for regeneration is a simultaneous attempt to distance his system from the New Divinity of Hopkins and Joseph Bellamy. Both had studied theology with Dwight's grandfather Jonathan Edwards and, after Edwards's death in 1758, had come to be regarded as his successors. Dwight was himself considered part of the New Divinity movement for most of his career and would always think of himself as firmly within the Edwardsean tradition. By the time he began preaching the sermons compiled in *Theology*, however, he would distinguish his own understanding of the role of the means of grace from the strict Calvinism of Hopkins. In an earlier controversy with Chauncy's friend and fellow Arminian Jonathan Mayhew, Hopkins had asserted not only that human beings are powerless to prepare for regeneration but that, when the unregenerated attempt to use these means, they actually become more guilty in God's eyes. Although Dwight would never openly question the doctrine of free grace as a central tenet of orthodox Protestantism, in the dozen or so sermons in *Theology* dealing with regeneration he would use the idea of self-examination to steer a course between Arminianism and New Divinity fatalism. Only God can effect regeneration, but, insofar as the means of grace lead naturally to spiritual self-examination and personal conviction of sin, he concludes, the way to salvation is "open, and equally open to all. . . . Nothing stands in his way, but his own impenitence and unbelief."[37]

36. Ibid., X, 878; Dwight, *Theology*, II, 432, 445.

37. Samuel Hopkins, *An Enquiry concerning the Promises of the Gospel* . . . (Boston, 1765), 124–125; Dwight, *Theology*, II, 218. On Dwight's proper place in the theological spectrum between New Divinity Calvinism and Arminianism, most scholars have concluded that Dwight began his career firmly within the New Divinity camp but, after taking over the professorship of divinity at Yale in 1795, developed a theology comparable to Arminianism; see Joseph Haroutunian, *Piety versus Moralism: The Passing of the New England Theology* (New York, 1932), chap. 9; Sidney Earl Mead, *Nathaniel William Taylor, 1786–1858; a Connecticut Liberal* (Hampden, Conn., 1967), 113–119; John R. Fitzmier, *New England's Moral Legislator: Timothy Dwight, 1752–1817* (Bloomington, Ind.,

At the same time, Dwight's insistence upon a vision of earthly life that is defined by epistemological limitations precludes the possibility that, even after receiving grace, men and women can ever be assured of this fact. Unlike those New Lights who had, since the Great Awakening, emphasized the conversion experience as a form of sanctification, Dwight would contend that regeneration occurs only at an ontological level, never accompanied by convincing signs either felt in the heart or understood by the intellect: "God administers his spiritual providence in such a manner, as to leave his children destitute of the Faith of Assurance, for their own good." Thus, life for the saint goes on much as it did before regeneration, characterized by the same proneness to sin and error, the same alienation from the sphere of the divine, the same need to struggle through continual self-examination: "the detection of his sins . . . the investigation of his duty. . . . looking daily into his heart . . . scrutinizing his life."[38]

With its emphasis upon a life of unending self-examination and moral struggle, Dwight's system of Christian redemption was still firmly within the Augustinian view of human moral life. The degree to which this vision is also drawing on the logic of Augustan satire was, perhaps, not as immediately recognizable. This connection has less to do with the subject matter of any par-

---

1998), 126–129. For Dwight as belonging to the wing of the New Divinity associated with Joseph Bellamy, see Stephen E. Berk, *Calvinism versus Democracy: Timothy Dwight and the Origins of American Evangelical Orthodoxy* (Hamden, Conn., 1974), chap. 4. For Dwight as the originator of the more "Arminianized" New Haven theology, see Conrad Cherry, *Nature and Religious Imagination: From Edwards to Bushnell* (Philadelphia, 1980), chap. 6; Annabelle S. Wenzke, *Timothy Dwight (1752–1817)* (Lewistown, N.Y., 1989), chap. 1. Precisely when Dwight began to move closer to an Arminian view of human agency in salvation is still a matter of speculation because, although he began preaching the sermons that make up *Theology* when he was pastor of Greenfield Hill (1783–1795), they were not written down until 1805, when the college hired an amanuensis to assist Dwight's failing eyesight; the extent to which the sermons evolved over time is uncertain. However, Dwight's early partnership with John Trumbull on "The Correspondent," in which Trumbull satirized Hopkins and Bellamy directly, suggests that even as a young man he was sympathetic toward criticism of the New Divinity (see Chapter 1, above).

38. Dwight, *Theology,* II, 533, III, 50.

---

ticular poem than with an implicit sense in several such poems that the function of satire is to lay bare unflattering truths that are nevertheless essential to moral or spiritual improvement. Within Augustan poetry proper, this necessity was presented as arising from the failure or unwillingness of religious leaders to preach such truths. In response to the rise of Latitudinarianism during the Restoration, for example, Pope's *Essay on Criticism* had described a crisis in which "*Pulpits* their *Sacred Satire* learn'd to spare, / And Vice *admir'd* to find a *Flatt'rer there!*" By the 1720s and 1730s, moreover, both Pope and Young were lamenting a similar crisis in which clergymen no longer told their parishioners what they did not want to hear. Part of Dwight's own purpose in *Theology* is to restore this element of satiric directness to its central position within practical religion. Thus, for instance, in the discourse on the duties of the clergy, Dwight reminds those students preparing for this profession that, whether "God or Man, the Law or the Gospel, Heaven or Hell, morality or piety, are the themes of his preaching," a responsible minister "will make the corruption of the human heart the foundation, on which all will be built."[39] Only by being made to recognize his or her own corruption, Dwight insists, will a sinner be prepared to undertake the hard spiritual struggle to conviction of sin, and thus to regeneration.

Dwight's insistence upon a theology that retains what Pope had called sacred satire, in turn, will provide the context in which the strongest form of criticism against any denomination or theological system will be to speak of it as "an easy, pleasant kind of religion," as he refers to Unitarianism at one point. Behind his positive system of regeneration in *Theology* lies the same momentous struggle over the meaning of Christianity that had begun during the Universalist controversy, with Dwight now speaking against a rising tide of new Pelagian voices declaring their theological liberation from the alienating doctrines of Augustinian moral theory. Thus, the great moral defense of Pelagian Christianity—that true religion will be saved from infidelity only by revealing the benevolence of God and the harmony and comfort of the universe—will signify in *Theology* an abandonment of the essential religious element of moral struggle.

The result will be, at best, a mere parody of Christian theology, what

39. Alexander Pope, *An Essay on Criticism* (1711), in Butt, ed., *Poems*, 161; Dwight, *Theology*, I, 502.

Dwight called in *The Triumph of Infidelity* the religion of smooth divines and, at worst, a Christian version of the very forms of infidelity that Chauncy and others had claimed to obviate. In rendering Christian doctrine consistent with some external standard such as reason or divine benevolence, he declares, "Many of those who have professedly received the Word of God in the Christian world have universally denied the real import of the book, which they have professed to believe. . . . The doctrines of the Gospel they have with one consent reduced to the level of mere natural religion." As in *The Triumph of Infidelity*, moreover, Dwight states that such doctrinal revisions issue chiefly from a desire to avoid the reality of human sinfulness and the necessity of reformation. In this sense, they contain an unrecognized or repressed desire for easy salvation that is made explicit only in Universalism:

> The heart relishes sin, and disrelishes reformation. Hence it devises various modes of quieting its fears concerning the anger of God, and securing itself from future woe. . . . For this purpose some persons become atheists, and deny the very Existence of God. Others become deists, and deny his Word and Character. . . . Others, still, adopt, for the same purpose, the scheme of Universalism; to something, very like which, in substance, all other schemes which I have mentioned, directly tend; whether perceived by those who embrace them, or not perceived.[40]

By the time Dwight was putting together the final version of his *Theology* sermons, Universalism was in a later stage of development, wherein Chauncy's self-proclaimed heirs would openly and optimistically accept the very conclusions about which Chauncy himself had remained somewhat reticent. Within only a few years of the appearance of *The Mystery Hid*, Universalists had already begun to declare their theology to be not merely a revision of a single doctrine but a radically new form of religion that would forever alter

---

40. Dwight, *Theology*, I, 458, II, 34, IV, 464–465. Dwight echoes the sentiments of the Smooth Divine passage from *The Triumph of Infidelity* in his discussion of the duties of the clergy in *Theology:* "Some shun every thing, which is unpopular; and utter only *smooth things;* such as they expect to be relished by their hearers; and satisfy themselves with the belief, that their congregations will receive nothing else, and that therefore nothing else will be useful to them" (IV, 255).

the future of Christianity. Dwight, in fact, had first glimpsed this development at the time he was composing *The Triumph of Infidelity.* He includes it in the narrative of the poem, when, at the end of Chauncy's long explanation of his doctrine, the aging divine looks beyond his own system and symbolically passes the torch to another man: "I've done my part; I've given you here the pith; / The rest, the bark and sap, I leave to S****" (733–734). Chauncy is referring here to William Pitt Smith, who in his 1787 publication, *The Universalist,* would identify his theological endeavor as part of a tradition begun by "the venerable CHAUNCEY," paying homage to this recently deceased "luminary of the church."[41] Yet the link between Chauncy and Smith in *The Triumph of Infidelity* goes beyond their shared belief in universal salvation. What Dwight glimpses in Smith's treatise is the beginning of Universalism's evolution into a religion that, although remaining Christian in name, would be openly more deistic than anything Chauncy himself would have imagined.

Smith follows closely the system of temporary punishment outlined in *The Mystery Hid,* but he is less concerned with doctrine as such than with his prediction that Universalism will ultimately resolve the crisis that has caused so many people to leave the church for deism and other infidel doctrines. Universalism, he writes, will first put an end to sectarianism, for the idea of universal future happiness will convince Christians that their doctrinal differences have no real import in the eyes of God. At the same time, it will provide a common language by which Christians and deists will finally come to understand each other. Those who follow the scriptural warnings of God's punishment of sinners can find no real objections to the punishment's being merely temporary. By the same token, the deists who accept the inherent rationality of a future state of perfection, but who reject the theological necessity of Christ, will be persuaded that Christ's role in salvation is no less rational, an instrument for God's moral ends in the same way the sun is an instrument for his natural ends. Far from being infidels, Smith declares, deists are men "of amiable characters, of sense, learning and morality," and their apostasy has always been a legitimate protest against an irrational system of Providence. The perfect marriage of reason and revelation offered by Universalism will inspire among

41. William Pitt Smith, *The Universalist; in Seven Letters to Amyntor* (New York, 1787), 3.

freethinkers a massive return to faith, creating a new Church of Christ that is more welcoming, peaceful, and rational than ever before.[42]

Between *The Triumph of Infidelity* and *Theology,* moreover, the further development of Universalism would unfold in the story of the emerging Universalist Church under the leadership of Hosea Ballou. Although Ballou's early career had been comparable to those of other itinerant Universalists, and his early theology consistent with the evangelical impulses of Murray and Caleb Rich, during the 1790s he would become increasingly attracted to other arguments for universal salvation, which, he believed, revealed more fully the rational foundations of the doctrine. In 1804, Ballou would publish his own system of Universalist theology, *A Treatise on Atonement,* which constituted a radical departure from his earlier influences, yet one that is strangely anticipated by the argument of *The Triumph of Infidelity.* In this work, Ballou endeavors to synthesize the arguments of two other works that he believed were particularly crucial to the Universalist movement: Chauncy's *The Mystery Hid* and Ethan Allen's *Reason, the Only Oracle of Man.*[43]

Organized around the traditional Protestant questions of the nature and consequences of sin and the necessity of atonement, Ballou's *Treatise* seems at first to have little in common with the deism of Ethan Allen. Yet the system Ballou constructs around his particular conception of atonement is unlike anything that had been argued from within the confines of Christian discourse. Although he follows Chauncy's argument that sin is the necessary re-

---

42. Ibid., 82.

43. Allen's influence on Ballou has been documented by Ernest Cassara, who points out that Ballou stated that his only aids in writing *A Treatise on Atonement* were "the Bible, Ethan Allen's *Oracles of Reason,* and my own reflections" (Cassara, *Hosea Ballou: The Challenge to Orthodoxy* [Boston, 1961], 194). This testimony notwithstanding, Cassara also shows that Ballou was familiar with *Salvation for All Men* (this title, in fact, may refer to *The Mystery Hid*) from at least 1797. Yet Ballou's use of Allen is particularly important because it forces modern readers to recognize the practical compatibility of discourses that at first glance may appear mutually exclusive. Ballou begins his career in the evangelical tradition of Murray and Caleb Rich, but he is able to incorporate Allen's explicit Enlightenment rhetoric, creating a text that, on one page, speaks of Christ's love and spirit in terms that evoke revivalism and, on the next, ridicules the idea of the literal truth of the Scriptures in the manner of the philosophes.

sult of God's allowing natural and moral evil to exist, he departs from Chauncy at the moment he describes the consequences of sin; he asserts with Allen that, if God is infinitely benevolent, there is no reason to conclude that he will punish mankind for a mere consequence of his own creation, even for a temporary period. Instead, the only consequence of sin is the guilt that issues naturally from one's rational faculties, a torment, he adds, that will exist only as long as a person's earthly life. Ballou's first radical move will thus be to imagine within the context of Christianity a future state that is more deistic than Allen's conception of a gradual rise from guilt to liberation: at the moment of bodily death, Ballou argues, human beings are instantly freed from the nature that gives rise to sin and guilt, and their souls assume a purely rational state in the blissful and eternal presence of the deity.

In a system where the only consequence of sin is a temporary experience of guilt, atonement seems hardly necessary. But Ballou fundamentally rewrites Christian theology by rejecting the traditional definition of atonement as a process by which sins are forgiven and the sinner made worthy in the eyes of God. Rather, in a grand act of reversal, he declares atonement to be the process by which God is accepted in the eyes of human beings. Because of God's omniscience and infinite mercy, he understands and has already forgiven our imperfections, making it unnecessary to reconcile ourselves to him. Instead, Ballou declares, the true atonement occurs when we reconcile God to ourselves: "God's love to us is antecedent to our love to him, which refutes the notion of God's receiving the atonement; but the idea that the manifestation of God's love to us causes us to love him, and brings us to a renewal of love, is perfectly consonant to the necessity of atonement."[44]

Following the logic of his inverted definition of atonement, Ballou's final radical departure from all previous versions of Universalism is to reconceive the role of Christ within Christianity. He asserts that the significance of Christ's life and death is purely symbolic and educational, a means of effecting the true atonement by attracting human beings to God's love. Ballou's Christology, in turn, has important implications for his understanding of the Christian religion as a whole, allowing him to take William Pitt Smith's earlier prediction of an age in which deists will return to the fold and declare that age to have already begun. Although Ballou speaks throughout the *Treatise* of the reli-

44. Hosea Ballou, *A Treatise on Atonement*, ed. Ernest Cassara (Boston, 1986), 120.

gion of Christ, he makes no distinctions between Christian and non-Christian on the basis of any particular belief—even the belief that Christ is instrumental to God's plan of redemption. Because the sole purpose of Christianity is to reconcile God to man, he argues, "the divine grace of reconciliation may be communicated to those who have never heard the name of a Mediator proclaimed, as the only way of life and salvation." "Even those . . . who reject Christianity altogether," he adds, may still "possess a good degree of this love, which is the spirit of life in Christ Jesus."[45] Thus, the new church of Christ that Smith had identified with the return of the deists emerges finally as a church in which no actual return is necessary, for many deists are already, in Ballou's sense of the phrase, "good Christians."

If Ballou's explicit act of reconfiguring the line between Christian and non-Christian represents a step no previous Universalist had taken, the idea of atonement from which his conclusion follows is never far from Chauncy's theology or its similar origins in Pelagian moral theory. Here, as in *The Mystery Hid,* human redemption is signified by the moment one realizes that the Augustinian vision of the world is a myth, that God rules the world according to rational and beneficent principles, and that whatever sense of alienation people have experienced is not simply their condition on earth but the result of the deceptions and errors that have for centuries obscured the truth of human moral capability. The appearance of Ballou's *Treatise* would in this sense confirm what Dwight had all along maintained in *The Triumph of Infidelity:* that, despite Chauncy's efforts to present a version of universal salvation that was consistent with the New England theological tradition, it was no longer possible to deny the ways in which Universalism tended to blur the line between Christianity and deism.

At the same time, however, the radical direction in which Ballou takes Universalism would pose a final, paradoxical problem in relation to Dwight's own theology. Ballou's unambiguous redefinition of Christianity would bear out Dwight's charge that Universalism constituted a Christian form of infidelity. Yet, as Chauncy had himself demonstrated years earlier in *The Benevolence of the Deity* and *Five Dissertations on the Fall of Man,* Pelagian assumptions such as benign Providence and the human capacity for rising in glory could themselves be synthesized with Christian thought in far less controversial ways

45. Ibid., 124.

than in Universalism. It would be far more difficult, moreover, to attack such assumptions as evidence of a co-opting of Christianity by infidel philosophers. Precisely for this reason, the greater challenge to Dwight's own theological position would be posed, not by infidelity as such, but by that more subtle transformation by which Pelagian assumptions of natural human virtue would come to be seen as essentially Christian in spirit.

Within the history of nineteenth-century religious thought generally, Chauncy's great moral defense of Universalism—that the crucial standard by which any religious doctrine should be measured is a general spirit of benevolence or goodwill—will prove to have more momentous consequences than the doctrine of universal salvation. According to this standard, Dwight's theology, unwavering in its insistence upon the frailty of human nature and the necessity of difficult moral struggle, will be rendered in the new discourse of Pelagian theology as an example of how orthodox divines vent their ill will or frustration toward their fellow human beings. The defining moment will be the publication of William Ellery Channing's "Moral Argument against Calvinism," within which such systems as Dwight's will be represented as the last vestiges of an outmoded theology that is not only false but detrimental to the progress of Christianity, a religion that "owes its perpetuity to the influence of fear in palsying the moral nature."[46] The effect of this representation will be registered within only a few years of Dwight's death in 1817, when his immediate theological successors, themselves engaged in a series of pamphlet wars over Unitarianism (1820–1825), will be forced to reconsider the moral overtones of their own adherence to Dwight's *Theology*.

Yet the way in which Dwight's more general theological assumptions, his particular synthesis of Calvinist theology and Augustan satire, would be contested in the decades following the publication of *The Triumph of Infidelity* was already evident in 1788. In that year, a version of the same benevolist argument was leveled against Dwight's satire in a review of the poem by Noah Webster. Although Webster—who might or might not have been aware that the poem was the work of his former Yale tutor Timothy Dwight—acknowledges that *The Triumph of Infidelity* is not without literary merit, he takes particular issue with the harshness of the satire directed against the poet's symbolic

46. William Ellery Channing, "Moral Argument against Calvinism" (1820), in *The Works of William E. Channing, D.D.*, 3d ed., 6 vols. (Boston, 1843), I, 218.

opponents. In one sense, of course, this is a form of the same backlash against satiric acerbity that had haunted the English Augustans in their own day. Yet Webster makes a special point of asserting that such "illiberal abuse" of men like Shaftesbury, Joseph Priestley, Chauncy, and Allen is inconsistent with the spirit of Christianity and that the man who wrote these lines "can hardly be a candidate for that heaven of love and benevolence which the scripture informs us is prepared for good men."[47] Here is a moment at which Webster speaks not merely as the symbolic first literary critic of the American Republic but as what will later prove to be the voice of a new Pelagian Christianity, delivering its verdict against the *"malevolent"* spirit of Augustan satire and the theological assumptions from which such a spirit arises.

47. Noah Webster, "Review of New Publications," *American Magazine,* I (1787–1788), 590.

CHAPTER 3

Progress and Redemption

Within the larger story of American Universalism in the two decades following the death of Charles Chauncy, the importance of an otherwise minor theological treatise such as William Pitt Smith's *Universalist* arises from the sheer exhilaration over the possibility of a new "age of Universalism." In this dawning era, not only Christianity but history itself would be imagined in a fundamentally new way. Smith celebrates the implications of universal salvation that Chauncy had at first been most hesitant to acknowledge, particularly those that concerned the doctrine's special role as a savior of Christianity, the one essential truth that would ultimately bring Christians and deists and skeptics together. As a result, Smith believed, one would not have to wait until the end of history or one's own earthly life to witness the redemption of the "brotherhood of all men." Only a few years or decades would be needed to register the effects of the revelation of God's plan for universal salvation, a full-scale awakening of human consciousness and virtue that would bring sweeping changes to virtually every aspect of human existence:

> These are the halcyon days of the church of Christ. Persecution dies, as if consumed "away by the moth"; superstition and ignorance shrink as "at the breath of his mouth, and before the brightness of his coming." The nations of the earth are gradually moulding into circumstances more favourable to the progress of truth. European courts grow ashamed of the cruel policy that once governed their councils, and adopt more refined and liberal sentiments. In places, where lately fire and faggot were esteemed the most conclusive arguments, we now find the pious, the learned and ingenious, honestly avowing their opinions, disseminating knowledge, searching the

entrails of superstition, and shaking the very foundations of fashionable orthodoxy. . . . To this happy country, men of all persuasions may resort, and worship the Universal Parent. No pretended infallibility is set up to decide in matters of conscience.[1]

If not for Smith's assertion that this vision of intellectual and political progress signals the "halcyon days of the church of Christ," this passage might well be mistaken for any of the more openly secular celebrations and predictions made a few years later by freethinkers like Thomas Paine and Condorcet. Despite its obvious theological differences, this passage shares with the great progressivist vision of the early years of the French Revolution not simply a belief in the progress of enlightenment but a corresponding conviction that mystification and tyranny would be banished from the face of the earth. Like these more radical figures, moreover, Smith articulates the sense of living at that singular moment in history when the secret of societal perfectibility is at last becoming available to human understanding. The name of that secret, for Smith as for countless others by the end of the eighteenth century, is purification, the idea that human knowledge will be cleansed of all of the myths and superstitions that have corrupted it in past ages. Yet, although this mystery has begun to be understood by more than an enlightened few, Smith adds, there remain those who stubbornly refuse to acknowledge its truth: until they do, "in vain shall we expect to see the golden cords of charity and love, binding the whole christian world in one amiable brotherhood, and one rational system of faith, conquering all opposition."[2]

In general terms, Smith's unmistakably religious language so closely resembles the otherwise secular discourse of unmasking superstition because of the long tradition of doctrinal reform and purification within Protestantism. Echoing the earliest reformers, Smith is at once able to assert his Christian faith while charging, with Voltaire or Holbach, that the most dangerous errors of the age have originated in one or another form of Christianity and that all intellectual and social progress begins with exposing and discarding such myths. At the same time, although versions of this argument had been

1. William Pitt Smith, *The Universalist; in Seven Letters to Amyntor* (New York, 1787), 71–72.

2. Ibid., 70.

advanced for centuries, they were perhaps never so commonplace as during the late eighteenth century, as is evident in the number of works designed to rewrite the history of Christianity—or, to borrow the title of Joseph Priestley's particular contribution to the genre, the history of the *corruptions* of Christianity.[3] The common purpose of such histories, whether written by an encyclopedist, a deist, or a self-proclaimed rational Christian, was to explain how Christianity had metamorphosed from a simple and essential system of beliefs about God and basic rules of moral conduct to a complex and superfluous set of doctrines that had all but obscured its pure and primitive truth.

Within this narrative, Christianity begins with the man, Jesus, preaching doctrines significant not so much for their originality as for their simplicity: indeed, he had purified the decalogue into only two commandments, to worship God and to love thy neighbor. Yet, by the time of the first generation of apostles, these basic tenets had already been corrupted, whether attributed, as in some versions of the story, to Paul's metaphysical system of grace or, in others, to the model of church government identified with Peter. In either case, such accretions led in turn to others, such as the myth of Christ's divinity or his ability to perform miracles, until the essence of Christianity was ultimately obscured by a very different message, one centered on an individual's dependence for redemption on the intervention of priests or on an arbitrary system of grace. To combat these corruptions, the work of the enlightened historian is, as Priestley puts it, to place this system in the *"refiner's fire,"* to purge it from the dross that has debased it; "and when it shall have stood this test, it may be presumed that the truth and excellency of it will never more be called in question." At the same time, as Priestley's own career suggests, this discourse of purification owes as much to science as to theology, particularly to the Enlightenment application of the principles of empiricism to the history of religious thought. The empiricist ideal of advancing knowledge, not by constructing new systems, but by rejecting the very notion of system-building and grounding knowledge on experience alone would be understood as the foundation for unmasking all forms of religious superstition. The oft-celebrated triumvirate of Francis Bacon, Isaac Newton, and John Locke—names virtually

3. Joseph Priestley, *An History of the Corruptions of Christianity* (1782), in John Towill Rutt, ed., *The Theological and Miscellaneous Works of Joseph Priestley*, 25 vols. (London, 1817–1832), V.

synonymous with the ideals of science and empiricism throughout the eighteenth century—would be held up by skeptics like Voltaire and D'Alembert as the patron forebears of their own more radical project.[4]

By the end of the century, this same identification of science and empiricism with the Enlightenment strategy of unmasking superstition would in turn allow certain orthodox or enlightened theologies to be presented not merely as consistent with science but, in fact, as issuing directly from scientific inquiry. In one example, Paine asserts that his particular brand of deism is the only religion in which human beings worship God by way of their scientific advancements—"The creator of man is the creator of science, and it is through that medium that man can see God, as it were, face to face." In another, Priestley derives his Socinian Christology, the belief in the simple humanity of Jesus, from his chemical experiments and materialist theory of the universe. As Priestley reasoned in *Disquisitions Relating to Matter and Spirit*, if what the metaphysicians called the "immaterial soul" amounted to nothing more than matter-in-motion then Jesus Christ could not have been anything more than a purely material, human creature.[5]

For those who shared the belief that science could reduce all knowledge to

4. Ibid., 4. Whereas Priestley concludes the essential doctrine of religion to be Unitarianism, others conclude it to be a version of deism (see Thomas Morgan, *The Moral Philosopher; in a Dialogue between Philalethes a Christian Deist, and Theophanes a Christian Jew* [1737], ed. Gunter Gawlid [Stuttgart-Bad Cannstatt, 1969]; and Voltaire, *Philosophical Dictionary* [1764], ed. and trans. Theodore Besterman [Harmondsworth, Eng., 1971]). In *The Age of Reason* (1794, 1795), Thomas Paine depicts Jesus as preaching not only a simpler theology but a radical set of political views, opposing both Jewish priests and Roman political officials; as a result, "this virtuous reformer and revolutionist lost his life" (Paine, *Collected Writings* [New York, 1995], 671). Only David Hume's contribution to the genre, *The Natural History of Religion* (1755), rejects the notion of an essential set of religious doctrines and advises the reader instead to take refuge in "the calm, though obscure, regions of philosophy" (Hume, *The Philosophical Works of David Hume*, 4 vols. [Boston, 1854], IV, 493). For the philosophes' application of the works of Francis Bacon, Isaac Newton, and John Locke, see Peter Gay, *The Enlightenment: An Interpretation*, I, *The Rise of Modern Paganism* (New York, 1966), 127–159.

5. Paine, *Age of Reason*, in Paine, *Writings*, 827; Joseph Priestley, *Disquisitions Relating to Matter and Spirit* (1777), in Rutt, ed., *Theological and Miscellaneous Works*, III, 218–221.

its bare essence, the great virtue of characterizing Christianity as superstition was that it seemed readily to explain why the progress of knowledge had been impeded for so much of human history. A host of eighteenth-century progressivists thus imagined a counter-Enlightenment, defined most precisely by Paine as a conspiracy of political despots and priests who sought to preserve control over the institutions of learning and to oppose the advancements of science that otherwise would have exposed their systems as mere myth. Such men, he writes, "could not but foresee that the continually progressive knowledge that man would gain, by the aid of science, of the power and wisdom of God, manifested in the structure of the universe, and in all the works of creation, would militate against, and call into question, the truth of their system of faith; and therefore it became necessary to their purpose to cut learning down to a size less dangerous to their project . . . the dead study of dead languages."[6]

Beyond its explanatory power, what made the theory of a counter-Enlightenment especially compelling was the corresponding notion that the particular truths that had been concealed by priests and despots—and so clearly revealed by science and empirical inquiry—were those that concerned the nature, interests, and capabilities of human beings. At the heart of the idea of a struggle between enlightened philosophers and their enemies lay the conviction that superstition serves to perpetuate a pessimistic view of human nature, as in Paine's remark elsewhere in *The Age of Reason* that the history of superstition is the story of man always being taught "to contemplate himself as an out-law, as an out-cast, as a beggar, as a mumper, as one thrown, as it were, on a dunghill, at an immense distance from his Creator." To the contrary, the synthesis of science and the essential doctrines of theology reveals, first and foremost, that human beings have been created for the purpose of moral, intellectual, and material progress and that science is the creator's way of providing for this development. Were this divine purpose only to be universally recognized, he adds, the human mind "would encrease in gratitude as it increased in knowledge. His religion or his worship would become united with his improvement as a man."[7]

In the years following the appearance of *The Age of Reason* in America,

6. Paine, *Age of Reason,* in Paine, *Writings,* 697–698.
7. Ibid., 685, 827.

the identification of intellectual enlightenment and moral progress would become a theme in dozens of pamphlets and orations, particularly by those associated with the popular Enlightenment groups and Democratic-Republican societies that had formed during the height of American enthusiasm over the French Revolution. For the most radical voices in this movement, such as Elihu Palmer—a prominent member of the Democratic Society of New York whose own career had taken him from orthodox Connecticut preacher to Universalist to founder of the New York Deistical Society—Paine's argument could be appropriated without toning down his emphasis on exploding the myths of revealed religion. In Palmer's 1797 Fourth of July oration, *An Enquiry Relative to the Moral and Political Improvement of the Human Species,* he argues that, although the American Revolution stands as the singular event in the struggle to abolish political despotism, what remains to be eradicated is the even more destructive "moral despotism" of priests who have long "pretended to hold a high and social intercourse with celestial powers, and to receive immediately from them the mandates by which man was to be directed in his conduct." Having established a "supernatural scheme with dogmas and principles of a very extraordinary and awful nature," in which "human virtue was considered of but little consequence," he adds, the result was that "the moral condition of man became truly deplorable." Yet, he warns, the day is coming when, "awakened by the energy of thought, inspired by the American revolution, man will find it consistent with his inclination and his interest to examine all the moral relations of his nature, . . . and to relinquish with elevated satisfaction, those supernatural schemes of superstition which have circumscribed the sphere of beneficial activity, for which Nature designed him."[8]

For those more hesitant to follow Paine and Palmer to an outright rejection of revealed religion, on the other hand, the same general argument could be made in purely moral and political terms, as in the 1796 address to the Society of Saint Tammany by Tunis Wortman, *An Oration on the Influence of Social Institution upon Human Morals and Happiness.* The question Wortman poses is not whether society will ultimately be perfected by advancements in the natural and moral sciences, for this is by now self-evident: "Human knowledge has

8. Elihu Palmer, *An Enquiry Relative to the Moral and Political Improvement of the Human Species; an Oration, Delivered in the City of New-York on the Fourth of July, Being the Twenty-First Anniversary of American Independence* (New York, 1797), 25–27.

already arrived to a degree of perfection that has exceeded the hopes of the most sanguine and enthusiastic visionary. Moral light has . . . diffused its invigorating influence throughout every department of social life, and exalted the human character to a state of splendid greatness and perfectibility, that no former age has ever yet realised or experienced." Instead, he addresses the denial of this truth by both political and religious leaders who insist that human nature is fixed, incapable of being reformed by education. This belief—what Wortman calls the "degradation and debasement of the human character"— threatens the future of the Republic: because this view is naturally attractive to those who favor a coercive government, it will serve as "a standing argument to justify the oppressions they have used, and the miseries and calamities they have occasioned."[9]

In works such as Palmer's and Wortman's, the Augustinian view of human nature is thus treated as ideology in the specifically eighteenth-century understanding of the term. This is ideology as a system of false consciousness used by an identifiable group of conspirators to promote its own interests in the guise of universal or absolute truth.[10] In Wortman's address to the almost exclusively Jeffersonian membership of the Tammany Society, this conspiracy

9. T[unis] Wortman, *An Oration on the Influence of Social Institution upon Human Morals and Happiness, Delivered before the Tammany Society, at their Anniversary* . . . (New York, 1796), 3, 6.

10. The distinction between the twentieth-century conception of ideology as a dynamic, autonomous historical force and the cruder Enlightenment version of the theory as a deliberate conspiracy, goes back to Louis Althusser's seminal essay, "Ideology and Ideological State Apparatuses." Beginning in the eighteenth century, he writes, philosophers began seriously to contend that the conditions of human existence had for much of human history been falsely represented by religion, law, and other institutions. In contrast to the increasingly complex theory of ideology that developed in the nineteenth and twentieth centuries, "the first answer (that of the eighteenth century) proposes a simple solution: Priests or Despots are responsible." "They 'forged' the Beautiful Lies so that, in the belief that they were obeying God, men would in fact obey the Priests and Despots, who are usually in alliance in their imposture, the Priests acting in the interests of the Despots or *vice versa*, according to the political positions of the 'theoreticians' concerned" (Althusser, *Lenin and Philosophy and Other Essays*, trans. Ben Brewster [London, 1971], 153–154).

was understood first and foremost as a Federalist plot to negate the effects of the Revolution by opposing not only the ideals of liberty, equality, and the rights of man but also the rational or scientific grounds for these ideals. Within this intellectual and political climate, Timothy Dwight would, in only a few years, appear as one of the leaders of the counter-Enlightenment, an American counterpart to the Scholastics and Jesuits before him—which is what his Republican opponents would have in mind when they referred to him as "the Pope of Federalism."

In specific terms, they portrayed Dwight as an opponent of political and social progress, using his position as president of Yale to poison the minds of Connecticut's youth with the political prejudices of his Federalist allies and the religious superstitions of his grandfather Jonathan Edwards; in short, he betrays liberty and reason to maintain and increase his own power. "Active, persevering, and undaunted, he proceeds to direct all political, civil, and ecclesiastical affairs," accuses one pamphleteer, John Cosens Ogden, before delivering the Enlightenment coup de grâce: "Science, he forsakes, and her institutions he prostrates, to promote party, bigotry, and error." And, as we have seen, one of the symbols of Dwight's continuing struggle to maintain political and ecclesiastical control was *The Triumph of Infidelity:* "Dr. Dwight will scourge with the scorpions of . . . polemic divinity, party politics, poetry, satirical writings, the Triumph of Infidelity, and the prejudices circulated by young men and young divines taught by him."[11]

In the image of *The Triumph of Infidelity* as a satiric scourge against all proponents of social and intellectual progress, we are able to recognize how a counter-Enlightenment served as a powerful interpretive lens through which the poem was read from the 1790s onward. At the same time, the central complication to this interpretation is also found in *The Triumph of Infidelity*. The narrative recounted in the poem, spanning the period from the time of Christ through the Reformation and the rise of the New Science, is itself a version of the same Enlightenment history in which human knowledge is gradually

---

11. [John Cosens Ogden], *A View of the New-England Illuminati: Who Are Indefatigably Engaged in Destroying the Religion and Government of the United States* (Philadelphia, 1799), 17; [Ogden], *An Appeal to the Candid, upon the Present State of Religion and Politics in Connecticut* (Stockbridge? Conn., 1798), 11–12.

purified from the dross of superstition and metaphysical excess. This common conceptual framework, in turn, reveals the point of contention underlying the poem's attack on so many Enlightenment figures and their doctrines: what is implied is, not some simple opposition to a universally held conception of "The Enlightenment," but an ideological struggle over the meaning of intellectual enlightenment itself. Dwight is thus not so much defending a religious tradition that is at that moment being unmasked as superstition or ideology as challenging the logic of these very categories. In doing so, he posits a crucial question about the Enlightenment that has since been raised in our own century: Did the assertions of Voltaire and Paine and others signify a liberation from centuries of false consciousness, or did their own vision of progress constitute simply a newer ideology, one that projected a set of beliefs and power relations favoring bourgeois individualism over supernal authority?

The immediate means by which *The Triumph of Infidelity* offers a competing vision of enlightenment is through the widely held idea of the harmonious coexistence of science and religion. Once again, the great symbol of this harmony is the triumvirate of Bacon, Newton, and Locke, here celebrated as much for their public adherence to Christianity as for their specific philosophical discoveries or innovations. At the same time, Satan's inverted tribute to these figures will constitute Dwight's attempt to reclaim them from the opposing historical narrative assumed by the philosophes. When Satan recalls his own infidel campaigns in the late seventeenth century, he also laments that his efforts were almost singlehandedly demolished by the empirical movement. As he acknowledges, the superior reasoning of such professed Christians as Locke and Newton served only to ridicule by comparison the pseudoscience of Restoration-era infidelity:

> Thro' nature's fields while cloud-borne Bacon ran,
> Doubtful his mind, an angel, or a man;
> While high-soul'd Newton, wing'd by Heaven abroad,
> Explain'd alike the works, and word, of God;
> While patient Locke illum'd with newborn ray,
> The path of reason, and the laws of sway;
>
> . . . .
>
> Pain'd, shrivell'd, gasping, from the forceful ray
> How crept my mite philosophers away?   (185–198)

In presenting empiricism as a movement essentially in the service of Christianity, Dwight is simply reasserting the standard argument of religious apologists going back to the original appearance of Locke's *Essay concerning Human Understanding* (1690) and Newton's *Principia* (1687): the explanation of the inward workings of the mind or the outward movement of the physical universe served ultimately to reveal the greater glory of God. "Piety has found / Friends in the friends of science, and true pray'r / Has flow'd from lips wet with Castalian dews. / Such was thy wisdom, Newton, childlike sage!" Cowper had written in *The Task* a few years earlier.[12] Yet, as the tone of Cowper's insistence also suggests, by this time a need had already arisen to defend this position against the opposing assertion that the empiricists' larger project was in its essence antireligious, that Newton's scriptural interpretations or Locke's *Reasonableness of Christianity* (1695) indicated only that these pioneers of scientific reasoning had wittingly or unwittingly stopped short of the full implications of their thought.

In *The Triumph of Infidelity*, Dwight responds to this argument by adding to this illustrious company of empiricists another name, George Berkeley, bishop of Cloyne, whose influence had been less far-reaching in America but whose work epitomized for Dwight the interdependence of religion and empirical thought. Although Berkeley's radical idealism represented a skeptical challenge to the belief in the material world, Dwight presents it in the poem as a conception of the universe that "In all events, and in all beings shew'd / The present, living, acting, speaking God" (193–194). More specifically, Berkeley's importance arises from his method in *A Treatise concerning the Principles of Human Knowledge*, which is entirely inductive. His idealism is rooted in the principle that the existence of external reality cannot be distinguished from perception, and it thus represents a direct extension of Locke's skepticism concerning the possibility of knowing the essence of material reality. At the same time, his skeptical approach to the question of the very existence of matter allowed him to illustrate the workings of God in a way that even Newtonian physics could not. If every idea or sensation issued directly from the mind of God, it was impossible to interpret the universe as a machine that could run without the constant supervision of its creator. As Berkeley explained, the reli-

12. William Cowper, *The Task* (1785), in John D. Baird and Charles Ryskamp, eds., *The Poems of William Cowper*, 3 vols. (Oxford, 1980), II, 169.

gious truth implicit in idealism is that "all things necessarily depend on Him as their Conservator as well as Creator . . . all nature would shrink to nothing, if not upheld and preserved in being by the same force that first created it."[13]

For Dwight, then, empiricism implies an underlying religious impulse, not simply in the insistence that the true end of science is to reveal the workings of the creator of the universe but in the belief that empirical inquiry is an act of resisting the temptation of what the eighteenth century condemned generally as "philosophical pride." One of the great virtues of depending upon observation and inductive reasoning, as opposed to constructing elaborate systems, Locke had said, is that, rather than being ruled by a view toward transcending the limits of human knowledge, the empiricist is satisfied to confine himself to the "knowledge which is most suited to our natural capacities."[14] This epistemological humility—drawing as it does upon the view of human earthly limitation lying at the heart of Dwight's theology—allows him to conceive of the structural relationship between the scientific and theological modes of inquiry in an even more radical way. In *The Triumph of Infidelity*, science and religion become virtually interchangeable, such that the approach to knowledge assumed in Dwight's conception of religion is understood as a kind of empiricism.

Dwight's comprehensive vision of a theological or Christian empiricism is all but lost to modern categories of science and religion, which becomes immediately evident in the poem when none other than Jonathan Edwards is presented as the great symbol of Dwight's philosophical ideal. Satan, turning from the state of Europe to that of America, curses Edwards as his "chief bane" and "apostolic foe" (353) and bitterly credits him for preventing deism and skepticism from taking hold in the colonies. Yet, although it is hardly surprising that this inverted tribute would be given to Edwards, the importance of Edwards is identified only incidentally with his role in the Great Awakening or in such doctrinal works as *Freedom of the Will* (1754) or *Great Christian Doctrine of Original Sin Defended* (1758). Far greater emphasis is given instead

13. George Berkeley, bishop of Cloyne, *A Treatise concerning the Principles of Human Knowledge* (1710), in A. A. Luce and T. E. Jessop, eds., *The Works of George Berkeley, Bishop of Cloyne*, 9 vols. (London, 1949–1957), II, 281.

14. John Locke, *An Essay concerning Human Understanding* (1690), *The Works of John Locke*, 10 vols. (London, 1812), III, 79.

to Edwards's least traditionally theological work, *The Nature of True Virtue*. Here Edwards reveals himself, as Satan puts it, as a "moral Newton." That is, just as Newton revealed the laws of motion in the physical world, Edwards uncovered the hidden workings of the moral world:

> He, in clear view, saw sacred systems roll,
> Of reasoning worlds, around their central soul;
> Saw love attractive every system bind,
> The parent linking to each filial mind;
> The end of Heaven's high works resistless shew'd,
> Creating glory, and created good.[15]   (357–362)

Even in this passage, where Dwight seems to be revealing a wholly unconventional set of assumptions about the relationship between religion and science, he is never far from the fundamental categories governing *The Triumph of Infidelity* as a whole. Nor are these categories essentially different from those governing the Enlightenment teleology of purification of knowledge. The em-

15. In *The Nature of True Virtue*, published posthumously in 1765, Jonathan Edwards defines true virtue as love or benevolence toward "being in general," a capacity that does not belong naturally to human beings but is invested in individuals by God as they grow spiritually. Because "being in general" is, for Edwards, synonymous with God, virtue consists of a total predilection toward God and goodness and, in its purest form, does not allow for a distinction between one's own personal happiness and that of others (Edwards, *The Nature of True Virtue*, with a foreword by William K. Frankema [Ann Arbor, Mich., 1960]). Thus, in *The Triumph of Infidelity*, Dwight presents Edwards as having discovered a force of virtue that is the moral equivalent of gravity: God, the center of the moral or spiritual system, draws beings toward him, causing the virtuous to revolve around his love.

In making such a claim for Edwards, Dwight is offering his own orthodox counterargument to similar analogies, found in a number of eighteenth-century English poems, depicting moral philosophers such as Shaftesbury or Ralph Cudworth as Newtons of the moral world. See, for instance, William Melmoth's praise of Shaftesbury in *Of Active and Retired Life:* "Not orbs he weighs, but marks, with happier skill, / The scope of actions and the poise of will, / In fair proportion here describ'd we trace / Each mental beauty, and each moral grace" (John Bell, ed., *Classical Arrangement of Fugitive Poetry*, 18 vols. [London, 1790–1797], I, 9).

phasis upon observing, in Newtonian fashion, only those systems that exist in nature is directly opposed to what Satan calls the "love of system" in his ironic tribute to Chauncy and Universalism. The same opposition between elaborate constructs of human pride and simple truths more humbly observed, moreover, is emphasized from the very beginning of the poem, with Satan's nostalgic recollection of the paganism of ancient Rome. The great power of the Roman Empire, Satan explains, lay not merely in its wealth or military might but in what he calls "The Pagan fabric of a thousand years; / The spells, the rites, the pomp" (40–41). The elaborate structure of superstition and empty ritual, he laments, was suddenly unmasked as such by the simpler and more rational doctrines of the early Christian church: "As sand-built domes dissolve before the stream, / As visions fleet upon th' awakening beam, / The structure fled" (45–47). In the same way, the conception of true Christianity as opposed to such systems, in turn, controls Satan's story of the usurpation of Christianity by the Catholic papal succession and its consequent liberation by Protestant reformers. The crucial point about the Reformation is that it was never simply a religious or doctrinal movement but an intellectual and political one as well, the end of what Satan calls his "glorious empire," in which the "veils" and "cobwebs" of Catholic theology gave way to a larger awakening: "The mind new sprang; rebudding virtue grew; / And trembling nations rose from death anew. / . . . / . . . / Where, long by wintry suns denied to rise, / Fair right and Freedom open'd on the skies" (123–128).

In presenting the history of Christianity in these terms, Dwight is drawing upon a historiography shared by his theological and ideological opponents. The depiction of the early church as the simple and rational antithesis to paganism, for instance, corresponds to the same ideal of a pure, primitive Christianity found in critiques of the modern church by Priestley, Thomas Morgan, and others. In the same way, the story of political and social liberation brought about by the Reformation corresponds to the tendency of religious skeptics to recast the history of the Reformation in purely sociological terms—the notion that Protestantism, while representing no great theological or philosophical breakthrough, signified the first challenge to the power of despots and priests. With Luther's initial resistance to papal authority, Voltaire had said, at least "a corner of the veil was lifted," and Paine would later credit the Reformation with breaking "the first link in this long chain of despotic ignorance," even as he would add that "this was the only public good the reformation did."[16] Dwight's strategy in *The Triumph of Infidelity* is thus to reabsorb this secular interpretation into his own traditionally religious historiography, presenting the Reformation as a return of the church to a theological essence long obscured by Catholicism.

The Triumph of Infidelity, then, while constituting on one level a defense of orthodox religion against Enlightenment skepticism, will simultaneously employ the same skeptical discourse within which religious doctrines are subject to interpretation as systems of delusion or manipulation. This discourse is most evident in the passage where Satan recalls that one of his most successful tools of undermining the cause of true religion has been the philosophical influence in Europe of the Society of Jesus. The special importance of the Jesuits in this context lies in their common eighteenth-century reputation as the emblem of what we have since come to call ideology. They had symbolized not only the priestcraft associated generally with the Catholic church but the more insidious practice of consciously employing various kinds of sophistry to protect and extend their own power, all the while deceiving ordinary people of their true spiritual conditions and interests. Satan has precisely this systematic deception in mind when he presents the Jesuits' theological and moral system as infidelity:

> Here Jesuitic art its frauds combin'd
> To draw ten thousand cobwebs o'er the mind,
> In poison'd toils the flutterer to enclose,
> And fix, with venom'd fangs, eternal woes.
> On sceptic dross they stamp'd Heaven's image bright,
> And nam'd their will-a-wisp, immortal light,
> Thro' moors, and fens, the sightless wanderer led,
> 'Till down he plung'd, engulph'd among the dead.   (311–318)

In describing "Jesuitic art" as drawing "cobwebs o'er the mind" and leading the "sightless wanderer" to treat as divine truth what is in reality no more

16. Voltaire, *Essaies Sur Les Moeurs* . . . , ed. René Pomeau, 2 vols. (Paris, 1963), II, 217 ("Après avoir décrié les indulgences, il [Martin Luther] examina le pouvoir de celui qui les donnait aux chrétiens. Un coin du voile fut levé"); Paine, *Age of Reason,* in Paine, *Writings,* 700.

than an ignis fatuus or "will-a-wisp," Dwight is employing two of the stock images of the philosophes' own discourse of unmasking. The same discourse, moreover, would be taken over by Karl Marx in his famous denunciation of religion as an opiate that dulls human consciousness to the reality of human alienation.[17] Yet Dwight uses a version of this critique to make a very different point. Although the Jesuits are portrayed as using a mask of religious doctrine to repress or deny a fundamental truth, in this case the truth that is being repressed is itself religious in nature. The specific "fraud" to which Satan refers in this passage—the act of stamping "Heaven's image bright" on "sceptic dross"—is the practice of interpreting moral and religious law known as *probabilism*, or *laxism*. This form of casuistry allowed a person to violate a given law if there existed any grounds for doubting its truth or application. As the critics of probabilism charged, such reasoning could easily be used as an ingenious way of rationalizing moral failure. We are thus able to glimpse an alternative conception of the ideological nature of certain religious doctrines: the reason "Jesuitic art" had so successfully deluded otherwise reasonable people, *The Triumph of Infidelity* suggests, is that its deception appealed to the aspect of human nature that was already prone to pride and self-delusion.

In redefining superstition in this manner, *The Triumph of Infidelity* opens the way for its most sweeping critique of Enlightenment rationalism, the notion that what has ostensibly been a movement toward freethinking has actually been characterized by the same tendencies long since exposed as superstition in their more obvious religious guises. This is the point, in fact, of the ex-

17. The image of the ignis fatuus, the deceptive light that appears over marshland owing to the combustion of gas, was particularly useful during the Enlightenment as a means of representing a given philosophical system as a false or dangerous "light" that prevents ordinary people from being truly enlightened. Thus, in the preface to *The System of Nature*, Holbach uses an image almost identical to Dwight's: "In short, man disdains the study of Nature, except it be partially: he pursues phantoms that resemble an *ignis-fatuus*, which at once dazzle, bewilder, and affright: like the benighted traveller led astray by these deceptive exhalations of a swampy soil, he frequently quits the plain, simple road of truth, by pursuing of which, he can alone ever reasonably hope to reach the goal of happiness" (Paul Thiry, baron d' Holbach, *The System of Nature; Or, Laws of the Moral and Physical World* (1770), trans. D. Robinson, 2 vols. in 1 [Boston, 1889], viii–ix).

tended passage satirizing Voltaire, a critique that differs from the attacks by Dwight's contemporaries in the important sense that Voltaire is never treated simply as an opponent of religion. The Voltaire whom Satan praises in *The Triumph of Infidelity* as one of his favorite infidels is not the withering voice of skepticism in *Candide* (1759) and *The Lisbon Earthquake* (1756); he is the representative Enlightenment figure of *The Philosophical Dictionary* (1764), whose satire of Christian superstition is presented alongside a positive argument reasserting an alternative set of pure or essential doctrines. Thus, Voltaire has undergone a religious conversion, not to deism or some other modern system, ironically, but, as numerous references in his *Dictionary* suggest, to an idealized conception of ancient Chinese religion as the great truth that has long been lost to the West:

> He, light and gay, o'er learning's surface flew,
> And prov'd all things, at option, false or true.
> The gospel's truths he saw were airy dreams,
> The shades of nonsense, and the whims of whims.
>
> .   .   .   .
>
> The Greeks, and Romans, never truth descried;
> But always (when they prov'd the gospel) lied.
> He, he alone, the blest retreat had smelt,
> The Well, where 'long with frogs, the goddess dwelt;
> In China dug, at Chihohamti's call,
> And curb'd with bricks, the refuse of his wall.   (263–276)

With its references to "The Well" and "the goddess" and the emperor Shih Huang-ti (Chihohamti), the last lines of this passage have been especially obscure to modern readers, but its immediate point is clear enough: in the name of philosophical freethinking, Voltaire has merely substituted one set of "airy dreams" for another. His fascination with China might have begun with the common Enlightenment use of Eastern philosophy as a perspective from which to point out the limitations of the Christian claim to absolute religious truth; but his preoccupation with finding an alternative to Christianity led him to suggest that Chinese philosophy is itself the way to true spiritual understanding. Or, in the symbolic terms of the passage above, Voltaire has persuaded himself that he has discovered the fabled well of truth in China, built by Shih Huang ti with the leftover bricks from his other celebrated accomplishment, the Great Wall. At the same time, the deeper critique of Voltaire's conversion is seen in the more subtle allusions suggested by these images, which call into question the claims to objectivity and philosophical progress implicit in Enlightenment freethinking generally. Those familiar with Chinese cultural history would recall that Shih Huang-ti was also legendary for ordering all of China's early literature to be burned; indeed, this moment is memorialized in Alexander Pope's *Dunciad* when he describes the history of dulness and Shih Huang-ti himself as the "god-like Monarch" who in "one bright blaze turns Learning into air." Similarly, the well of truth, as the passage makes clear, is also the well inhabited by the frog from a famous fable from the *Chuang-Tzu*, who vainly purports to understand the outside world from his own limited perspective of peering at a section of the sky from the depths of the well.[18]

The limited perspective to which these allusions point is the same limitation addressed elsewhere in *The Triumph of Infidelity:* pride-in-consciousness as it reconstructs the universe around an image of its own central importance, which Dwight presents as the basis of all forms of infidel philosophy. At the same time, through such passages Dwight begins to describe this limitation in the explicit terms of religious faith. Appropriating the argument used by critics of religion—that its claim to rationality is compromised by its reliance on faith or imagination—Dwight suggests that the same critique is applicable to systems in which religion is explicitly rejected. As he will later assert in *The Nature, and Danger, of Infidel Philosophy,* even in the case of outright atheism,

18. Alexander Pope, *The Dunciad* (1728), in John Butt, ed., *The Poems of Alexander Pope: A One-Volume Edition of the Twickenham Text with Selected Annotations* (New Haven, Conn., 1963), 754–755. The fable of the frog in the well involves a conversation between a turtle, who expresses joy over living in the sea, and a frog, who is bewildered because his only view of the world is through the top of the well. This story is mentioned several times in the *Chuang-Tzu*, as, for instance, in this proverb: "You can't talk to a frog in a well about the sea . . . because it is cramped inside its hole. . . . You can't talk to hole-in-the-corner scholars about the Way, because they are constricted by their doctrines" (Chuang-tzu, *The Seven Inner Chapters and Other Writings from the Book Chuang-tzu,* trans. A. C. Graham [London, 1981], 145). Dwight's allusion to this fable thus underscores the irony of Voltaire's claims to philosophical independence.

"the difficulties and embarrassments to faith are lessened neither in number, nor in degree. On the contrary, they are multiplied, and enhanced."[19] This same conclusion had been reached in *The Triumph of Infidelity* in the satiric portrait of the Infidel of Modern Breed. Although this persona is meant to symbolize those in America who most closely adhered to the still-novel materialism of La Mettrie and Holbach—a conception of the world that rejected any form of deity—the modern infidel views human material reality as "theological," describing himself as

> Made, not to know, or love, the all-beauteous mind;
> Or wing thro' heaven his path to bliss refin'd:
> But his dear self, choice Dagon! to adore;
>
> . . . .
>
> His soul not cloath'd with attributes divine;
> But a nice watch-spring to that grand machine,
> That work more nice than Rittenhouse can plan,
> The body; man's chiefest part; himself, the man.   (575–584)

This is materialism not as religion merely but as ancient mythology, newly revived as a veneration of the human physical self. As opposed to worshiping the "all-beauteous mind" of God, the modern infidel treats the "grand machine" of the human body as his "choice Dagon" or idol (referring to the pagan god of the Philistines from the First Book of Samuel). Neither is this charge simply an example of the common metaphor used by religious figures, describing the flesh as an object of idolatry; rather, the passage as a whole is directed at the metaphysical impulses already at the heart of the otherwise bare materialist theories of Holbach, Helvétius, and La Mettrie. In specific terms, the image of the body as an elaborate timepiece "more nice than Rittenhouse can plan" is a direct allusion to the image used by La Mettrie to illustrate how the human body, while on one level purely matter, could transcend mere materiality by virtue of the perfection bestowed upon it by nature. "The human body is a watch, a large watch constructed with such skill and ingenuity, that

19. Timothy Dwight, *The Nature, and Danger, of Infidel Philosophy Exhibited in Two Discourses, Addressed to the Candidates for the Baccalaureate, in Yale College* (1798), in Dwight, *Sermons*, 2 vols. (New Haven, Conn., 1828), I, 359.

---

if the wheel which marks the seconds happens to stop . . . all the others go on running," he had declared enthusiastically in *Man a Machine*. He added: "Nature is no stupid workman. She creates millions of men, with a facility and a pleasure more intense than the effort of a watchmaker in making the most complicated watch."[20] The satiric force of the modern infidel passage is thus directed at an emerging materialist metaphysics in which God is displaced by nature as the externally ordained source of order in the universe.

This notion of eighteenth-century materialism as metaphysical and even theological can be easily lost within the modern understanding of materialism. More than any other Enlightenment system, materialism has come to be seen as fearlessly antimetaphysical, singularly willing to posit a universe composed of only atoms moving according to their laws, independent of anything like a guiding spirit. Indeed, this same fearlessness is the basis of Marx's later insistence that only by going to the level of materialism can one then recognize the degree to which other explanations of the universe are ideologically constructed. What is addressed in the passage on the Infidel of Modern Breed, however, is an aspect of eighteenth-century materialism that would distinguish it from its later forms: the assumption that, even in the absence of a controlling deity, the universe, sustained by a Newtonian ideal of cosmic order, could still be imagined in terms analogous to the concept of Providence. One encounters this vision in *The System of Nature*, for example, when Holbach, normally the voice of uncompromising demystification, drifts into a language that sounds remarkably religious, as when he imagines Nature's rhapsodic address to humankind: "O thou . . . who, following the impulse I have given you, during your whole existence, incessantly tend towards happiness, do not strive to resist my sovereign law. Labour to your own felicity; partake without fear of the banquet which is spread before you, and be happy; you will find the means legibly written on your own heart."[21]

Holbach's ability to imagine a kind of Providence without a God arises from the particular way in which the Newtonian conception of natural regularity and predictability implied a greater capacity first to comprehend and then to

20. Julien Offray de La Mettrie, *Man a Machine* (1748), trans. Gertrude C. Bussey (La Salle, Ill., 1953), 141, 145.

21. Holbach, *System of Nature*, trans. Robinson, 332.

apply the knowledge of the laws of nature. This possibility, in turn, allows even the materialist conception of man—as nothing more than a finite amalgam of carbon and nitrogen and oxygen—to appear as an indication, not of human degradation or meanness, but, paradoxically, of a new transcendence, the capacity to step back from one's material finitude and harness it for the good of society at large. The crucial corollary of eighteenth-century materialism is that the mind is a moral tabula rasa, capable of being determined to a precise degree by studying the principles of human behavior and learning to control the environment in which such behavior can be shaped. Thus, as the argument would be advanced particularly by Helvétius, the great scientific and political progress of the Enlightenment also carried with it the promise of a new kind of human transcendence, the possibility of reshaping human behavior and human motivation according to the ideals of an enlightened society.[22]

What one encounters in the satire of materialism as a virtual theology of man, in short, is Dwight's initial and still somewhat murky glimpse of Pelagianism in its latest and what would soon prove to be its most powerful guise: the faith in the power of enlightened intellectual and political institutions to create an environment so perfect that the machinery of human moral nature could ultimately be perfected. As seen in the orations of Elihu Palmer and Tunis Wortman, this vision is as optimistic as anything that had been advanced by the Shaftesburian or benevolist strain of Pelagianism; yet, paradoxically, it would now be reasoned from an opposing set of assumptions— not by denying or minimizing the more instinctual or base aspects of human nature, but by rendering these characteristics morally innocent or even beneficial in practice. Thus, for instance, self-interest, once understood as a poten-

---

22. In *De l'homme* (*On Man, His Intellectual Faculties, and His Education* [1772]), Claude Adrien Helvétius argues that virtually all human problems could be solved by a system of education. The notion of transcendence as a function of stepping back from the materiality or finitude of human beings constitutes Michel Foucault's conception of the "birth of man" in *The Order of Things*. With the appearance of the human sciences—biology, economics, philology—man becomes a finite object of empirical study, limited by his lifespan, his particular cultural history, and the scarcity of wealth for which he is destined to toil. Yet, in the very act of producing knowledge about himself, he is able to transcend this finitude. (Foucault, *The Order of Things: An Archaeology of the Human Sciences*, ed. R. D. Laing [New York, 1973], 314).

tially dangerous human impulse, would now be seen as both wholly rational and capable of bringing hitherto unseen benefits to society at large. The most famous example of an institution able to systematically reshape society in this manner, of course, is the capitalist marketplace as imagined by Adam Smith. Within Smith's formulation, competing self-interests could be transformed into a universal political and economic benefit. Not only would the market allow otherwise opposing needs and interests to be mutually fulfilled, but commercial activity could bring entire nations together and, in doing so, promote an atmosphere of mutual sympathy that would result in a more charitable and benevolent world. As Phineas Hedges, in an address to his own local democratic-republican society in 1795, explained:

> In a free government, commerce expands her sails; prompted by a spirit of enterprize and a desire of gain, men venture the dangers of a bosterous [sic] ocean, in pursuit of new commodities. An acquaintance with man hence results. He participates of the pleasures and miseries of his species; he feels for all that suffer, he assists their wants, his heart melts into affection, and the rough impenetrable particles of the monk and barbarian, dissolve into the sympathising heart of a citizen of civilized life.[23]

Yet this vision of the marketplace would represent human nature in Pelagian terms at a deeper level still. Beyond nullifying the otherwise deleterious effects of self-interest, it would render self-interest as a virtue in itself. Thus, in response to Bernard Mandeville's earlier characterization of the marketplace as deriving public benefits from private vices, Smith would argue that such so-called private vices were in fact wholly reasonable and even complimentary aspects of human nature. Indeed, the invisible hand of the capitalist marketplace works so well, he would conclude, because self-love causes people to enter into good bargains.[24] Such rational self-interest would then

23. Phineas Hedges, *An Oration, Delivered before the Republican Society of Ulster County and Other Citizens: Convened at the House of Daniel Smith, in the Town of Montgomery, for the Purpose of Celebrating the Anniversary of American Independence, the 4th of July, 1795* (Goshen, N.Y., 1795), 11.

24. Adam Smith, *The Theory of Moral Sentiments* (1759), ed. D. D. Raphael and A. L. Macfie (Oxford, 1976), 308–314; Smith, *An Inquiry into the Nature and Causes of the Wealth of Nations* (1776), ed. R. H. Campbell and A. S. Skinner, 2 vols. (Oxford, 1976), I,

allow for the other great moral advantage built into capitalism: as long as the system as a whole was reasonable and fair in its workings and dispensations — justly rewarding virtue and industry and punishing dishonesty and sloth—it would continue to reinforce the advantages of virtue until, finally, such behavior would become second nature to all members of the society.

Far from being limited to the marketplace or the economic sphere alone, moreover, this logic of moral transformation would also be applied to another modern social institution that seemed to guarantee the moral regeneration of its members—the American Republic as it would increasingly be envisioned in the decades following the Revolution. More than merely an ideal form of government, the Republic would be celebrated as the ideal political environment within which the collective character of its citizens could be redeemed after suffering under the tyranny of British rule. As the theory was presented by Wortman, for instance, monarchy harms the moral character by "placing the interests of mankind in a state of perpetual variance with their virtues and their duties," whereas republican government works immediately to restore the faith of its citizens in fair government, thus reuniting public virtue with individual self-interest. And, as in the logic of capitalism, this ideal political environment would ultimately have even more far-reaching effects through social mimesis. Not only would the political environment of the new Republic create a more peaceful, prosperous, and virtuous society than any in history but, insofar as it then served as an example for the rest of the world, it also promised a hitherto unimagined period of worldwide moral and social progress. "Under this happy modification of social life," Wortman concluded, "we can only expect to arrive at that ultimate state of perfection of which the human character is susceptible." "The final hopes and expectations of mankind are placed upon the universal establishment of this salutary system of government."[25]

This is not the conception of the republic, importantly, that had been assumed in the English Opposition or Country tradition and later appropriated by countless anti-British pamphleteers in the years leading up to the Revolu-

---

26-27. For the significance of this newer understanding of self-interest and the marketplace during the early republican period, see Joyce Appleby, *Capitalism and a New Social Order: The Republican Vision of the 1790s* (New York, 1984), 31–32.

25. Wortman, *Oration*, 18, 24.

tion. That had been a conception of republican society as permanently imperiled by the natural tendency toward luxury, greed, and corruption. This republic, in contrast, was part of an opposing ideology of America's special regenerative power, as imagined, for instance, by Crèvecoeur in *Letters from an American Farmer*. For Crèvecoeur, composing such famous essays as "What Is an American" in the years just prior to the Revolution, the essence of America even under British rule lay in what he called its "invisible power" to transform so many wretched emigrants from European monarchies into virtuous and industrious citizens. This metamorphosis begins at the moment the emigrant is presented with a political and economic environment that is eminently rational, one that clearly rewards industry and virtue with increasing degrees of prosperity: "The American ought therefore to love this country much better than that wherein either he or his forefathers were born. Here the rewards of his industry follow with equal steps the progress of his labour; his labour is founded on the basis of nature, self-interest; can it want a stronger allurement?"[26]

Such moments reveal the ideological transformation of Shaftesburian Pelagianism from moral philosophy into political theory. One can glimpse in Crèvecoeur's passage the logic of Shaftesbury's argument that an essentially

---

26. [M. G. St. J. de Crèvecoeur], J. Hector St. John, *Letters from an American Farmer and Sketches of Eighteenth-Century America* (1782), ed. Albert E. Stone (Harmondsworth, Eng., 1986), 69, 70. This moral logic is assumed throughout the *Letters*. For instance, Crèvecoeur likens the effect on an immigrant's state of mind soon after arriving in America to a kind of resurrection: "If he behaves with propriety, and is faithful, he is caressed, and becomes as it were a member of the family. He begins to feel the effects of a sort of resurrection; hitherto he had not lived, but simply vegetated; he now feels himself a man because he is treated as such" (82). Similarly, in his celebration of the American system of laws, he suggests that the very knowledge of such laws can effect a similar transformation: "By what invisible power hath this surprising metamorphosis been performed? By that of the laws and that of their industry. The laws, the indulgent laws, protect them as they arrive, stamping on them the symbol of adoption; they receive ample rewards for their labours; these accumulated rewards procure them lands; those lands confer on them the title of freemen, and to that title every benefit is affixed which men can possibly require. This is the great operation daily performed by our laws" (69).

reasonable or positive cosmology naturally inspires a tendency toward moral virtue. The same logic, importantly, would run through Charles Chauncy's belief in the implicit virtue simply of professing the doctrine of universal salvation—except that here the regenerative vision of a harmonious universe has been reconceived as American society itself. Despite Crèvecoeur's own later misgivings about the Revolution, moreover, the same argument would in the aftermath of American independence allow for a conception of the new Republic as a utopia, recalling the earlier projections of America's future from the "rising glory" poems of the Revolutionary period. At the same time, this vision was now understood to be grounded in reason rather than mere aspiration, the inevitable result of creating a political environment that naturally encourages virtue in its citizens.

On the other side of the Atlantic, Richard Price would draw an almost identical conclusion about the power of the American Republic to transform human nature. As he would assert in his *Observations of the Importance of the American Revolution,* the great significance of American independence is that it has put into place a form of government "more equitable and liberal than any that the world has yet known." This government would then serve as the foundation for "an empire which may be the seat of liberty, science and virtue, and from whence there is reason to hope these sacred blessings will spread, till they become universal." Such predictions of America's fulfilling its social and political potential on the world stage would, in turn, provide the basis for the even more openly transcendent prospect of America as the leader of the universal progress of society. Thus, for instance, as Joel Barlow would imagine it in an address celebrating the Fourth of July, 1787:

> Under the idea of a permanent and happy government, every point of view, in which the future situation of America can be placed, fills the mind with a peculiar dignity, and opens an unbounded field of thought. . . . [T]he blessings of a rational government will invite emigrations from the rest of the world, and fill the empire with the worthiest and happiest of mankind; while the example of political wisdom and felicity here to be displayed will excite emulation through the kingdoms of the earth, and meliorate the condition of the human race.[27]

27. Richard Price, *Observations on the Importance of the American Revolution, and the Means of Making It a Benefit to the World* (Boston, 1784), 4; Joel Barlow, *An Oration, De-*

The significance of the American Revolution and the newly independent United States here lies in the promise of something even more far-reaching, a natural and steady progress of history moving humanity toward a state of perfection. Equally attractive about this logic of universal progress for figures like Price and Barlow, moreover, was the implicit sense in which it seemed to explain in rational or scientific terms what had previously been asserted only by millennial prognosticators. Thus, for instance, as Barlow would elsewhere put it, "such a state of peace and happiness as is foretold in scripture and commonly called the millennial period, may be rationally expected to be introduced without a miracle." The same logic would, within a decade, be made even more explicit in William Godwin's *Enquiry concerning Political Justice* and Condorcet's *Sketch for a Historical Picture of the Progress of the Human Mind*. Both works suggest in no less rational or scientific terms that even the once unimaginable ideal of human moral perfectibility follows simply from observing the steady intellectual and material advancements of previous ages and recognizing a law of historical progress no less apparent than the law of gravity in planetary motion. "The sole foundation for the belief in the natural science is this idea, that the general laws directing the phenomena of the universe, known or unknown, are necessary and constant. Why should this principle be any less true for the development of the intellectual and moral faculties of man?" concludes Condorcet. "Is it possible for us to contemplate what [man] has already done, without being impressed with a strong presentiment of the improvements he has yet to accomplish?" asks Godwin, before asserting, "There is no science that is not capable of additions; there is no art that may not be carried to a still higher perfection."[28]

Even as this secular historiography would dispense with its specifically theological language, it would remain fundamentally religious, retaining in

---

livered at the North Church in Hartford, at the Meeting of the Connecticut Society of the Cincinnati, July 4th, 1787 (Hartford, Conn., 1787), 20.

28. Joel Barlow, *The Vision of Columbus* (1787), in William K. Bottorff and Arthur L. Ford, eds., *The Works of Joel Barlow*, 2 vols. (Gainesville, Fla., 1970), II, 342; Marie-Jean-Antoine-Nicholas de Caritat, marquis de Condorcet, *Sketch for a Historical Picture of the Progress of the Human Mind* (1794), trans. June Barraclough (New York, 1955), 173; William Godwin, *Enquiry concerning Political Justice and Its Influence on Morals and Happiness* (1793), ed. F. E. L. Priestley, 3 vols. (Toronto, 1946) I, 118–119.

its narrative structure the same salvational teleology of earlier Christian millennialism. Indeed, even the most radically secular or self-consciously scientific forms of Enlightenment progressivism contained a hidden theological element. Yet, if the deeper relationship between millennial and utopian historiographies is easier to recognize from the hindsight of our own time, it was not entirely missed in the last years of the eighteenth century. Dwight, for example, felt the need to draw a clear distinction between his own millennial beliefs, taken as a matter of doctrine from works such as Edwards's *History of the Work of Redemption* (1773), and the idea of human perfectibility imagined during the height of the French Revolution by Godwin and Condorcet. "I am of the opinion that the Millennium is not to come all at once, but is to alleviate the evils of mankind by degrees," he would explain in a classroom discussion at Yale. "All this will take place; but when we have done, it will be as far from the perfectibility which fools talk of, as the mite from a man, and an oyster from a whale." [29]

Neither is Dwight simply defending his own religious millennialism against an emerging secular version of the same progressive story; rather, as his concluding remark suggests, he is advancing a more general critique against the notion of human perfectibility as a false ideal of transcendence underlying Enlightenment progressivism. The first error of believing in a future in which the human moral character can be radically transformed, he insists, is that it demands the believer place faith in something that history has shown empirically to be illusory. The perfectibility of the human character, he asserts in *Theology*, is the singular idea to which schools and religions and philosophies have been dedicated; yet, for all of that, human history has mocked every attempt to create a society uncorrupted by self-interest and greed and the desire for power: "Shall we believe that the schemes of modern philosophy will accomplish what all preceding philosophers, and men much wiser than philosophers, what the Word of God, the Redemption of his Son, and the

29. Theodore Dwight, Jr., ed., *President Dwight's Decisions of Questions Discussed by the Senior Class in Yale College, in 1813 and 1814* (New York, 1833), 331–332. Ernest Lee Tuveson made clear the religious underpinnings of this progressive historiography in *Millennium and Utopia: A Study in the Background of the Idea of Progress* (1949; reprint, Gloucester, Mass., 1972) and *Redeemer Nation: The Idea of America's Millennial Role* (Chicago, 1968).

communications of his Spirit, have never yet accomplished? . . . When Men become immortal by medicine and moral energy, according to the dreams of the same philosophy, they may perhaps become perfect by the proposed schemes of its discipline."[30]

In the immediate background of Dwight's symbolic attack against the Enlightenment ideal of human perfectibility, then, stands an older struggle between two opposing religious conceptions of the meaning of human history, both originating in early Christian thought. For Dwight, speaking in defense of Augustinian historiography, the meaning of history lies outside its limits in the timeless and transcendent sphere of the *nunc-stans*, in relation to which even the most crucial episodes of human progress must be acknowledged as passing and illusory, an aspect of the dimension of man's fallen state. Behind the Enlightenment vision of human perfectibility, on the other hand, stands the alternate spiritual impulse to invest the events and patterns of the *saeculum* with a divine or cosmic significance of their own. This tendency would serve as the underlying ideological continuity between an older scriptural millennialism—including, importantly, that of Dwight's Puritan forebears—and the radically secular utopianism of Barlow, Condorcet, and their ideological heirs in the nineteenth century, who would proclaim that humanity could reasonably expect a future period of earthly redemption that was already prefigured in the political, intellectual, and scientific advancements of the present.[31]

30. Dwight, *Theology*, I, 497.

31. J. G. A. Pocock points out that the Augustinian distinction between the nunc-stans and the saeculum arose in response to the millennialism of late antiquity. In opposition to the official church of Rome, some marginal Christian sects began to interpret events according to eschatological counterhistories that placed themselves at the center. Augustine, attempting to prevent the simple equation of history and eschatology, argued that, because the saeculum must always be acknowledged as the dimension of man's fall—understood in moral and epistemological terms—any attempt to identify specific historical events with scriptural prophesy or to read into such events the unfolding of some unquestionable millennial narrative must be viewed with skepticism. "It could not be denied that God was present and active in secular history," Pocock writes; "all that was denied was that we could identify secular events with the fulfillment of his purposes" (Pocock, *The Machiavellian Moment: Florentine Political Thought and the Atlantic Republican Tradition* [Princeton, N.J., 1975], 36). Tracing the ten-

Against this notion of a divine principle of progress moving all aspects of society ever forward, Dwight would continue to counterpose the Augustinian insistence upon a moral nature that is permanent and unredeemable inside history. Yet this insistence would carry important implications in the context of his own more limited optimism concerning the possibility of intellectual enlightenment and social or political improvement. First and foremost, it would imply a fundamental distinction between mere material progress and the far loftier ideal of human moral progress. More important, it would raise certain ominous questions about the ways in which such material advancements might be used by a human race still flawed in its moral nature. "That the world has materially changed, and is still changing, in many important particulars, cannot be questioned," he acknowledges in *The Nature, and Danger, of Infidel Philosophy*. "But whether these particulars are either profitable, or honourable, may well be questioned. That the knowledge, or the happiness, of mankind has been increased by the change is yet to be proved. We have not yet put off the harness, and our time for rational *boasting* is, therefore, not arrived."[32]

At the same time, this negative strategy in *The Triumph of Infidelity* of revealing Enlightenment progressivism to be the superstition of the modern age is always accompanied by an alternative notion of a true enlightenment. Dwight's own continued attempt to define this alternative in positive terms will characterize much of his writing from the early 1790s and, in particular, the high point of his public career as a poet, *Greenfield Hill* (1794). In this poem, Dwight will articulate his most optimistic hopes for the future of the American Republic, one that enthusiastically welcomes all of the specific examples

---

sion between these opposing tendencies through several centuries, Pocock shows that, by the seventeenth century, Puritanism had all but eroded the Augustinian distinction between history and eschatology, the nunc-stans and the saeculum, as Puritans both in Britain and America interpreted their own specific struggles within detailed millennial narratives. Such millennial visions, despite their obvious theological content, can be seen to constitute the ideological origins of modern secular progressivism, which emerges at the moment the saeculum is invested with a significance that elevates it above the level of the dimension of man's fall.

32. Dwight, *The Nature, and Danger, of Infidel Philosophy*, in Dwight, *Sermons*, 2 vols. (New Haven, Conn., 1828), I, 350.

of scientific, material, and political progress celebrated by his opponents, while remaining fundamentally skeptical of the belief that these instances together signify some larger promise of human transcendence inside history. Concerning scientific and material advancements, Dwight presents his view in explicit terms in the seventh and final section of the poem. Here the speaker encounters, in the classical genius loci tradition running through eighteenth-century English poetry, the Genius of the Sound—a spirit who rises from Long Island Sound to predict America's future in largely the same terms one encounters in the progressivist poems of Barlow and Philip Freneau.

Because of the similarity between the image of America in part 7 of *Greenfield Hill* and that found in Barlow's *The Columbiad* (1807), in fact, the Dwight of *Greenfield Hill* has long been interpreted as a voice of America's unquestionable millennial destiny, distinguished from Barlow only by his more explicit references to religion. Just as Barlow would illustrate the progressive course of history in *The Columbiad* by paying homage to specific inventions and technological advancements—the compass and the printing press, for instance—Dwight presents an image of America in *Greenfield Hill* in similarly technological terms, including such inventions as Benjamin Franklin's lightning rod and David Bushnell's submarine, themselves emblems of future scientific achievements that will "ease the load, that lies on human life." Yet even the Genius of the Sound, Dwight's great prophet of optimism, who will carry *Greenfield Hill* to its resoundingly uplifting conclusion, stops far short of suggesting that such advancements will have anything but a limited effect overall. Indeed, this point is made at a moment of withering irony. After cataloging such recent achievements and predicting a future in which "Columbian science" will "see all nature own it's magic force," the Genius of the Sound acknowledges the fleeting nature of these achievements: science can "Redress the ravage of encroaching clime, / Change the sad curse, rebuild the waste of time," but, ultimately, it can only "Protract man's date, bid age with verdure bloom, / And strew with flowers the journey to the tomb."[33]

33. Timothy Dwight, *Greenfield Hill* (1794), in William J. McTaggart and William K. Bottorff, eds., *The Major Poems of Timothy Dwight (1752-1817), with a Dissertation on the History, Eloquence, and Poetry of the Bible* (Gainesville, Fla., 1969), 520–521. It is important in this context to distinguish between the predominant attitude toward millennialism in Dwight's writing from 1781 to 1798 and an opposing apocalyptic position

This same limited enthusiasm toward scientific inventions will characterize Dwight's posthumously published *Travels in New England and New York*,
but with a crucial additional point about the prospect of continued material
or technological progress in a world in which human moral nature remains
permanently flawed. Among the stories Dwight tells in the course of describing his annual summer journeys through New England is the invention of the
cotton gin by Connecticut native and Yale graduate, Eli Whitney. Although
Dwight praises the cotton gin as an ingenious and useful invention in and of
itself, he then turns to the story of Whitney's subsequent legal troubles over
the cotton gin patent as a parable of the persistence of greed and corruption
in an otherwise advancing age. Because of the loopholes in Georgia's patent
laws and the blatant conflict of interest of so many officers of that state's court

---

he would take during two separate periods in response to specific political and social
events. Between 1798 and 1801, Dwight would fall back on apocalyptic historiography
to understand the combined threats of Jeffersonian Republicanism, French Revolutionary radicalism, and the imagined conspiracy of the Illuminati. See, for example,
Timothy Dwight, *The Duty of Americans, at the Present Crisis, Illustrated in a Discourse,
Preached on the Fourth of July, 1798* (New Haven, Conn., 1798); and Dwight, *A Discourse
on Some Events in the Last Century* (New Haven, Conn., 1801). After this period, Dwight
would return to a more cautious stance toward interpreting current events in light of
scriptural prophecy until the threat of the War of 1812, which he and other Federalists
strongly opposed. See, in this context, Timothy Dwight, *A Discourse, in Two Parts, Delivered July 23, 1812, on the Public Fast* (New Haven, Conn., 1812); and Timothy Dwight,
A Discourse, in Two Parts, Delivered August 20, 1812, on the National Fast (New York, 1812).
Those, such as Ernest Tuveson, Marc L. Harris, and Deitrich Buss, who treat Dwight
as a voice of American millennialism in an unqualified way, base their conclusions on
a selective reading of his work, usually emphasizing the works mentioned above, the
earlier "rising glory" poems of his youth, or the complex final section of *Greenfield Hill*.
See Tuveson, *Redeemer Nation*, chap. 4; Harris, "Revelation and the American Republic:
Timothy Dwight's Civic Participation," *Journal of the History of Ideas*, LIV (1993), 449–
468; Buss, "The Millennial Vision as Motive for Religious Benevolence and Reform:
Timothy Dwight and the New England Evangelicals Reconsidered," *Fides et Historia*,
XVI (1984), 18–34. Useful here is William C. Dowling's remark that the millennial strain
in Dwight's poetry "operates simultaneously to diminish the importance of the earthly
millennium" and serves always as a "warning against any misguided millennialism"
(Dowling, *Poetry and Ideology in Revolutionary Connecticut* [Athens, Ga., 1990], 68).

---

system, he writes, "The machine was converted into a political engine, and demagogues rose into popularity by unfounded and vociferous declamation against this species of right and the law which was made for its protection." Thus, he concludes, many people were made rich by the cotton gin, but Eli Whitney was not among them.[34]

Dwight would not live long enough to witness firsthand the even more destructive effects brought about by the use of Whitney's machine—the massive expansion of a cotton industry that exploited human slavery for its labor—but an earlier passage from *Greenfield Hill* suggests that he would hardly have been surprised. In this passage, in which Dwight's speaker is lamenting the existence of slavery in the New World generally, he makes the particular point that scientific or intellectual progress might be mobilized to justify such an indefensible practice. In particular, with the emergence of such pre-Darwinian theories of human evolution as those introduced by Henry Home, Lord Kames, and James Burnett, Lord Monboddo, whites could now defend slavery from so-called scientific precepts, arguing that Africans constituted a more primitive state of human development:

> Thus slavery's blast bids sense and virtue die;
> Thus lower'd to dust the sons of Afric lie.
> Hence sages grave, to lunar systems given,
> Shall ask, why two-legg'd brutes were made by HEAVEN;
> HOME seek, what pair first peopled Afric's vales,
> And nice MONBODDO calculate their tails.[35]

The same concept of human nature and human earthly existence that determines Dwight's mixed response to scientific and material improvement also serves as the basis for his view of social and political progress in the poem. The

34. Timothy Dwight, *Travels in New England and New York* (1821–1822), ed. Barbara Miller Solomon, with the assistance of Patricia M. King, 4 vols. (Cambridge, Mass., 1969), II, 197.

35. Dwight, *Greenfield Hill*, in McTaggart and Bottorff, eds., *Major Poems*, 404. Kames's conception of human evolution is found in *Sketches on the History of Man* (1774). Monboddo's proto-evolutionary views in *Of the Origin and Progress of Language* (1773–1792) were more controversial in that he asserted that the orangutan was actually a class of the human species.

belief that a machine or invention can somehow bring about a more fundamental advancement of society emerges, in fact, as one example of the problem of trusting in the transformative power of machinery in general, such as
the assumed workings of a political or economic theory designed to guarantee a stable or peaceful society. Once again, this is a critique that is qualified
by a more limited enthusiasm toward a number of the specific policies and
reforms that have been associated with Enlightenment progressivism. Thus,
for instance, in the extensive endnotes to *Greenfield Hill*, Dwight advocates at
some length on issues ranging from prison reform and the curtailment of capital punishment to the expansion of public libraries. Similarly, in the poem
itself, he speaks for enlarging the role of government policy: "Here too, her
scope shall Policy extend, / Nor to check crimes be still her single end. / Her
hand shall aid the poor, the sad console, / And lift up merit from it's lowly
stool." At the same time, however, Dwight places greater emphasis in this
poem and in his other writings from the same period on combating what he
calls elsewhere in *Greenfield Hill* "politic visions," abstract theories that seemed
to promise sweeping and automatic results from a given set of reforms or
changes in policy.[36]

36. Dwight, *Greenfield Hill*, in McTaggart and Bottorff, eds., *Major Poems*, 518.
Dwight's career as an educator, particularly his presidency of Yale, would be characterized by the same, more complex response to Enlightenment progressivism. On the
one hand, he would warn against believing that the fundamental limitations of human
historical existence can be transcended; on the other, he would respond enthusiastically to specific scientific advancements and social and political reforms. In the area
of science, Dwight's administration at Yale is remembered, for instance, for establishing a professorship of chemistry, America's first department of geology and miner-
alogy, and a department of medicine (which became the Yale Medical School shortly
before his death), and for acquiring the "Gibbs cabinet," a collection of thousands of
mineral specimens that immediately made New Haven a world center for geological
study. For more on Dwight's influence on scientific development at Yale, see Chandos
Michael Brown, *Benjamin Silliman: A Life in the Young Republic* (Princeton, N.J., 1989),
207–209, 263–264. For a discussion of Dwight's general influence on American science,
see Kathryn Whitford and Philip Whitford, "Timothy Dwight's Place in Eighteenth-
Century American Science," American Philosophical Society, *Proceedings*, CXIV (1970),
60–71.

Such promises are addressed directly in a speech delivered in 1795 entitled *The True Means of Establishing Public Happiness.* Dwight's strategy in this work is to engage such theories of large-scale social transformation by placing them inside a historical narrative that he insists is, not progressive or linear, but cyclical. Drawing on the Polybian historiography of the rise and fall of nations, he asserts that every successive age has defined the means necessary for establishing and preserving a peaceful and prosperous society. Yet what is usually assumed to constitute such means—wealth, material improvements, intellectual innovations—have had no lasting effect, and even the most powerful empires have collapsed under the weight of their own corruption. Thus, he states, using the two great examples of this pattern, "Greece became a Giant in war, in science, and in arts; but was still an infant in moral improvement, and useful policy," whereas the citizens of Rome, for all their civic innovations, were in moral terms "distinguished with little advantage from various nations whom they contemptuously styled barbarians."[37]

At such moments, Dwight is invoking the language of classical republicanism as it had been generally revived in the Revolutionary and early republican periods, first as an attempt to escape the inevitable historical cycle that seemed to promise Britain's impending downfall and then as a reminder of the difficulty of sustaining their own republican government. The first prin-

---

In the area of social reform, Dwight is remembered, first, for his experiment in co-educational schooling in the two academies he ran prior to the Yale presidency. In both schools, boys and girls were taught the same subjects in the same classroom; more important, the subjects Dwight taught were regarded not merely as preparatory for college but as an alternative to it, which is evident in the number of students Dwight's Greenfield Hill Academy drew from Yale during the 1780s (see Ezra Stiles, *The Literary Diary of Ezra Stiles, D.D., LL.D., President of Yale College,* ed. Franklin Bowditch Dexter, 3 vols. [New York, 1901], II, 422–423, 438). Dwight is also credited with abolishing the notorious "fagging system" at Yale, which allowed upperclassmen to discipline younger students and use them, effectively, as servants (see Charles E. Cuningham, *Timothy Dwight, 1752–1817: A Biography* [New York, 1942], 254–256).

37. Timothy Dwight, *The True Means of Establishing Public Happiness: A Sermon Delivered on the 7th of July, 1795, before the Connecticut Society of Cincinnati* (New Haven, Conn., [1795]), 11.

ciple of classical republicanism had always been that a republic can successfully stave off its corruption and downfall only by preserving public virtue, the collective orientation of its citizens toward the common good and against the natural tendency to place their private interests first. Dwight's emphatic corollary to this principle, expressed here and throughout his writings from the 1790s, will be that public virtue can never be sustained by such indirect or secondary means as creating a particular social or political environment. Rather, he asserts simply, "The primary means of originating and establishing happiness, in free communities, is . . . the formation of a good personal character in their citizens."[38] This is, to be sure, the standard discourse of republican virtue found everywhere in American thought and writing from this period; at the same time, such a phrase as "the formation of a good personal character" will, for Dwight, always carry the specific meaning of direct moral intervention in the lives of individual citizens.

This emphasis on individual morality as the foundation for sustaining a peaceful and stable republic, moreover, illustrates a crucial difference between the standard eighteenth-century conception of public virtue and Dwight's own. In contrast to the invocation of public virtue as primarily a collective or abstract cultural force, Dwight treats public virtue as nothing more than an aggregate of individual moral virtue, which he defines in *The True Means of Establishing Public Happiness* as "the Love of doing good" and "mental energy, directed steadily to that which is right." As such, he will insist, virtue can be achieved only by way of the same rigorous internal struggle that he described in *Theology* as the means of moral and spiritual improvement, in this case directed against the natural tendency to be ruled by self-interest in one's public or civic life. This theme will run through virtually all of Dwight's writings in the years following the ratification of the Constitution, from his 1791 election sermon, *Virtuous Rulers a National Blessing*—"The governing disposition of a ruler . . . must necessarily lead him to a faithful, uniform pursuit of the public interest, in preference to any private one, and to seek the good of millions rather than his own"—to the special emphasis in *The True Means of Establishing Public Happiness* on sustaining virtue by means of a necessary struggle: "The whole cultivation of virtue is a conflict with vice; but the war-

38. Ibid., 12.

fare is honourable, and the victory fruitful in advantage, beyond the reach of computation."[39]

Such sentiments as these, in turn, help explain Dwight's mixed reaction to the Constitution as a solution to the problems facing the Republic during the Confederation period. On the one hand, as he had written in the 1787 poem "Address of the Genius of Columbia, to the Members of the Continental Convention," Dwight believed that the creation of a federal government was necessary to offset those threats to stability arising from "the private interests of each jealous state." The makeup of the Constitution, moreover, as a system of checks and balances intended to impede the spread of corruption from one branch of government to another, was similarly attractive in the way it seemed to be grounded in the Augustinian view of human nature. Indeed, Dwight's own perspective on the need for such a system of government might be found in Alexander Hamilton's remarks in *The Federalist*, No. 6: "Have we not already seen enough of the fallacy and extravagance of those idle theories which have amused us with promises of an exemption from the imperfections, weaknesses, and evils incident to society in every shape? Is it not time to awake from the deceitful dream of a golden age, and to adopt as a practical maxim for the direction of our political conduct, that we . . . are yet remote from the happy empire of perfect wisdom and perfect virtue?" Yet almost immediately after it became evident that the Constitution would be ratified, Dwight would draw upon these same assumptions as the basis for a more cautious view of the Constitution, particularly if it should be taken as a blueprint for sustaining a peaceful and stable society. Thus, only a year after urging the representatives to draft the document, he would publish the "Address to the Ministers of the Gospel of Every Denomination in the United States." Here he would warn that the new Constitution, however indispensable as a purely negative system of restraint, "will neither restore order, nor establish justice among us, unless it be accompanied and supported by morality, among all classes of people."[40]

39. Ibid., 14, 32; Timothy Dwight, *Virtuous Rulers a National Blessing, a Sermon Preached at the General Election, May 12th, 1791* (Hartford, Conn., 1791), 16.

40. "Address of the Genius of Columbia, to the Members of the Continental Convention," in Elihu Hubbard Smith, ed., *American Poems, Selected and Original* (1793), ed. William K. Bottorff (Gainesville, Fla., 1966), 59; J. R. Pole, ed., *The American Constitu-*

As indicated by this open letter to the American clergy, the Dwight who would insist upon the difficult work of sustaining public virtue would also emerge in the 1790s as an outspoken advocate for the public role of (and, not surprisingly, the public support for) the clergy as moral monitors of a society otherwise ruled by popularly elected leaders. As he would argue in *Virtuous Rulers a National Blessing*, as long as the clergy remained outside the marketplace of public opinion that governed elections—necessarily independent of the pressures faced by politicians to flatter the pride of their constituents—they would be in a unique position to acknowledge the reality of moral weakness among the people. Such an office, he would remind his election-day audience, is "eminently necessary to so frail, and so forgetful a being, as man." Dwight's social and political vision for America would thus be rooted in two corresponding beliefs: first, citizens served the public good only by resisting their natural inclination toward self-interest, and, second, they needed regularly to be reminded of this duty, preferably by members of the clergy. The great challenge to this view, accordingly, would be the argument going back through Adam Smith and Francis Hutcheson to Shaftesbury that self-interest properly understood is necessarily united with the common good. For those attracted to this view, the suggestion that individuals did not naturally have the best interests of the Republic in mind risked being characterized as what Tunis Wortman would call "the degradation of the human character." In the same way, Dwight's insistence that public virtue required the monitory role of the clergy risked being attacked as an example of what Elihu Palmer would call the "moral despotism" of priests.[41]

For Dwight, on the other hand, the Pelagian assumption that enlightened self-interest could represent the means to public happiness would amount merely to an illusory formula for rendering the struggle against self-interest all but unnecessary. "In this age of innovation, visionary philosophers . . . have discovered, that men are naturally wise and good, prone to submit to good government," he warned the graduates in his first Yale commencement speech: "You will find every man pleased, not merely to be free, but to tyran-

---

tions, for and against: The Federalist and Anti-Federalist Papers (New York, 1987), 146; Timothy Dwight, "Address to the Ministers of the Gospel of Every Denomination in the United States," *American Museum*, IV (1788), 30.

41. Dwight, *Virtuous Rulers*, 7; Wortman, *Oration*, 6; Palmer, *Enquiry*, 25.

nize." Indeed, this is a shift from the confident voice of *The Triumph of Infidelity* and even the still hopeful tone of *Greenfield Hill,* and it reflects the evolution of Dwight's conception of his ideological adversaries. The promise of easy or automatic redemption, even in its most recent guise as the doctrine of human perfectibility, had hitherto seemed to represent only the reveries of a few idle philosophers, never the foundation on which an actual polity could be built. Yet, by the mid-1790s, Dwight became convinced of a very different and more frightening possibility. The new faith in human perfectibility was now one of the founding principles of the French Revolution, which, far from heralding a new age of virtue and reason, drowned these very ideals in blood:

> In the treatises, laws, and measures, brought into being in that nation, during its late wonderful struggle to become free, the people were uniformly declared to be good; honest; virtuous; influenced only by the purest motives; and aiming only at the best ends. These very people, at the same time, were employed in little else, except unceasing plunder, uniform treachery, the violation of all laws, the utterances of all falsehood, the murder of their King, Nobles, Clergy, and the boundless butchery of each other.[42]

In an important sense, Dwight's campaign of public attacks against French Revolutionary radicalism as the last and most frightening form of eighteenth-century Pelagian thought would prove successful; in the wake of the Reign of Terror, the ensuing European wars, and the rise of Napoleon Bonaparte, this view of the French Revolution as an empty utopianism degenerating into violence would quell a great deal of the earlier American enthusiasm toward the French Revolution. Yet, although this critique would effectively block or impede the new progressivist ideology in its most radically utopian forms, it would have far less of an effect on the equally progressivist vision of Jeffersonian democracy. Even as the voices of the new party forming around Jefferson would embrace an identical moral language of individual human virtue and capability, they would also continue to draw upon the same republican and Country vocabulary as that spoken by Timothy Dwight. The emerging Jeffersonian opposition could thus represent themselves as committed only to the preservation of a simpler, more virtuous republic. Indeed, one needed only to

42. Dwight, "On the Duties of a Professional Life" (1796), in Dwight, *Sermons,* I, 303; Dwight, *Theology,* I, 499.

look to Jefferson's famous idealization of agrarian virtue in *Notes on the State of Virginia*, it would seem, to recognize the new party as the true heirs to classical republicanism and Country ideology: "Those who labor in the earth are the chosen people of God, if ever he had a chosen people, whose breasts he has made his peculiar deposit for substantial and genuine virtue. . . . Corruption of morals in the mass of cultivators is a phænomenon of which no age nor nation has furnished an example."[43]

From Dwight's perspective, of course, Jefferson's republic of agrarian virtue would appear as just another imaginary formula for automatic regeneration, grounded in the same Pelagian assumptions as all other blueprints for a utopian society and differing only in it unique emphasis on resisting rather than embracing the effects of scientific and material progress. Yet this idealized image, steeped as it was in an ancient language connecting agriculture to simplicity and moral rectitude, would nonetheless lend itself to an emerging conception of American opposition politics that pitted a Jeffersonian Country party against a perceived Court party or monied interest controlling Washington's presidency. The imagined leader of this faction would be Alexander Hamilton, who, despite his own ideological underpinnings in classical republican theory, would find himself being characterized as a modern embodiment of Sir Robert Walpole, building a new Robinocracy around such policies as the national bank and the funding of the national debt.[44] The political controversies originating during the administrations of Washington and Adams would thus be fought against the backdrop of competing claims to a common

43. Thomas Jefferson, *Notes on the State of Virginia* (1787), ed. William Peden (Chapel Hill, N.C., 1955), 164–165.

44. For a description of Jeffersonian democracy as a later articulation of Country Ideology, in which Hamilton is represented as a modern Walpole, see Lance Banning, *The Jeffersonian Persuasion: Evolution of a Party Ideology* (Ithaca, N.Y., 1978). This interjection was the basis for the exchange of articles between Banning and Joyce Appleby during the 1980s over the true ideological lineage of classical republicanism. See Banning, "Jeffersonian Ideology Revisited: Liberal and Classical Ideas in the New American Republic," *William and Mary Quarterly*, 3d Ser., XLIII (1986), 3–19; Appleby, "Republicanism in Old and New Contexts," ibid., 20–34; Appleby, "Introduction: Republicanism in the History and Historiography of the United States," *American Quarterly*, XXXVII (1985), 461–473.

language of republican virtue, luxury, and corruption, within which would be contained fundamentally different assumptions about human nature and the course the new Republic should follow. For Dwight and other Federalists, the essence of classical republicanism lay in its steady insistence that a peaceful and virtuous republic could only be achieved by way of a collective struggle of individuals willing to sacrifice self-interest for the greater good. For the emerging voices of Jeffersonian democracy, on the other hand, for whom individual citizens were far more capable of aligning their own interests with the public good than has long been assumed, the real danger to a stable and virtuous republic lay in the possibility that the liberties of individual citizens would be constrained or even denied by a powerful class of emerging American aristocrats.

The great ideological victory of Jeffersonian democracy will arise from its capacity to synthesize the older language of republican virtue with the newer language that celebrated the virtues and capabilities—while cautiously guarding the rights and liberties—of man. Within this synthesis of Pelagianism and republicanism and Lockean liberalism, the Federalists' appeal to traditional values and beliefs will be rendered as part of an aristocratic conspiracy to undo the sweeping social and political advancements brought on by the American Revolution. The perceptions of how Federalists might carry out this plot will be various. In some cases, it will be the Federalist clergy attempting to deny the rights of the individual conscience by preventing a separation of church and state; in others, Federalist leaders will be said to impede the natural capacities of human beings by persuading them that they are morally unfit to handle their liberty and intellectually unfit to bring about significant social progress. Thus, Federalism will come to be regarded as merely an outmoded system of political superstitions, with Timothy Dwight as its pope, overseeing a conspiracy to forestall the day in which American citizens will universally enjoy the liberty and rights that will constitute their political salvation.

CHAPTER 4
The Theology of Man

If there is a single moment in Dwight's poetic career that registers his own realization that the literary and ideological warfare he had waged would likely prove a losing cause, it is "An Extract from 'The Retrospect,'" a four-hundred-line response to the French Revolution that would constitute at once his last substantial poem and his final poem on a political subject. He had written "The Retrospect" in 1796 and 1797 but chose not to publish it until 1801, when he offered it as the New Year's poem in the *Mercury and New-England Palladium*, the Federalist newspaper Dwight had helped to organize. "The Retrospect" was an unconventional choice because it did not, in the tradition of New Year's poetry, address events or issues specific to the previous year. As he explains in the introduction, he decided to submit the poem because its subject matter was "not so entirely worn out of the minds of our countrymen, as to be uninteresting."[1] This is, of course, an understatement, for Dwight no doubt believed that the poem was especially fitting for the year that marked both the turn of the new century and the impending Democratic-Republican takeover of the presidency. In his view, only a poem that addressed the events and aftermath of the French Revolution could make sense of the more widespread phenomenon of the last years of the eighteenth century, which he characterized as the spread of Jacobinism throughout Europe and into America.

"The Retrospect" begins with the speaker standing atop an Alpine summit

1. Timothy Dwight, "An Extract from 'The Retrospect,'" *Mercury and New-England Palladium* (Boston), Jan. 3, 1801. Hereafter citations to this poem will refer to the line numbers and will be made parenthetically in the text.

and looking down at the state of Europe in the wake of the Revolution, all the while being consoled by a guiding spirit who sadly confirms the speaker's worst fears: "With soft compliance smil'd the form again / 'Vain are thy hopes,' he cried, 'thy sighs are vain; / See vice, now quicken'd borne on dragon wing, / With forky tongue, and thrice envenom'd sting'" (1-4). The historical background of such despair is familiar enough to modern readers: the great republican ideals of the early years of the Revolution have given way to the violence and mass executions of the Reign of Terror, the bloody massacres at Nantes and Lyons, the military campaigns of the French army under the command of a young Napoleon Bonaparte. Yet, beyond this despair, there is also from the outset a deep sense of bewilderment over what is, for Dwight, a far more difficult phenomenon to comprehend, namely, that the revolutionary fervor has not abated with the outbreak of violence but has in fact increased and spread from France to other European countries. This problem is posed by the first vision revealed to the speaker, that of an ordinary Italian shepherd witnessing the conquest of his country by Bonaparte's army. Hitherto his life had been peaceful and innocent—"His veins of milk, and soul of harmless love" (17)—but, since the army's arrival, he has been transformed into an enraged champion of Bonaparte's cause:

From sleep and death he wakes to life unknown,
And glows with thoughts, and wishes, not his own;
Through the rous'd nerves he feels the clarion thrill,
His bosom throbs, his veins with horror chill,
From sparkling flames his phrenzied eye-balls roll,
And Freedom's mania races through his soul.
Aghast, he sees a newborn Caesar rise,
And grasp at all beneath Italian skies;
Aghast he sees the crimson ensigns play,
Fire sweep the fields, and ruin cloud the day;
"To arms" he hears th' immeasurable cry—
"Live, and be free; we conquer, or we die."   (27-38)

Most immediately, the purpose of this passage is to explain how someone like this peasant, with no personal or national interest in Republican France or its military campaigns, could be willing to kill or die for what is at bottom merely the ambition of a "newborn Caesar." Yet, in larger terms, this is Dwight's first attempt to make sense of the momentous ideological force he here calls "Freedom's mania," the same inexplicable rage that had first arisen a few years earlier in revolutionary France. Dwight begins to suspect that his earlier ideological warfare had been misdirected, that he had all along been mistaken about the most powerful threat to political or social stability. As we have seen, Dwight's writings up to this point had been an extension of the argument in *The Triumph of Infidelity:* the principle threat to moral life was a form of moral slumber, and the corresponding threat to the Republic, understood within the ideological framework of classical republicanism, was the belief that public happiness could be maintained with little or no sacrifice of individual self-interest, without the necessary struggle against complacency. Yet, in "The Retrospect," Dwight glimpses for the first time a threat more analogous to enthusiasm than to backsliding: unlike the slow, gradual process by which those with otherwise good moral intentions are ultimately corrupted, the "mania" described in these lines is a mass conversion to an altogether new moral logic, within which even violence can be viewed as necessary for the greater good of humankind. The corresponding political threat to this moral conversion is thus the possibility of a new totalitarian regime capable of passing itself off as anti-authoritarian, with a powerful individual such as Bonaparte arrogating to himself the authority to determine the greater good.

The initial response of "The Retrospect" is to present this phenomenon as an example of what we have since come to call false consciousness, described in the passage above as a new set of "thoughts and wishes" imposed on the shepherd, inspiring actions he would hitherto have regarded simply as madness. Yet, in making such an assertion, Dwight is mounting a broader counterattack against the popular identification of the Revolution and its subsequent events with the Enlightenment claim to have cleared away the systems of mystification that had deluded all previous ages. This assumption had been behind the more general emphasis upon secularization and anticlericalism at the height of the Revolution; importantly, it also gave Bonaparte's conquest of Rome a certain symbolic value for proponents of the Revolution both in Europe and America. Thus, for instance, Philip Freneau could interpret this event as a universal victory of liberty and reason, in which Rome, the historical center of civic and religious despotism, has suddenly undergone an intellectual awakening: "Superstition's dark inveterate train / Turns pale, and sickens at their blasted reign, / And hosts reviving, round the standard throng, / Exult, and wonder how they slept so long."[2]

The Italian shepherd from "The Retrospect," awakening from the "sleep and death" of feudal oppression, corresponds closely to Freneau's reviving hosts, but with one important difference: he does not awaken to a consciousness free from ideological control; rather, he exchanges one kind of conscious "sleep" for another. Yet, although the "thoughts and wishes" rushing through his mind are no more "his own" than those that had formerly prevented him from questioning his subjection to despotic rule, they appear as a sudden glimpse of truth and thus provide a perspective of enlightenment from which he recognizes the older form of ideology. The result, Dwight suggests, is a potentially more dangerous ideology that is characterized by both shame and intense hatred toward the sources of his earlier enslavement, and that leads inevitably to thoughts of violence: "The shame, he felt, the general bosom fires; / His rage, the rage of all the world inspires; / Round the portentous chief the millions throng, / And blood, and death, and ravage, swell the song" (41-44).

In this notion of an ideology that appears in the guise of a liberation from authoritarian control, Dwight will discover, in turn, a crucial means of confronting the more general problem posed by the French Revolution, particularly for those who had followed the written accounts of its progress throughout the 1790s. In its earliest period, it had appeared as a sign of a large-scale awakening of the republican spirit that had begun with the American Revolution. Indeed, some of the most outspoken voices of the anti-French sentiment of the late 1790s, such as Noah Webster and Jedediah Morse, had celebrated what they believed to be France's liberation from the shackles of despotism. Yet, as Dwight would recall looking back on these years in *Travels in New England and New York,* it was precisely this sense of liberation and enlightenment that obscured the brutal reality of the Revolution at the moment the reports from France turned to executions and massacres. "Even the crimes at which this world was lost in astonishment," he would write, "were by the audacity

2. Philip Freneau, "On the Invasion of Rome" (1796), in Fred Lewis Pattee, ed., *The Poems of Philip Freneau: Poet of the American Revolution*, 3 vols. (Princeton, N.J., 1902), III, 135.

and decision with which they were perpetrated surrounded with a gloomy luster which dazzled and deluded the spectator." "Actions which a few years before would have mocked all utterance, now passed over the tongue with moderate censures and reluctant severity. Robespierre, Danton, and Carrier . . . were mentioned not only without infamy and horror, but at times with satisfaction and applause."[3]

Dwight gets at this problem in "The Retrospect" by focusing on the specific aspect of the revolutionary fervor that is already most familiar to him, the connection between the larger Enlightenment discourse of unmasking, taken over directly by the revolutionaries during the anti-Catholic purges and the assembly of the National Convention, and the Enlightenment infidelity he had been combating since the time of *The Triumph of Infidelity*. As the still-familiar symbols remind us—the Republican Calendar that replaced the seven-day week with the "decade," the renaming of Notre Dame as the Temple of Reason, the signs placed at cemeteries declaring "death is an eternal sleep"—the ideological aim of the Revolution had been to overthrow not merely the tyrants but the structures of belief that justified their authority and to create in their place a wholly secular and rational culture. Yet, although this aim had been a cause for alarm for those who, like Dwight, worried about the social and political effects of infidelity—"I own to you, I know not what to make of a republic of thirty million atheists," John Adams had written in 1790—infidelity alone could not fully account for the atmosphere of enthusiasm surrounding this antireligious sentiment.[4] Dwight will thus discover a more comprehensive explanation by drawing upon his earlier argument in *The Triumph of Infidelity*. In a grand act of symbolic reversal, he presents this new secular ideology, not as a denial or rejection of religion, but as a displacement of an older theology with a new one that takes the paradoxical form of radical secularization. Yet, far from being purified of the vestiges of superstition, he will assert, this new religion is characterized by its own strict creed, icons of devotion, and empty ritual:

3. Timothy Dwight, *Travels in New England and New York* (1821–1822), ed. Barbara Miller Solomon, with the assistance of Patricia M. King, 4 vols. (Cambridge, Mass., 1969), IV, 267–268.

4. John Adams to Richard Price, Apr. 19, 1790, in C. F. Adams, ed., *The Works of John Adams; Second President of the United States*, 10 vols. (Boston, 1850–1856), IX, 563–564.

See thrice ten millions, burning to be free,
Bow to a cap, and fall before a tree;

. . . .

With Egypt, bend before a calf, or cat,
Jesus dethrone, and deify Marat;
To heaven's own altar the foul strumpet raise,
And roar in frantic hymns her tainted praise.   (57–74)

The specific irony highlighted in this passage is that, for all of the claims of the French National Convention to have purified reason from the myths of the past, Jacobinism has within a few short years degenerated into mere ritual religion, reviving many of the characteristics of the very superstitions it had ostensibly swept away. In the devotion paid to the liberty cap, the liberty pole, or a woman dressed as the "Goddess of Reason," Dwight suggests, the Republican *citoyens* and *citoyennes* are never closer to the ancient Egyptian worship of calves or cats. As in *The Triumph of Infidelity*, moreover, the purpose here is not so much to turn the charge of superstition back onto those who had similarly attacked Christianity; more important, it is to comprehend an otherwise unprecedented phenomenon from within existing categories of thought. Other critics of the cult of reason, such as Noah Webster in his 1794 treatise *The Revolution in France*, had emphasized this explanatory point. In this work, Webster sought to undeceive those who, like himself, had been blinded to the true nature of the Revolution by those who represented it as the culmination of an awakening to reason and truth after centuries of ideological slumber. To examine this new allegiance to reason, he asserts, is to recognize the persistence of certain myths and rituals that recall the idolatry of ancient civilizations such as Egypt. "The passion of the Egyptians will be called *superstitious* perhaps," he writes, "but it is the object that is changed, and not the principle." "Our people are perpetually exclaiming '*Liberty is the Goddess we adore,*' and a cap is the emblem of this Goddess. Yet in fact there is no more connection between *liberty* and a *cap*, than between the Egyptian deity Isis, and just notions of God; nor is it less an act of *superstition* to dance round a cap or a pole in honor of *liberty*, than it was in Egypt to sacrifice a bullock to Isis."[5]

5. [Noah Webster], *The Revolution in France, Considered in Respect to Its Progress and Effects* (New York, 1794), 23.

Within the literature surrounding the French Revolution, this image of Jacobinism as a revival of ancient superstition would be used on both sides of the Atlantic as a purely satiric point, as in Thomas Moore's indictment of modern democracy in general, for instance—"Which courts the rabble's smile, the rabble's nod, / And makes, like Egypt, every beast its god!" As is suggested in Webster's reference to the passion underlying such veneration, moreover, critics could also draw a direct relationship between the implicit irrationality of such idolatry and the irrational violence committed in the name of reason, as in the following excerpt from the *Anti-Jacobin Review and Magazine:* "But still, of France, I don't despair, / For *true religion* triumphs there. / They have, my Lord, a strange machine / They call the *holy guillotine*, / On which they place the sinner blinking, / To teach them *their true way of thinking.*" The more general argument, meanwhile, that Jacobinism must be treated first and foremost as a form of religion, would survive to become, by the middle of the nineteenth century, a legitimate historical interpretation, such as in Alexis de Tocqueville's highly influential work, *The Old Régime and the French Revolution.* The great strength of Tocqueville's analysis lies in his providing, alongside the various social and economic explanations of the Revolution, a clear explanation of the theological underpinnings of the revolutionaries' radically secular ideals. He would be the first to explain in systematic terms that, at the moment the traditional forms of divinity were swept away, there remained an alternative conception of divinity in human beings:

> When religion was expelled from their souls, the effect was not to create a vacuum or a state of apathy; it was promptly, if but momentarily, replaced by a host of new loyalties and secular ideals that not only filled the void but (to begin with) fired the popular imagination.
>
> For though the men who made the Revolution were more skeptical than our contemporaries as regards the Christian verities, they had anyhow one belief, and an admirable one, that we today have not; they believed in themselves. Firmly convinced of the perfectibility of man, they had faith in his innate virtue, placed him on a pedestal, and set no bounds to their devotion to his cause. . . . Of this passionate idealism was born what was in fact a new religion.[6]

6. Thomas Moore, "Epistle VII to Thomas Hume, Esq., M.D.," in Moore, *The Poetical Works of Thomas Moore, Esq.,* 2d ed. (New York, n.d.), 169; "Original Criticism,"

From Tocqueville's historical vantage point, the new theology of man could be regarded as an admirable one, for he would be able to see precisely what his work would teach subsequent generations of readers to see, the relativity of exchanging one ideological universe for another. To those like Dwight, however, encountering this phenomenon at the height of the Revolution, such an idealization of man as the sole source of divinity in an otherwise secular universe appeared only in a threatening or demonic aspect. For Dwight, the theology of man constituted not simply a devotion to man as an abstract or metaphysical entity but a devotion to man as a material being whose primary purpose for existence was the satisfaction of physical or material needs. Dwight had treated this form of self-worship at length in *The Triumph of Infidelity* in the portrait of the Infidel of Modern Breed, the materialist who openly embraced a view of the world in which the purpose of human existence was merely "to couple, eat, and die" (587). The same point will be made in "The Retrospect" with regard to the members of the Jacobin mob, acting out their own rituals of self-worship and thus lowering themselves to similar depths: "Proud to be brutes, their souls to death consign, / And, brutelike, live to couple, and to dine" (59). Yet, against the backdrop of the Terror and the massacres under Georges Jacques Danton and Jean Baptiste Carrier, Dwight would glimpse a deeper connection between such a descent into the material level of existence and the tendency toward brutality and violence. Thus, the irony surrounding the Revolution was that the attempt to elevate man to the level of divinity had in fact transformed men and women into "Beings form'd in fiercest wrath to man, / And shap'd and featur'd on the human plan; / With souls if souls they were, to naught allied, / But rage, and lust, and butchery, and pride" (101–104).

As frightening as this vision would be, even more frightening would be Dwight's growing perception of the connection between Jacobinism in France and the party then forming around Thomas Jefferson and other proponents of the French Revolution, which spoke an identical language of liberty and the rights of man. This fear is expressed when, near the end of "The Retrospect," the speaker's guiding spirit turns from the state of Europe to that of America and finds a Republic threatened by its growing devotion to the same abstract principles: "Thy sons most free, some unknown freedom claim, /

Anti-Jacobin Review and Magazine, I (1798), 546; Alexis de Tocqueville, *The Old Régime and the French Revolution* (1856), trans. Stuart Gilbert (Garden City, N.Y., 1955), 156.

That dwells in dreams or vibrates in a name: / Thy sons, most blest, their real bliss forget, / And sigh for blessings of a fairy state" (359–360). At the same time, the mood that pervades the conclusion of "The Retrospect" is equally significant for what it reveals about Dwight's own literary career; he begins to acknowledge a sense of hopelessness about the future of the Republic that he had scarcely permitted himself before. Despite the ever present threats to the Republic in *The Triumph of Infidelity* and even in *Greenfield Hill* (1794), America had still always represented the world's best hope for a virtuous and peaceful republic. Yet the image of America presented in "The Retrospect" is one in which this hope has been all but destroyed by the frenzy of violence:

> Here Gallia's self-inspir'd, Vesuvian flame
> Burns furious in ten thousand sons of shame;
> Phrenzy, destruction's bosom in his hand,
> Stands pois'd to sweep each blessing from the land;
> With lowering eyeball marks religion's cause,
> And foams, and gnashes, at the name of laws.   (297–302)

The significance of this moment in Dwight's poetic career might best be understood, in turn, in the context of its place within the Augustan tradition as a whole, for Dwight reaches largely the same conclusion in reference to America that such poets as Oliver Goldsmith and especially William Cowper had reached decades earlier in reference to Britain. In the same way that *The Task* (1785) had demanded to be read as an elegy on Augustan values—a final lament that the satiric warfare of John Dryden, Jonathan Swift, and Alexander Pope had lost and that England was sinking under the weight of luxury and corruption—"The Retrospect" signals the mournful end of Dwight's poetic struggle for the preservation of public virtue in America. Thus, whereas his earlier poetry had implicitly opposed any misguided notions that looked to Providence for immediate salvation outside the sphere of human moral struggle, in the final lines of this poem Dwight's speaker offers only a prayer of desperation that the hand of God might somehow intervene where human beings have failed: "O thou, the source of truth, and joy refin'd, / The gracious father of lost human kind, / . . . Extend thy hand, the maddening millions save; / And snatch a world from an untimely grave!" (399–404).

With the conclusion of "The Retrospect," Dwight's ideological warfare against the forces of infidelity will undergo a crucial shift, marked, most immediately, by a move away from poetry into polemical prose. More specifically, he moves from the confident Augustan voice of *The Triumph of Infidelity* and *Greenfield Hill* to the fierce and thundering tone of a New England jeremiad, particularly heard in such works as *The Duty of Americans, at the Present Crisis* and *A Discourse on Some Events of the Last Century* (1801). Dwight will draw upon the depiction of French revolutionary ideology from "The Retrospect" as a new religion now attracting American converts and begin to imagine the struggle against infidelity as, literally, a religious war between the forces of traditional Christianity and those of Jacobinism. As in the case of his earlier poetry, the audience of such works is assumed to possess the collective power to decide the future of the Republic. Yet this is no longer an abstract moral or religious choice between virtue and complacency; it is a choice between two fully realized religions competing for loyalty. He warns against the proponents of the new American Jacobinism, "For what end shall we be connected with men, of whom this is the character and conduct? . . . Is it that our churches may become temples of reason, our Sabbath a decade, and our psalms of praise Marseillois hymns? Is it, that we may change our holy worship into a dance of Jacobin phrenzy, and that we may behold a strumpet personating a Goddess on the altars of JEHOVAH?"[7]

By the time Dwight would express this more urgent sense of a Jacobin threat to American religion, he would have already come across an account of recent historical events that would confirm in concrete detail his earlier view of the dangers of radical republicanism and infidel philosophy. This is the story of the Bavarian Illuminati, which Dwight first mentions in a concluding footnote to the 1797 sermon *The Nature, and Danger, of Infidel Philosophy*. Soon after the manuscript had gone to press, he explains, he encountered a book describing a decades-long plot to bring about a series of revolutions throughout Europe similar to that in France, an overthrow of existing governments, and a large-scale eradication of Christianity. "All this is to be done under the pretence of enlarged Philanthropy, and of giving mankind liberty and equality," he cautions. "By this mask is carefully concealed the true end, which is . . . a

7. Timothy Dwight, *The Duty of Americans, at the Present Crisis, Illustrated in a Discourse, Preached on the Fourth of July, 1798* (New Haven, Conn., 1798), 20.

complete subjugation to these Philosophers; a subjugation of mind as well as of body."[8]

The book to which Dwight is referring is John Robison's *Proofs of a Conspiracy against All the Religions and Governments of Europe*, the first of several books and pamphlets published in America that attempted to prove that the connection between Enlightenment skepticism and the French Revolution had been far more direct and deliberate than previously supposed. Robison argues that the Revolution had originated with a group of political radicals and religious skeptics known as the Bavarian Illuminati, who had first disseminated their views throughout Europe by infiltrating the Masonic societies and converting their members into advocates of political and religious revolution. According to this theory, the conspiracy had first been conceived in the early eighteenth century by the philosophes and their allies but had not been put into action until the 1780s, when the Illuminati began secretly to spread from Germany to France. There they eventually joined with the Jacobin clubs to guide them in their revolutionary activities. At the same time, as Robison and others warned, this was only the beginning of a larger scheme to overthrow all of the governments of Europe and America and to rebuild them in the image of the French Directory.[9]

8. Timothy Dwight, *The Nature, and Danger, of Infidel Philosophy Exhibited in Two Discourses, Addressed to the Candidates for the Baccalaureate, in Yale College* (1798), in Dwight, *Sermons*, 2 vols. (New Haven, Conn., 1828), I, 380.

9. The Bavarian Illuminati was, in fact, a real organization, founded in 1776 by Adam Weishaupt, professor of canon law at the University of Ingolstadt. Weishaupt's reasons for forming the society were in some ways as ambitious as those later attributed to him: to use the group as a means of propagating Enlightenment ideals and opposing what he called political and ecclesiastical tyranny. Modeled largely after the Freemasons—with levels of membership based on one's "degree of Enlightenment"—the Illuminati had a sizable membership within a decade of its founding. In part because of this growth, the society became a threat in the eyes of Bavarian elector Carl Theodore and was officially suppressed in 1786. Yet the demise of the actual order contributed to the growing myth of its secret influence: in the aftermath of an inquest of former members, testimony about Weishaupt's grand ambitions were gradually transformed in common discourse into secret plans believed to be then already under way. In the wake of the French Revolution, two major works appeared to expose the conspiracy, John Robi-

The Illuminati theory gained immediate popularity in America in late 1797 and early 1798, after the tide of public opinion had turned against the French Revolution amid the XYZ affair and the threat of a Franco-American war. Yet, for Federalists like Dwight, Jedediah Morse, and others, the theory would have a greater value, not least because it provided a single historical narrative that connected Voltaire and Jean-Jacques Rousseau with Robespierre and Jefferson. This narrative, moreover, imposed a degree of rationality onto a series of events that otherwise challenged existing categories of thought. Far from constituting a symptom of irrational or paranoid thought, as it has sometimes been characterized, belief in the Illuminati plot actually helped to explain historical causes and effects within common Enlightenment assumptions, particularly about the projection of false consciousness onto the masses. Indeed, the Illuminati theory applied the same reasoning to the actions of philosophes and revolutionaries as had earlier been used by figures such as Paine and Joel Barlow to account for the inaction of the oppressed masses prior to the French Revolution, that of a systematic delusion imposed on unsuspecting people by an identifiable group of power-hungry men. The appearance of Robison's *Proofs of Conspiracy* would merely confirm Dwight's growing apprehension registered in "The Retrospect" and elsewhere that, behind the revolutionaries' ideology of individual liberty, lay a hitherto unrecognized authoritarianism.[10]

---

son's *Proofs of a Conspiracy against All the Religions and Governments of Europe, Carried on in the Secret Meetings of Free Masons, Illuminati, and Reading Societies* . . . (London, 1797) and the Abbé Barruel's *Memoirs, Illustrating the History of Jacobinism*, 4 vols. in 2 (London, 1797). The latter supplied the narrative of the conspiracy theory, explaining how a plan that was originally conceived in the early part of the century by philosophes like Voltaire and Denis Diderot had gradually spread through the ranks of the Freemasons. The plot was further revised by the more radical Illuminati, and, in the years just prior to the Revolution, communicated to the Jacobins, who put it into action. For a history both of the actual Illuminati and of the myth of its role in the French Revolution, see Vernon Stauffer, *New England and the Bavarian Illuminati* (New York, 1918).

10. The Illuminati theory had long been interpreted as an example of a tradition of American political paranoia (following Richard Hofstadter's essay, "The Paranoid Style in American Politics," in Hofstadter, *The Paranoid Style in American Politics, and Other Essays* [New York, 1965], 3–40). This view was all but put to rest by Gordon S.

The Illuminati scare would prove short-lived, but Dwight would continue to draw upon its controlling narrative of deliberate subterfuge and popular delusion to explain the rise of the Democratic-Republican party and the subsequent election of Jefferson. Although Dwight, as a Congregational minister, would avoid speaking about Jefferson or the election directly, he would nevertheless make his views known. Directing his critique, not at Jefferson directly, but at the general movement centered on the slogans of liberty and the rights of man, Dwight would thus suggest that Jeffersonian democracy was a manifestation of the same mass deception perpetuated in Europe by philosophes and Illuminati. Describing the most recent strategy of such groups in *A Discourse on Some Events of the Last Century*, for instance, he states that "their own cause they now artfully, and with complete success, blended with that of liberty; and, although the union was unnatural and monstrous, yet they were easily able to prevent this fact from being discerned, even by some sagacious eyes, during the moment of popular phrenzy. This junction was clearly the most politic single step, which they have ever taken." [11] At the same time,

---

Wood ("Conspiracy and the Paranoid Style: Causality and Deceit in the Eighteenth Century," *William and Mary Quarterly*, 3d Ser., XXXIX [1982], 401–441). Wood argued that, although the French Revolution would later influence the way Western thought would explain such mass popular movements, those witnessing the events in the 1790s were predisposed to an explanation that accorded with an idea of "autonomous, freely acting individuals who are capable of directly and deliberately bringing about events through their decisions and actions" (409), thus making reasonable the existence of an identifiable cabal of perpetrators. For an analysis of the other element of the Illuminati theory, the explanation of mass popular deception by these perpetrators, see Amos Hofman, "Opinion, Illusion, and the Illusion of Opinion: Barruel's Theory of Conspiracy," *Eighteenth-Century Studies*, XXVII (1993), 27–60.

11. Timothy Dwight, *A Discourse on Some Events of the Last Century* (New Haven, Conn., 1801), 24. During the period following the XYZ affair, the Illuminati theory enjoyed its widest popularity, and even George Washington, himself a Freemason, expressed concern over Illuminati infiltration of Masonic lodges. Because of this assumed relationship between "Illuminism" and masonry and the resulting suspicion directed at members of various lodges, the theory soon lost its appeal and became the object of a counterattack. Those like Jedediah Morse and Dwight were accused of using the Illuminati theory as part of a conspiracy of their own against their Jeffersonian opponents (see, for example, [John Cosens Ogden], *A View of the New-England Illuminati:*

the special poignancy of this remark derives from the timing of Dwight's delivery of the *Discourse* in early January 1801. As with the publication of "The Retrospect" only a few days earlier, the great unmentioned fact giving meaning to Dwight's statement is that the Federalists have been defeated and the presidency will soon be taken over either by Jefferson or by another notorious Democrat, Dwight's own cousin Aaron Burr. In this veiled sense, then, Dwight would render his verdict on the election of 1800 as the victory of the new theology of man, the symbol of an actual triumph of infidelity in America.

Yet, despite the sense of unmitigated defeat felt by Dwight and others after Jefferson's election, he would not follow the persona from "The Retrospect" toward utter hopelessness and despair. Indeed, the extent to which Dwight would continue to believe in the power of satire to intervene can be seen in the decision to revive, at least briefly, his satiric campaign against infidel philosophy. In the months following Jefferson's inauguration, Dwight would publish in the *Mercury and New-England Palladium* a serialized prose satire entitled "Morpheus," which focuses specifically on the notion of human perfectibility and the possibility of an earthly utopia as the dominant ideology of the new administration. Using the familiar form of a dream vision, the narrator of "Morpheus" recounts his travels through a newly transformed America—a place, he explains, that was once called "The Country of Instruction" but has since been renamed "The Land of Nod" because so many of its leaders "have spent their lives in nodding, or dreaming, while they were awake." In particular, the narrator describes the "City of Perfectibility," a utopian polis presided over by none other than William Godwin, whose futile attempts to put the philosophy of his *Enquiry concerning Political Justice* (1793) into practice provides the basis of the satiric narrative. In one sense, the "Morpheus" essays employ the familiar criticism against metaphysical or speculative excesses found everywhere in eighteenth-century satire. Godwin himself emerges here as a version of Swift's Laputan philosophers as he reveals his utter inexperience

_____

Who Are Indefatigably Engaged in Destroying the Religion and Government of the United States [Philadelphia, 1799]). Versions of the Illuminati theory have been revived since 1800: in the nineteenth century, it was invoked as part of the more general suspicion of Freemasons, and even today it survives as one example of popular conspiracy discourse in America. See Steven C. Bullock, *Revolutionary Brotherhood: Freemasonry and the Transformation of the American Social Order, 1730–1840* (Chapel Hill, N.C., 1996).

with such things as agriculture and physical labor: "As he had never ploughed anything before, except metaphysical fields, which he had always taken care to have smoothed and mellowed to his liking; plain farmer's ploughing in rough fields must be supposed to have been attended with several inconveniences, not the less agreeable because they were new." The chief target of the "Morpheus" essays, however, is the Enlightenment assumption of human moral innocence understood as the shared political philosophy of Godwin and the new president, also known to Federalists as the "American Condorcet." Thus, the City of Perfectibility—perhaps itself an emblem of the new federal capital—fails precisely because of its founder's gross miscalculations of the responses of actual people, forcing the fictional Godwin to deal with unforeseen crimes and conflicts, including, at one point, being tarred and feathered by his own followers.[12]

12. Timothy Dwight, "Morpheus," *Mercury and New-England Palladium*, Nov. 24, Dec. 8, 11, 1801. In addition to Godwin, Dwight also satirizes Mary Wollstonecraft in two essays entitled "Morpheus, Part 2." Addressing a crowd in the City of Perfectibility, Wollstonecraft is accused by a female member of the audience, first, of basing her feminism on an erroneous belief that all men are tyrants and, second, of using feminism to reject traditional sexual mores (Mar. 5, 9, 1802). Chandos Michael Brown argues that the satire in these essays is rooted in the same critique as that leveled against Godwin and others, that its chief object of attack is the displacement of an older moral order based on duty and subordination of self-interest with a new assertion of individual desire and aspiration as the center of human existence. Brown also points out that "Morpheus, Part 2" appeared as part of a general backlash against Wollstonecraft that came in the wake of Godwin's 1798 publication of *Memoirs of the Author of "The Rights of Women,"* which confirmed rumors of her reputed sexual license (Brown, "Mary Wollstonecraft; or, The Female Illuminati: The Campaign against Women and 'Modern Philosophy' in the Early Republic," *Journal of the Early Republic*, XV [1995], 389–424). This image of Wollstonecraft as a moral threat helps to explain why Dwight, who was a pioneer in women's education and whose views on the subject corresponded in many ways to Wollstonecraft's, would single her out for satiric response. Indeed, like the Wollstonecraft of *Thoughts on the Education of Daughters* (1787) and *Vindication of the Rights of Woman* (1792), Dwight denounces the educational system that cultivates reason in men but only refinement in women. "It is evidently high time that women should be considered less as pretty, and more as rational and immortal beings," he writes in the *Travels* (ed. Solomon, IV, 336; see also I, 372–375). This position guided

Within the body of Dwight's writings after 1801, however, the "Morpheus" essays appear as an anomalous satiric utterance in a shift not only away from satire but from explicit commentary on national or international trends. Instead, Dwight would orient himself chiefly toward the preservation of New England as the last bastion of piety and public virtue in a world elsewhere falling victim to the delusions of radical democracy and the theology of man. During this period, for instance, he would begin keeping the journal of his annual travels through New England and New York as a conscious attempt to record the character of the region in the face of rapid historical change. More important, he would redirect the struggle he had begun in *The Triumph of Infidelity* away from the earlier strategy of direct rhetorical engagement with the various forms of Enlightenment secularism and progressivism and toward the more limited emphasis upon revitalizing Christianity as a means of defense. To glance at the titles of some of Dwight's later publications is to recognize the measure of this shift: *The Charitable Blessed* (1810), *The Dignity and Excellence of the Gospel* (1812), "Lectures on the Evidences of Divine Revelation" (1810–1813), "On the Manner in Which the Scriptures Are to Be Understood" (1816).[13]

Most immediately, Dwight would cultivate religious devotion through revival. The years between 1800 and Dwight's death in 1817 would mark one of the most intense periods of religious revivalism in Connecticut and elsewhere, and Dwight would himself lead a series of revivals at Yale. Gradually he would come to be known by his students less for the thundering tones of commencement speeches like *The Nature, and Danger, of Infidel Philosophy* than for the quiet intensity of revival sermons such as *The Harvest Past*. As one

---

his own coeducational academy at Greenfield Hill in the 1780s, where boys and girls were taught not only the same curriculum but one that was reputed to rival Yale in academic rigor (see Leon Howard, *The Connecticut Wits* [Chicago, 1943], 207).

13. Dwight's new emphasis after the election of 1800 on preserving New England rather than leading America is evident in a letter to Jedediah Morse concerning the formation of the *Mercury and New-England Palladium* as a voice for Federalism. Describing the renewed sense of purpose among Federalists since the late election, he concludes, "I think N. England will be saved from ruin" (Dwight to Morse, Dec. 21, 1800, Morse Family Papers, 1799–1868, Yale University Library, New Haven, Conn.). For a discussion of the *Travels* as representative of an inward turn toward New England, see Kenneth Silverman, *Timothy Dwight* (New York, 1969), 130–136.

of the most prominent members of the Congregationalist clergy, moreover, Dwight would lead the way in the various missionary and reformist activities that are generally regarded as the social arm of the Second Great Awakening. He would serve, for instance, on the editorial board of the *Connecticut Evangelical Magazine* and later help to create the *Panoplist, and Missionary Magazine;* he would preside over the Connecticut Religious Tract Society; he would even assist Thomas Gallaudet in founding the first American school for the deaf. In this context, Dwight's ostensible retreat from broad political and ideological struggle must also be viewed as exemplifying what has since been called the principal means by which the church maintained its social influence in the age of Jefferson and Andrew Jackson.[14]

Dwight's emphasis on strengthening the church as an institution during these years is equally evident in his more than two decades of training and placing the next generation of Yale Congregationalists. Among the list of clergymen trained by Dwight were revivalists and reformers like Lyman Beecher and Asahel Nettleton and theologians like Nathaniel W. Taylor, who would later hold the Dwight Professorship in the new Yale Divinity School. It is in this capacity that Dwight would also play a role in the controversy over Unitarianism, which, although taking place chiefly after his death, would pit his own Calvinist colleagues and successors against the theological heirs to the Arminian tradition earlier represented by Charles Chauncy. Indeed, after the controversial election of the Unitarian Henry Ware as Harvard's Hollis Professor of Divinity in 1805, Dwight would work to unite New Divinity men and more moderate Calvinists to found a competing seminary in Andover and would preach the opening sermon in 1808. Two years later, Dwight would send his former student Jeremiah Evarts to work with Jedediah Morse as editor of the *Panoplist,* thus bringing together the two men who would later initiate the Unitarian controversy in the pages of that same magazine.[15]

14. For Dwight's involvement in missionary and reform organizations, see Charles Roy Keller, *The Second Great Awakening in Connecticut* (New Haven, Conn., 1942), chaps. 5, 7; Stephen E. Berk, *Calvinism versus Democracy: Timothy Dwight and the Origins of American Evangelical Orthodoxy* (Hamden, Conn., 1974), chap. 9.

15. Following Chauncy's death in 1787, most Arminian Congregationalists remained uncertain about the merits of Chauncy's scriptural proof of universal salvation. Even

To be sure, Dwight would continue to express his concerns about the future of America—during the War of 1812, he would briefly return to the rhetoric he had employed in *The Duty of Americans, at the Present Crisis* and *A Discourse on Some Events of the Last Century*—but nearly two decades of revivals would make Dwight more optimistic in his last year of life than at any time since the election of Jefferson. In a series of essays entitled "Observations on the Present State of Religion in the World," published less than six months before his death, he would write, "I am constrained to believe a new era in the moral concerns of man to have commenced; and anticipate from this period a new order of things in the affairs of our world, in which the Religion of the Gospel will rise in all its majesty, beneficence, and glory, to the astonished, and delighted view of mankind." For Dwight, as for numerous other Congregationalists, the era of infidelity appeared to be over: "The present has been emphatically styled by the age of Bibles and Missionaries," declared a member of the Fairfield County Bible Society in that same year, adding: "The atheism of Voltaire and his associates, is gone down, almost with their dust to the grave. The blasphemies of Paine are remembered only to be abhorred." Yale graduates like Lyman Beecher would look back to their college years in the 1790s and, seeking to account for the decline in fashionable religious skepti-

those who were attracted to the doctrine chose not to make it a central element of their theology, and it was supplanted by anti-trinitarianism as the crucial doctrinal revision separating the Boston liberals from the Calvinists. After this time, Calvinists and Unitarians coexisted uneasily within the Congregational Church until the controversy began with Evarts's 1815 publication of "Review of American Unitarianism," a work intended finally to expose the existence of a Boston Unitarian movement. After this, pamphlets were exchanged on both sides between 1815 and the mid-1820s by such figures as William Ellery Channing, Andrews Norton, Leonard Woods, Henry Ware, and Nathaniel W. Taylor. By the end of the 1820s, the denominational schism was complete, as individual churches chose to remain Congregationalist or declare themselves Unitarian. For Dwight's role in the formation of the Andover Seminary and his placement of Jeremiah Evarts on the *Panoplist, and Missionary Magazine*, see Berk, *Calvinism versus Democracy*, 178–183. Conrad Wright's *Beginnings of Unitarianism in America* (Boston, 1955) remains the authoritative study of the theological origins of Unitarianism; for Chauncy's relationship to later Arminians and Unitarians, see 196–199.

cism, would give much of the credit to President Dwight's relentless public warfare.[16]

Yet, even as Dwight would be remembered as the symbol of a triumph *over* infidelity in the first decades of the nineteenth century, during this same period many of the assumptions governing Dwight's ideological warfare would come under attack. Foremost among these assumptions, not surprisingly, would be the perceived association between irreligion and the more general sympathy for either the French Revolution or the Jeffersonian party. Dwight's charge might be credited with halting the influence of the relatively small number of Republicans who enthusiastically followed their French counterparts in identifying the cause of liberty with eradicating the vestiges of religious superstition—the few unabashed supporters of Paine after the public outcry over *The Age of Reason,* for instance, or the members of Elihu Palmer's New York Deistical Society. This identification of Jefferson with infidelity would, however, prove far less powerful against the greater number of Jeffersonians who were not only loathe to give up their religious affiliations but who were already insisting that the ideals of liberty and the rights of man were necessarily intertwined with the essential doctrines of Christianity. The most powerful counterattacks against Dwight and the Federalist clergy would thus be articulated in religious as well as social or political terms.

Even during the height of the clergy's anxiety over the existence of a party of American Jacobins wholly sympathetic to the iconoclastic objectives of the French Revolution, the possibility had existed for a direct Democratic countercharge that the true threat of irreligion lay with those Federalists who, under the pretense of defending a more traditional social and religious order, were in fact intending to restore to power a new American aristocracy. Indeed, the accusation that such aristocrats secretly held skeptical or atheistic views had been advanced directly in an anonymous poem of 1795 entitled *Aristocracy: An Epic Poem,* a work that might accurately be described as thematically and structurally the Democratic-Republican answer to *The Triumph of Infidelity.* In the poem's preface, the author begins by defending those members of Demo-

16. Timothy Dwight, "Observations on the Present State of Religion in the World," *Religious Intelligencer,* I (Sept. 14, 1816), 245–246; "Second Annual Report of the Directors of the Fairfield County Bible Society," ibid. (Oct. 19, 1816), 331; Barbara M. Cross, ed., *The Autobiography of Lyman Beecher* (1864), 2 vols. (Cambridge, Mass., 1961), I, 27.

cratic societies who have been "stigmatized with the opprobrious epithets of Anarchists and Disorganizers," arguing that such accusations themselves illustrate the influence of a "spirit of Aristocracy" and, particularly, the work of a "dangerous Coalition" that exists "to destroy the general influence of the people." The larger narrative of the poem, accordingly, tells the story of this hidden coalition, and, though it leaves off after only two books, it recounts the group's initial formation by a character named "Aristus" and his subsequent alliance with a mysterious European envoy. Yet the rhetorical power of *Aristocracy* arises from the way in which, like *The Triumph of Infidelity*, it renders this aristocratic threat in symbolic form by making Satan the controlling presence of the story. And, although the Satan of *Aristocracy* is decidedly more Miltonic as he addresses his minions from his throne in Pandemonium, he does allude directly to Dwight's Satan when he lays out his plan to use Aristus and his circle of would-be aristocrats to bring the American Republic once again under his control:

> Beneath my yoke see Europe sinking low,
> And Asia stoop, and feeble Afric bow:
> O'er half the western world my sway extends,
> And slowly yielding, now the other bends.
>
> .   .   .   .
>
> But, lo! to Hell more pleasant prospects shine,
> And fair Columbia hastens to be mine.
> Even now, immers'd in dark surrounding shade,
> ARISTUS roams, the spirit and the head.
> His mighty soul now labours to extend
> My spreading sway, himself my dearest friend.[17]

17. *Aristocracy: An Epic Poem* . . . (Philadelphia, 1795), iii, 14–15. One of the most remarkable characteristics of this poem is that it is presented not merely as a symbolic unmasking of a general conspiracy of American "aristocrats" but as proof of an actual plot. In the preface, the presumed author of the poem states that he is, in fact, only the "editor" and that the poem was written by one of the conspirators: "The Author of this work was, as acknowledged therein, concerned in one of those plots against the liberties of the people. . . . The manuscript, which probably was never intended for publication, at length passed into my hands" (iv–v). As a result, the editor is forced to explain, first, why the author of the poem would have described himself and his

At such moments in *Aristocracy,* the great ideological counterpoint to the argument of *The Triumph of Infidelity* is that the true demonic threat facing America is aristocracy as much as infidelity. Or, more precisely, the threat of irreligion commonly identified with radical democracy can be traced, in fact, to the aristocratic tendencies of the Federalists. Drawing upon the common eighteenth-century literary conception of the European aristocracy—and, particularly, the figure of "rake aristocrat" who is both morally reprobate and entirely skeptical in religion—the poem presents Aristus and his circle as men who possess the same air of sophisticated amorality as their European counterparts, but who acknowledge such beliefs only to each other. Thus, they adhere completely to a Hobbesian moral reality in which self-interest is the wellspring of all moral actions—"Yes, let the rich abjure, the poor despise," Aristus proclaims, "'Tis *Self* alone which charms each mortal's eyes." At the same time, they admit their willingness to adopt any guise that will elevate them in the minds of the vulgar populace, whether this involves the pretense to Christianity, which Aristus calls the "dream" of "Priests, and men priest-ridden," or to republican disinterest: "While we, who vary as each coming day, / In different forms shall public will display— / And strive, beneath this mask of patriot zeal, / Our proud aspiring wishes to conceal."[18]

In the context of the party wars of the 1790s, the significance of a poem like *Aristocracy* lies in its clearing ideological space for a more formidable attack against the Federalist clergy as a body of would-be aristocrats whose pretense to virtue or religious orthodoxy served merely as a tool for social or political control. In New England, this attack would come in the specific form of a counteroffensive to the Bavarian Illuminati scare, a series of pamphlets proposing to uncover the existence of a "New England Illuminati," directed at Dwight and other orthodox Congregationalist leaders. As one writer explains, this organization was formed in the 1760s by the disciples of Jonathan Edwards as a means of limiting theological study to New Divinity doctrines. More recently, under the leadership of President Dwight—"the head of the

---

colleagues as villains and admit their motives are wholly selfish and demonic and, second, why a person who, in one passage, acknowledges the skepticism or atheism of himself and his fellow conspirators would, in another, describe them as under Satan's influence (vi).

18. Ibid., 11–12.

Illuminati"—they have undertaken the next phase of their plot, to undermine the progress of liberty by exerting their influence over politics: "Courting the rich men, and directing the politics of the country in every period, they had united a formidable body with them among the laity, who received votes and preferments at the will of the clergy. This united phalanx it was dangerous to attack." Since then, another pamphleteer writes, the leaders of the New England ecclesiastical establishment have mounted a two-pronged attack. On one front, they have attacked religious dissenters in a manner that recalls the sneers of the Jewish priests against the early Christians, "because they had neither purse nor scrip, and because their leader was poor." On the other, they have waged war against republicanism itself, "because it cherishes that *liberty of conscience, which is inconsistent with ecclesiastical dominion . . . and because it contends for an equality of civil rights, which is fatal to the pretentions of those, who want more than their share.*" [19]

As the references to the early church suggest, such sentiments belong not to Jeffersonian Republicanism merely but to the more particular synthesis of radical republicanism and evangelical Protestantism that would characterize American religious dissent from the 1790s onward. By appealing to such ideals as civil liberty and social equality, an entire generation of radical sectarians and itinerant preachers—Lorenzo Dow, Billy Hibbard, Elias Smith, and others—was able to distinguish their own, more self-consciously primitive forms of Christianity from the "modern Pharasaism" represented by the Standing Orders. This was never merely a social or political critique but one that carried always a crucial theological element. It was based on the assumption that certain doctrines or religious practices, because of their consistency with egalitarianism or the rights of man, were more consistent with Christ's true message. In turn, the campaign against Dwight and the Congregational Standing Order, beyond simply constituting a democratic challenge to ecclesiastical authority, became a struggle over the true meaning of Christianity, as, for instance, in Simon Hough's 1792 attack against the Congregationalists' insistence upon the necessity of a college-educated clergy:

19. [Ogden], *A View of the New England Illuminati*, 7; Abraham Bishop, *Proofs of a Conspiracy, against Christianity, and the Government of the United States* (Hartford, Conn., 1802), 32, 48.

As there were witnesses for God in the Jewish church, and those were generally poor and despised; so there has been in the gospel church much the same . . . ; and in your conduct you as much resist the Holy Ghost as the Jews did; for you reject the poor if they teach truth, and will have none but the learned and worldly wise, no more than they; nay you deny the power of the Holy Ghost, to furnish men for teachers, unless they are college learnt, and in so doing you despise Christ and his Apostles, for they were not college learnt; . . . nor can you discern the things of God, by your worldly wisdom, any more than they could.[20]

At the same time, Hough is simply providing a more explicitly social or political articulation of the argument used throughout the eighteenth century to demonstrate the inherent benevolence of certain doctrines. Indeed, a similar identification of social equality with the essence of Christ's teaching had been used to contrast Universalism—which seemed to reveal most vividly the equality of all men in God's eyes—with the inherently hierarchical doctrine of eternal damnation. Even Chauncy, who can hardly be called a radical egalitarian, recognized the relationship between his doctrine and the emerging universalist vision of the Republic as proclaimed by writers like Crèvecoeur: "Where is the man so destitute of benevolence, so bereft of humanity," he asks, "as not to bid God-speed to an attempt, intended to establish it as a revealed truth, that . . . before the scene of providence is finally shut up, [eternal salvation] shall be the portion of all men, of whatever nation, character, colour, station, or condition?" This same implication could then be adopted by populist Universalists and presented along specifically class or party lines, as in John Murray's assertion in 1798 that only universal salvation affirms that all men are truly created equal: "*Our* gospel, is *glad tidings of good things* unto *all people;* the other gospel is *glad tidings* of *good things,* to *some* people, supposing them *better* than *others,* and *sad tidings* of *bad things* to the *greater part of mankind.*"[21]

20. [Simon Hough], *An Alarm to the World* . . . (Stockbridge, Mass., 1792), 22. For a discussion of the theological dimension of the dissenters' appeal to liberty and equality, see Nathan O. Hatch, *The Democratization of American Christianity* (New Haven, Conn., 1989), 44–46.

21. Charles Chauncy, *The Mystery Hid from Ages and Generations, Made Manifest by the Gospel-Revelation; or, The Salvation of All Men the Grand Thing Aimed at in the Scheme*

Aside from the particular egalitarian claims of Universalists, however, distinctions between aristocratic and democratic denominations could be made over a number of issues, perhaps most notably those of religious toleration and the separation of church and state. To defend the existence of an established church in Connecticut or Massachusetts, or even to assume that one's own doctrines represented the standard of orthodoxy, seemed to violate not only the principle of equality but, more important, the right of ownership over one's conscience. This right would be invoked both by members of newer sects—Freewill Baptists, Shakers, the Christian Connection—seeking to challenge the authority of established clergy and by individual believers finding it necessary to define their own personal creeds, independent of the competing claims of existing sects. This conception of religious freedom cannot be understood simply as belonging to the discourse of toleration running roughly from John Locke to Joseph Priestley, as a practical policy intended to hasten the purification that will ultimately unite all believers around a common set of doctrines. Rather, this is toleration as an end in itself, a new pluralistic vision of individual creeds, each understood as possessing its own self-contained truth.

In its most radical form, this notion of a fully individualized conscience would render virtually meaningless Dwight's conception of the conscience as a window to the *nunc-stans* perspective. Nowhere is this effect more evident than in the redefinition of infidelity itself. As Paine would declare in *The Age of Reason,* insofar as one's obligation as a believer is simply to be faithful to the dictates of one's conscience, "Infidelity does not consist in believing, or in disbelieving: it consists in professing to believe what [one] does not believe." For a freethinker like Paine to define infidelity as essentially self-referential was one thing; for a professed Christian to do the same would be another, for Christianity necessarily demanded a belief in an external standard of divine or absolute truth.[22] Yet, among Universalists such as William Pitt Smith and

---

of God . . . (1784), ed. Edwin S. Gaustad (New York, 1969), 13; John Murray, *Universalism Vindicated: Being the Substance of Some Observations on the Revelation of the Unbounded Love of God* (Charlestown, Mass., [1798]), 45.

22. In *A Letter concerning Toleration* (1689), John Locke states that it is impossible for any denomination, including the established church, to prove that its own doctrines are those of the true church. Thus, toleration is understood as a way of living peacefully

Hosea Ballou, the redefinition of infidelity along the lines of Paine's would be possible because the doctrinal definition of Christianity was being displaced by a looser definition that Ballou had called the "spirit" of Christianity. By this sense, he would assert, even a deist might be considered a good Christian. Yet it is also clear in *A Treatise on Atonement* that a good Christian might reasonably be accused of infidelity, for, to insist that one's particular doctrines constitute divine truth is a sure sign that one does not possess this Christian spirit:

> All the religion in our world, founded on the partial principles of man's inventions, pointing out particular modes of faith and forms of worship, is from carnal man. Discord and contention ensue; wars and fightings are the consequences; hatred, wrath, strife, emulation, and rivalship, rage in the minds of those who possess this spurious religion. . . . How miserable has religion made mankind! But, says the reader, it was sin that you were to tell

---

in a world in which the truth belongs "only to the Supreme Judge of all men, to whom also alone belongs the punishment of the erroneous" (*The Works of John Locke*, 10 vols. [London, 1812], VI, 19). This understanding would survive within Joseph Priestley's teleology of doctrinal purification as a means by which "every remaining corruption of Christianity [will] be removed, and nothing will be found in it that any unbeliever, any Jew, or Mahometan, can reasonably object to" (Priestley, *A General History of the Christian Church* (1802–1803), in John Towill Rutt, ed., *The Theological and Miscellaneous Works of Joseph Priestley*, 25 vols. [London, 1817–1832], X, 534). At the same time, insofar as Locke's formulation depended on the notion that one's beliefs, however true or false in reality, must be treated as property, it would open the way for dissenters increasingly to locate the essence of religion within the individual conscience. Thus, by the end of the eighteenth century, some believers (such as Lucy Mack Smith, mother of Mormon founder Joseph Smith, and Abner Jones, cofounder of the Christian Connection) would insist upon being baptized or ordained only as Christians, independent of the particular tenets of any denomination (see Hatch, *Democratization*, 40–43).

This characterization of toleration as itself a creed would be later criticized by Lyman Beecher as a new absolutism in the guise of relativism. During the controversy leading up to the 1818 disestablishment of religion in Connecticut, Beecher included the following verses in a satiric essay entitled "The Toleration Dream": "Some tolerate virtue, some tolerate vice, / Some tolerate truth, some tolerate lies, / Some tolerate religion, some tolerate none, / And the test of all faith is their TOLERATION" (Cross, ed., *Autobiography of Beecher*, I, 290).

the consequences of, not religion. I tell you, kind reader, that the religion of which I speak, is opposed to every degree of the spirit of life in Christ Jesus, which has ever been revealed to mankind, and, therefore, is sin.[23]

For Ballou, doctrinal considerations can no longer legitimately be used to exclude a particular set of beliefs from the category of Christianity. At the same time, Ballou's assertion that sectarianism is antithetical to "the spirit of life in Christ Jesus" posits a new category of "practical infidelity," defined as a violation by a professed Christian against the faith's true spirit of toleration. Not surprisingly, this same identification of practical infidelity with intolerance would be used during the controversy over religious establishment and separation of church and state, with Dwight and the Congregationalist clergy being accused of "conspiring, not against the name, form and profession, but against the spirit and temper of christianity." The same charge could be leveled more generally against Calvinism not simply because it was the particular theology professed by the Standing Order but because of the political implications of designating a small number of people as the elect and persuading the majority of their innate powerlessness to pursue redemption. Or, as the itinerant preacher Lorenzo Dow would put it in a satirical hymn, to tell one sinner that "he's decreed / Unto eternal bliss" and another that "he is doom'd to miss" is to deny to both the liberty of seeking their own salvation: "The first he bindeth fast in pride, / The second in despair; / If he can only keep them tied, / Which way he does not care."[24]

The criticism that Calvinism amounted to a practical violation of the spirit of Christianity would be heard not only from outside the Congregationalist establishment (leading up to the unseating of the Connecticut Standing Order in 1818) but, in the last years of Dwight's life, from within its ranks, by the body of Unitarians who had up to that point preferred to remain discreet in their heterodox beliefs. Although the Unitarian conflict would recall in some ways the dynamic of the earlier Universalist controversy—centering on a largely anonymous group of Boston liberals who had come to deny cer-

23. Thomas Paine, *The Age of Reason* (1794), in Paine, *Collected Writings* (New York, 1995), 666; Hosea Ballou, *A Treatise on Atonement* (1805), ed. Ernest Cassara (Boston, 1986), 43.

24. Paine, *Age of Reason*, in Paine, *Writings*, 666; Bishop, *Proofs of a Conspiracy*, 66; Lorenzo Dow, "There Is a Reprobation Plan" (1814), in Hatch, *Democratization*, 229.

tain orthodox tenets—the crucial difference would lie in the way in which the Unitarians, once exposed by Morse and Evarts, would succeed in transforming the doctrinal argument into a moral debate over the implications of adhering to a Calvinist conception of God and man. The high point of the debate would come in William Ellery Channing's famous "Moral Argument against Calvinism," in which he would explicitly assert that Calvinism is mere ideology—that it "owes its perpetuity to the influence of fear in palsying the moral nature" and that it "has passed its meridian, and is sinking, to rise no more." Yet Channing would raise the same moral argument at a much earlier point in the controversy in the "A Letter to the Rev. Samuel C. Thacher." The primary purpose of this open letter, addressed to one of Channing's Calvinist friends, was to defuse the controversy and to convince Congregationalists that their doctrinal differences were not a good enough reason for splitting the denomination. At the same time, Channing would not refrain from suggesting that, although certain doctrinal differences are largely insignificant, others—specifically those having to do with what Chauncy had called "the comfort of God's creatures"—were the real determiners of whether a denomination was worthy of the name Christian. "We consider the errours which relate to Christ's person as of little or no importance," he would declaim, "compared with the errour of those who teach, that God brings us into life wholly depraved and wholly helpless, that he leaves multitudes without that aid which is indispensably necessary to their repentance, and then plunges them into everlasting burnings and unspeakable torture, for not repenting." For Channing, the immorality of professing such views about God and man is more clearly incompatible with the essence of Christianity than even to deny that God and Christ are one.[25]

So far as Dwight had always been considered an indirect participant in the Unitarian controversy, moreover, it comes as no surprise that, even after his death, he would be held up as a symbol of the unwavering Augustinian moral position assumed in Calvinism. This moment would come, appropriately, in the midst of an exchange of treatises on the subject of human nature between

25. William Ellery Channing, "The Moral Argument against Calvinism" (1820), *The Works of William E. Channing, D.D.*, 6 vols. (Boston, 1843), I, 218, 240; Channing, "Letter to the Rev. Samuel C. Thacher" (1815), in Sydney Ahlstrom and Jonathan S. Carey, eds., *An American Reformation* (Middletown, Conn., 1985), 82.

Henry Ware and Leonard Woods, theology professors, respectively, at the Unitarian Harvard Divinity School and the Calvinist Andover Seminary. Woods, attempting to sidestep the Pelagian moral argument identifying one's view of human nature with a greater or lesser degree of goodwill, appeals to an argument he hoped would be accepted by both sides, that human moral weakness seems to be an obvious empirical fact: "Regulating ourselves by the maxims of BACON and NEWTON, we inquire, not . . . whether this or that thing can be reconciled with the infinite wisdom and goodness of God,—but simply, *what is fact? What do we find from observation and experience?*" To provide the necessary evidence, Woods refers to the recently deceased Doctor Dwight's practical experience as an educator, quoting from a passage in *Theology* in which Dwight states that, after thirty years of teaching children, "I cannot say with truth, that I have seen *one*, whose native character I had any reason to believe to be virtuous; or whom I could conscientiously pronounce to be free from . . . evil attributes." Yet, as Woods would discover, this appeal could be discounted by Ware simply as a case of Dwight's own inability to recognize virtue in his fellow human beings: "Such is the black picture of the youthful character given us by one of our most distinguished orthodox divines, and which meets with the unqualified approbation of Dr. Woods." Indeed, he suggests, this picture might well be explained by Dwight's own moral influence on his students. Noting that Dwight also acknowledges in *Theology* that younger children appear more naturally virtuous than older children and adults, he asks, "If, from being amiable and well disposed at first, children become otherwise or less so under the hand of instruction and discipline, it would certainly seem natural for parents to inquire . . . how far it may be attributed to fault or defect in the mode in which the moral education is conducted." Thus, the belief that human moral weakness constitutes an empirical, objective fact would be circumscribed within this new moral logic as arising merely from a subjectivity predisposed to finding moral evil in the human heart.[26]

By the time Ware would deliver his verdict on Dwight's view of human

26. Leonard Woods, *Letters to Unitarians Occasioned by the Sermon of the Reverend William E. Channing* . . . (Andover, Mass., 1820), 27; Woods, *A Reply to Dr. Ware's Letters to Trinitarians and Calvinists* . . . (Andover, Mass., 1821), 42; Henry Ware, *Answer to Dr. Woods' Reply, in a Second Series of Letters, Addressed to Trinitarians and Calvinists* (Cambridge, Mass., 1822), 23, 25.

nature, the extent to which the Pelagian moral vision had come to exert a permanent influence on Congregationalist theology would be measured not so much by the number of Unitarians affirming Ware's conclusion as by the number of Calvinists—including Dwight's own favorite students, Lyman Beecher and Nathaniel W. Taylor—who would find it increasingly difficult to defend the doctrine of Original Sin as it had traditionally been defined. Taylor's conviction would be that he agreed more with the Unitarian than the Calvinist in the Woods-Ware controversy. This stance would lead the "Dwight Professor of Didactic Theology" to develop what would come to be known as the New Haven theology, a far more Arminianized and Pelagianized explanation of Calvinist doctrine than his teacher would ever have been willing to accept. To be sure, the New Haven theology would, at least in its early years, retain the Calvinist language of human depravity, but only as a way of describing specific actions or moral choices rather than the essential moral tendencies of human beings. Yet, if Taylor's revisions would be representative of how nineteenth-century Congregationalists would gradually redefine Calvinism for an age more in line with Channing's contention that "society is going forward in intelligence and charity, and of course is leaving the theology of the sixteenth century behind it," the corresponding legacy of Dwight's earlier warfare against Chauncy and Universalism would be an environment in which no successive doctrinal revision, however benign at first glance, would ever go unremarked.[27]

27. Channing, "Moral Argument against Calvinism," *Works*, I, 240. For Taylor's redefinition of depravity as a characteristic of actions rather than human nature, see Nathaniel W. Taylor, *Concio Ad Clerum: A Sermon Delivered in the Chapel of Yale College, September 10, 1828* (1828), in Sydney E. Ahlstrom, ed., *Theology in America: The Major Protestant Voices from Puritanism to Neo-orthodoxy* (Indianapolis, Ind., 1967), 214–222. Several religious historians have considered Dwight's differences with the New Divinity as leading directly to Taylor's "Arminianized" explanation of Calvinism; see Joseph Haroutunian, *Piety versus Moralism: The Passing of the New England Theology* (New York, 1932), chap. 9; Sidney Earl Mead, *Nathaniel William Taylor, 1786-1858; a Connecticut Liberal* (Hamden, Conn., 1967), 113–119; Annabelle S. Wenzke, *Timothy Dwight (1752-1817)* (Lewiston, N.Y., 1989), chap. 1; Conrad Cherry, *Nature and Religious Imagination: From Edwards to Bushnell* (Philadelphia, 1980), chap. 6. At the same time, Beecher writes in the *Autobiography* that, at the end of his life, Dwight saw the direction Taylor

Within this contested theological field, even Dwight's own successors such as Taylor and Beecher would come under attack by a more conservative wing of Calvinists. Taylor, for instance, would be forced to defend the New Haven theology against the charge of rejecting tenets essential to Calvinism by Bennet Tyler (another of Dwight's theology students). Beecher, then president of Cincinnati's Lane Theological Seminary, would in 1835 be tried for heresy on similar grounds. Yet the logic of *The Triumph of Infidelity*, in which a single doctrinal revision signals nothing less than a fundamentally altered conception of reality, would not be lost on the Unitarians. The subsequent pressures by those forces intending to purify their theology of the remaining vestiges of "mere historical Christianity"—the most memorable example being Ralph Waldo Emerson's Divinity School address (1838)—would ultimately lead many former radicals to become nostalgic for a theology grounded in something more than the inexorable progress of human wisdom. Thus it is that Andrews Norton, who had made his name during the Unitarian controversy in a discourse assailing the Calvinists' attempts to define the crucial line separating orthodox from heterodox, would revive the argument of *The Triumph of Infidelity* in response to the emerging transcendentalism of Emerson, George Ripley, and others. As Norton would charge in the 1839 address, *A Discourse on the Latest Form of Infidelity*, "At the present day there is little of that avowed and zealous infidelity, the infidelity of . . . acknowledged enemies of our faith, which characterized the latter half of the last century"; yet infidelity has now assumed a different form, one that is "distinguished by assuming the

---

was taking his theology and disapproved, creating a tension between the two (Cross, ed., *Autobiography of Beecher*, I, 241). Similarly, given Dwight's emphasis in *Theology* that the foundation of all preaching should be the corruption of the human heart, it appears he would have stopped far short of Taylor's redefinition of depravity. Moreover, Taylor's opponent in the controversy over the New Haven theology, Bennet Tyler, frequently invoked Dwight as firmly within the orthodox tradition of Congregationalism. At the opening of the rival, conservative Hartford Theological Seminary, Tyler declared that the seminary "stands for the doctrines which have been held in New England for generations by Edwards and Bellamy and Dwight" (Curtis Manning Geer, *The Hartford Theological Seminary, 1834-1934* [Hartford, Conn., 1934], 64). See also Bennet Tyler, *Letters on the Origin and Progress of the New Haven Theology; from a New England Minister to One at the South* (New York, 1837), 101, 108, 137, 168.

Christian name, while it strikes directly at the root of faith in Christianity, . . . by denying the miracles attesting the divine mission of Christ."[28] To be sure, Norton's standard for defining the essence of Christian faith is different from Dwight's; in the absence of the Trinitarian doctrine that Christ is a part of God, Norton appeals to the necessary truth of Christ's miracles as the distinction that separates Christ from humankind and Christianity from a mere ethical system. Yet the attempt to locate a crucial line between religious and secular systems places Norton at a later point in a story that had included Nathaniel W. Taylor's and Leonard Woods's opposition to the younger Norton and Dwight's opposition to Chauncy and Universalism.

In general terms, such passages reveal the degree to which the collective memory of open avowals of deism and atheism from the period of Dwight's own campaign against infidelity would continue to serve as the point of reference for a variety of new radical movements during the 1820s and 1830s, from transcendentalism and Fourierism to the communitarianism of New Harmony and elsewhere. Among Dwight's more immediate theological successors, moreover, the same cultural memory would provide the basis for an increased suspicion during this period that their earlier celebrations of a triumph over infidelity and the dawning of an age of missionary and Bible societies had been premature, that the revolutionary infidelity of Condorcet and Paine and Elihu Palmer had never completely disappeared, and that it was in fact being revived in a new Jacksonian celebration of populism and the common man. It is against this background that Lyman Beecher would revive the voice of the anti-Jacobin Dwight—the Dwight of *The Nature, and Danger, of Infidel Philosophy* and "The Retrospect"—as a means of combating a new synthesis of radical politics and religious skepticism in the movement centered on Robert Dale Owen, Frances Wright, and the emerging Workingman's parties.

Beecher's *Lectures on Political Atheism,* for example, was first delivered in direct response to Frances Wright's 1829 appearances in Boston and dedicated to "the working men of our nation." As his dedication suggests, the purpose of the lectures is to win back the working classes to Christianity by identifying true republicanism with piety and dissociating it from the skepticism

28. Andrews Norton, *A Discourse on the Latest Form of Infidelity; Delivered at the Request of the Association of the Alumni of the Cambridge Theological School, on the 19th of July, 1839* (Cambridge, Mass., 1839), 8–9, 11.

and anticlericalism with which it had been associated since the 1790s: "Infidels are republicans in theory and in tongue, but not in deed and truth," he warns, echoing almost verbatim the Dwight of 1801. By the same token, behind Beecher's insistence throughout the lectures on the need to ground one's political vision in a higher, supernatural order is the same nightmare vision glimpsed by Dwight in "The Retrospect" of a mass conversion to a materialist metaphysics in which fundamental moral laws and even the value of life itself are rendered meaningless. Thus, his most emphatic point will be that to embrace the new "political atheism" is never simply a matter of altering one's opinions; one must replace the conception of man as a "free, accountable, immortal mind, acting under the responsibilities of eternity," with one that "reduces man to the insect of day, and renders murder an event of no more magnitude than the killing of fly." "'What is it to kill a man?'—said one of these atheistic philosophers, while the work of death was going on, and blood was flowing from the guillotine as from an inexhaustible fountain,—'Only to change the direction of a few ounces of blood.'"[29]

For Beecher, who would continue to revise the *Lectures* and deliver them regularly throughout his career, the struggle on which the future of the Republic depended would remain one of preserving Christian piety and morality against a new generation of freethinkers and radicals. For a growing number of fellow evangelical Protestants, on the other hand, the real struggle involving Christianity would center on the issue of how fervently those who had initiated the age of revivals and reforms would now take up abolitionism as the next great social reform. In this context, indeed, the tendency of clergymen like Beecher to focus on temperance or the protection of the Sabbath would

---

29. Lyman Beecher, *Lectures on Political Atheism* (1852), *Works of the Reverend Lyman Beecher*, 3 vols. (Boston, 1852–1853), I, 95, 99–100, 136. As in Chandos Michael Brown's analysis of Dwight's satire of Mary Wollstonecraft (see note 12, above), Lori D. Ginzberg argues that Beecher's opposition to the religious skepticism represented by Owen and Wright cannot be separated from Wright's protofeminist challenge to the constraints of women's lives. Thus, Beecher's fear of a social and political philosophy oriented, not toward some higher or eternal order, but to self-interest alone would also include a corresponding fear of women's rejecting traditional gender roles (Ginzberg, "'The Hearts of Your Readers Will Shudder': Fanny Wright, Infidelity, and American Free Thought," *American Quarterly*, XLVI [1994], 195–226).

appear as a dwindling of the Second Great Awakening into the mere preservation of middle-class morality and outward signs of piety. In direct contrast, a new generation of reformers would appropriate Beecher's emphasis upon directing oneself according to a higher calling and demand that Christians confront what was increasingly being called the "national sin" of slavery.

Among this new generation of Christian abolitionists would be Yale classmates Elizur Wright and Amos Phelps, whose religious conversions and commitment to reformist ideals had led them to the abolitionist movement. They would take seriously the notion of slavery as America's national sin and would view such partial solutions as gradual abolition or African colonization as a direct violation of God's call for immediate repentance. "Under the government of God, as exhibited in this world, there is but one remedy for sin, that is available only by repentance evidenced by reformation," warns Wright in *The Sin of Slavery, and Its Remedy*. "There is no such thing as holding onto sin with safety." Wright's call for immediate repentance and reform, at whatever the cost to slaveholders and others, recalls Dwight's earlier rejection of the compatibility of self-interest and social progress. At the same time, there would arise in this context a need to account for why, in the face of such an obvious sin, so many clergymen in the North as well as the South remained indifferent. Thus, Phelps, pastor of Boston's Pine Street congregation (who was himself ostracized for his involvement in the antislavery movement) would find his answer in what Dwight had called the problem of smooth divines:

> I know that ministers, like other men, are sometimes turned aside from duty by fear, or self-interest, or some other motive; that, too often, they are covetous of a good living . . . or cowardly . . . ; and that this is specially apt to be true, when duty calls them to encounter a vitiated public sentiment, which tolerates and gives respectability to some prevalent sin. Still these same ministers are the *hinges* of public sentiment. Let them get right, and then, let them muster the courage to meet that vitiated sentiment, and, with all its blustering, it will soon yield.[30]

30. Elizur Wright, *The Sin of Slavery, and Its Remedy; Containing Some Reflections on the Moral Influence of American Colonization* (New York, 1833), 39; Amos A. Phelps, *Lectures on Slavery, and Its Remedy* (Boston, 1834), 15.

The idea that the clergy is paralyzed by fear or self-interest will account for the portrait of Lyman Beecher, derived from the antislavery protests at Lane Seminary, as one who had betrayed his own cause by rejecting as too extreme the call for the immediate abolition of slavery. For instance, in William Lloyd Garrison's treatment of Beecher in the pages of the *Liberator*, Beecher's campaign against political atheism is presented not merely as irrelevant in the face of a greater social problem but as stemming from a more insidious blindness to the moral depravity and practical infidelity that pervades the system of slavery. "The Dr. undertakes to 'glance at some of the perils which threaten us,' but the existence of slavery is not in the catalogue," Garrison writes.

> "The prevalence of Atheism" first attracts his notice. But is not the slave-system practically based upon Atheism? Does it not, in effect, dethrone God, dehumanize man, blot out free agency, and overturn the moral government of the universe? . . . But the Dr. continues: "The form of this skepticism is a philosophy which *treats the mind of man as though it were mere matter.*" . . . A perfect portraiture of the slave system of the South, which treats millions of human bodies, intellects, minds and souls, as "mere matter," goods and chattels, marketable commodities!"[31]

For Garrison, slavery is thus doubly representative of infidel philosophy as Dwight had characterized it in the 1790s: it elevates certain human beings to the position of arbitrating the fate of one's fellow men while reducing others to the level of mere matter.

The paradox surrounding Garrison's angry denunciation of Beecher in this passage is that, even as he takes as his primary target Beecher's campaign against infidelity—and thus his direct ideological inheritance from Timothy Dwight—Garrison is also echoing the Dwight of *The Triumph of Infidelity*. Beyond Garrison's assertion that slavery constitutes a form of practical infidelity, his choice of Beecher as his particular object of attack is grounded in Dwight's earlier contention that the clergy function as satiric monitors of their society, that they fail when they refrain from preaching difficult truths, and that they best serve the cause of religion and public virtue when they hold a mirror up to an otherwise unacknowledged evil. This same insistence both explains Garri-

31. William Lloyd Garrison, "Lyman Beecher," *Liberator* (Boston), July 23, 1836.

son's sense in this passage of being betrayed by such a prominent religious leader and will continue to inform Garrison's writings even as he gradually moves away from the religious orthodoxy of his earlier career. Thus will Garrison continue to sound not merely like a revivalist preacher but one engaged in the same satiric warfare earlier waged by Dwight against the superstitions and false gods that persist in deluding the American populace: "We are an idolatrous people, and worship many gods. . . . 1st. The MOLOCH OF SLAVERY, in whose presence we tremble exceedingly, and to whom we cause our children to pass through the fire. 2nd. PARTY, the Baal of Selfishness, upon whom we rely for all our honors, preferments, and successes. 3rd. *The GODDESS OF LIBERTY*, an imaginary deity, to whom we pay superstitious honors, and whom we devoutly worship in the abstract. . . . These be thy Gods, O Columbia!"[32]

To see Garrison's target in this speech as the same abstract or delusional devotion to liberty that Dwight had been among the first to expose in his time is thus to recognize the legacy of Dwight's satiric campaign in the nineteenth century. It extends beyond the question of religion as such to what has since been described as the ideology of Jacksonian America, the celebration of equality and the common man even in the face of slavery. Insofar as Dwight had understood the act of ideological unmasking as a particular function of poetry or satire, moreover, we are in turn able to trace the hitherto unremarked influence of such poems as *The Triumph of Infidelity* and "The Retrospect" on the body of abolitionist literature that included, perhaps most prominently, the antislavery poetry of John Greenleaf Whittier. In Whittier's poems, especially, notwithstanding their stylistic differences from the Augustan tradition within which Dwight had been writing, we encounter a revival of the Augustan preoccupation with accounting for mass deception or dulness, in this sense the unwillingness or inability of most Americans to acknowledge the seriousness of slavery as a national evil. In the comic or satiric register of a poem like "The Haschish," then, is Whittier's own attempt to explain in imaginary terms the same problem of popular ideological delusion with which Dwight had engaged decades earlier in "The Retrospect." Yet, whereas Dwight had accounted for this phenomenon using the eighteenth-century image of superstition, Whittier calls upon an image more represen-

32. William Lloyd Garrison, "Fourth of July in Providence," ibid., July 28, 1837.

tative of the Romantic period, that of the drug-induced "vision." Although the hemp plant is said to produce mysterious hallucinations in the mind—"Of Dervish or of Almeh dances! / Of Eblis, or of Paradise, / Set all aglow with Houri glances!"—it is powerless, he writes, in comparison to the cotton plant, the "Haschish of the West," for distorting the reality of its users:

> The preacher eats, and straight appears
> > His Bible in a new translation;
> Its angels negro overseers,
> > And Heaven itself a snug plantation!
>
> .   .   .   .
>
> The noisiest Democrat, with ease,
> > It turns to Slavery's parish beadle;
> The shrewdest statesman eats and sees
> > Due southward point the polar needle.[33]

The view that slavery has the power to lull Americans into a collective state of moral slumber will, in turn, suggest in the more solemn, negative register that is usually associated with Whittier's verse that American society has long since dwindled into the shrunken moral world of pride and greed and self-interest that Dwight had warned against in *The Triumph of Infidelity*. In religious terms, this is the world depicted in the poem "Official Piety," in which Whittier confirms Dwight's deeper fear that religious institutions will become a front for Satanic manipulation: "Satan is modest. At Heaven's door he lays / His evil offspring, and, in Scriptural phrase / And saintly posture, gives to God the praise / And honor of the monstrous progeny." The same moral world is identified more generally as modern America in the opening lines of "For Righteousness Sake," a poem that immediately brings to mind the common influence of Cowper on both Dwight and Whittier. Here the system of slavery is understood, not as a persistent example of sin that tarnishes an otherwise still-redeemable society, but as a single manifestation of a society given over wholly to selfishness and superficial materialism, masked by empty gestures toward religious duty: "The age is dull and mean. Men creep, / Not walk; with

---

33. John Greenleaf Whittier, "The Haschish" (1854), *The Complete Poetical Works of Whittier: Cambridge Edition* (Boston, 1975), 315, 316.

---

blood too pale and tame / To pay the debt they owe to shame; / Buy cheap, sell dear; eat, drink, and sleep / Down-pillowed, deaf to moaning want; / Pay tithes for soul-insurance; keep / Six days to Mammon, one to Cant."[34]

Beyond their connection to the cause of abolition, moreover, such poems bring to light the general observation made by Lawrence Buell that the larger satiric themes of *The Triumph of Infidelity*, far from simply fading away in the early nineteenth century in the face of an emerging Romanticism, would survive during the American Renaissance in the body of satire directed at "the sugary surface of American optimism." Thus, even a writer like Henry David Thoreau, whose transcendentalist leanings might otherwise seem to place him at the opposite end of the moral and theological spectrum from Dwight, will become the voice of protest in his own time against the same ideology of inevitable human progress that had survived its earlier radical association with Godwin and Condorcet to become, by the middle of the nineteenth century, one of the commonly accepted truths of the day. "We are told today that civilization is making rapid progress; the tendency is ever upward; substantial justice is done even by human courts; you may trust the good intentions of mankind," he would write in his journal in 1852. "How many have heard speak with warning voice? Utter wise warnings? The preacher's standard of morality is no higher than his audience. He studies to conciliate his audience and never to offend them."[35]

34. John Greenleaf Whittier, "Official Piety" (1853), "For Righteousness Sake" (1855), ibid., 315, 317–318.

35. Lawrence Buell, *New England Literary Culture from Revolution through Renaissance* (Cambridge, 1986), 96; Bradford Torrey and Francis H. Allen, eds., *The Journal of Henry David Thoreau*, 14 vols. (Salt Lake City, Utah, 1984), III, 321–322. Thoreau's role as a critic of the progressivism of the period goes back to the beginning of his career. In a review of one of the countless volumes published at the time predicting just such a utopian future, John Adolphus Etzler's *Paradise within the Reach of All Men, without Labour, by the Powers of Nature and Machinery . . .* , 2d. ed., 2 vols (London, 1842)—which, as the title suggests, emphasized the socially transformative power of technology—Thoreau follows the distinction Dwight had made in *Theology* between those, like Etzler, who imagine a future paradise in which society's ills will be alleviated by material or technological improvements, and those, like himself, who insist that "a moral reform must take place first, and then the necessity of the other will be superseded" (Thoreau, "Para-

In Thoreau's words may also be heard the critique, going back through Whittier, Garrison, and Dwight himself to the satires of Pope and Edward Young, of the dwindling of religious leaders into a class of flatterers and sycophants. Thus, paradoxically, as mainstream American theology continued to move in the direction of Taylor, Channing, and Horace Bushnell, social activists and literary figures with no particular religious stake would regard the purpose of their own work as filling the void left by an older generation of clergymen-satirists. This implicit function is especially evident in Nathaniel Hawthorne's "The Celestial Railroad," his satiric retelling of John Bunyan's *The Pilgrim's Progress,* in which Christian's lonely pilgrimage from the City of Destruction to the Celestial City has been transformed into a comfortable and fashionable railroad excursion, with all of the obstacles that attended his original journey removed. Although readers of Hawthorne's fiction have tended to emphasize the story's satiric jab at his transcendentalist contemporaries, that accounts for only a small part of the story's critique of a society given over wholly to the Pelagian assumptions of human innocence and divine benevolence, and for which religious life has lost all sense of the difficulty and struggle that characterized it in Bunyan's time. To this extent, then, "The Celestial Railroad" appears as a revival of the satiric argument of *The Triumph of Infidelity* at a later period in American religious and philosophical history. Yet an even closer connection to Dwight's poem emerges in the suggestion that this large-scale conversion to the Pelagian myth may well represent Satan's ultimate triumph.

This point is sustained throughout the story, from the moment that Hawthorne's narrator discovers that, beyond the construction of the railroad itself, the greatest difference between Christian's pilgrimage and his own is that it no longer involves a struggle against demons such as Beelzebub or Apollyon. Such demons have since reached an "understanding" with the Director of the Railroad and are now employed as baggage handlers and engineers, which the narrator praises as indicative of "the liberality of the age," proving "that all musty prejudices are in a fair way to be obliterated." Nor do the pilgrims who accompany the narrator—"parties of the first gentry and most respectable people of the neighborhood," he points out, echoing another of Dwight's

dise (to be) Regained" [1843], in Thoreau, *Reform Papers,* ed. Wendell Glick [Princeton, N.J., 1973], 46–47).

themes—encounter the kind of internal struggle experienced by Bunyan's archetypal Christian. Indeed, for the purpose of avoiding such struggle, they are attended on their journey by such characters as Mr. Smooth-It-Away, a figure who, like the Smooth Divine or even Chauncy himself in *The Triumph of Infidelity*, reassures them against any apprehensions they may have, including the momentary torments of conscience the narrator experiences as he travels through the Valley of the Shadow of Death. Ultimately, of course, Mr. Smooth-It-Away reveals himself as a Satanic figure and, importantly, in the specific sense emphasized in *The Triumph of Infidelity*, as a deceiver whose most powerful means of deception is to deny the very existence of hell (or, as Hawthorne's narrator calls it, Tophet). Thus, as they travel past the mouth of the infernal region, Mr. Smooth-It-Away "took occasion to prove that Tophet has not even a metaphorical existence," which the narrator recalls at the end of the story when he realizes that this is precisely where the Celestial Railroad had all along been heading: "The impudent Fiend! To deny the existence of Tophet, when he felt its fiery tortures raging within his breast!"[36]

Within the symbolic system governing Hawthorne's fiction, to deny the existence of hell or Satan is none other than to deny that earlier Puritan insistence upon the evil within the human heart. In this sense, "The Celestial Railroad" provides a useful vantage point to look back not only on *The Triumph of Infidelity* but the larger campaign against infidelity. By the end of Dwight's life, the war he had waged against irreligion appeared to have been won in the narrow sense of its successfully defending Christianity against the skepticism of Voltaire and Paine, Godwin and Condorcet. At the same time, the new possibility glimpsed by Hawthorne, Garrison, Whittier, and others at midcentury is that this very triumph might all along have masked a deeper process by which religion had become synonymous with mere respectability and moral life with ease and complacency. In Hawthorne's updated version of Bunyan's Vanity Fair, the most immediate difference is that "every street has its church, and . . . the reverend clergy are nowhere held in higher respect."[37] Thus, "The Celestial Railroad" is less a revival of the argument of *The Triumph of Infidelity* than a confirmation of the possibility first imagined by Dwight at the end

36. Nathaniel Hawthorne, "The Celestial Railroad" (1843), in Hawthorne, *Selected Tales and Sketches*, ed. Michael J. Colacurcio (New York, 1987), 320, 324, 335.

37. Ibid., 327.

---

of the poem in his own satire of "decent" or respectable Christianity: "The decent Christian threw his mask aside, / And smil'd, to see the path of heaven so wide, / To church, the half of each fair Sunday, went, / The rest, in visits, sleep, or dining, spent; / To vice and error nobly liberal grew; / Spoke kindly of all doctrines, but the true" (761–766).

In our own time, the temptation may be to trace the legacy of Dwight's war against infidelity in religious terms alone, emphasizing a continuing struggle between evangelical Protestantism and the forces of secularization, with successive generations of Dwights and Beechers continuing to denounce the presence of infidelity and atheism in newer and more diverse guises. Yet, although this is indeed an important story, to look back upon *The Triumph of Infidelity* from the perspective of Hawthorne, Thoreau, and Whittier is to recognize another equally important story that has yet to be told in significant detail. Therein what Dwight had identified as the essence of infidelity, an emerging ideology of comfort and human self-worship, would appear to a later generation as becoming so widespread and powerful as to have co-opted much of Christianity for its own purposes. This is a story, in turn, in which the satiric voice of *The Triumph of Infidelity* would survive its own earlier moment of religious controversy to become the basis of a later tradition in American literature, to treat with satiric condemnation any of the subsequent forms of the American tendency to want to believe only the best about ourselves.

APPENDIX A
The Triumph of Infidelity

To Mons. de VOLTAIRE.

SIR,

YOUR Creator endued you with shining talents, and cast your lot in a field of action, where they might be most happily employed: In the progress of a long and industrious life, you devoted them to a single purpose, the elevation of your character above his. For the accomplishment of this purpose, with a diligence and uniformity which would have adorned the most virtuous pursuits, you opposed truth, religion, and their authors, with sophistry, contempt, and obloquy; and taught, as far as your example or sentiments extended their influence, that the chief end of man was, to slander his God, and abuse him forever. To whom could such an effort as the following be dedicated, with more propriety, than to you. The subject it celebrates is the most pointed attack upon your old enemies; an attack more happily devised, at least, than any of yours; as yours were more advantageously concerted than the efforts of any of your predecessors. Reasoning is an unhappy engine to be employed against Christianity; as, like elephants in ancient war, it usually, in this case, turns upon those who employ it. Ridicule is a more convenient weapon, as you have successfully evinced; but ingenious misinterpretation is a still more sure and effectual annoyance; for the sword and javelin, however keen, may be dreaded and shunned, while the secret and deadly dirk is plunged to the heart of unsuspecting friendship, unhappily trusting the smooth-faced assassin. Accept then, as due, this tribute of acknowledgement from the

WRITER OF THIS POEM.

Audies, & venient manes haec fama sub imos.

The Triumph of Infidelity

ERE yet the Briton left our happy shore,
Or war's alarming clarion ceas'd to roar,
What time the morn illum'd her purple flame,
Thro' air's dread wilds the prince of darkness came.
A cloud his gloomy car; his path around,
Attendant whirlwinds gave a fearful sound,
Before him dragons wound their bloody spires;
Far shot behind him death's Tartarean fires:
To image Heaven's high state, he proudly rode,
Nor seem'd he less than hell's terrific God.   (10)
While, full before him, dress'd in beauteous day,
The realms of freedom, peace, and virtue lay;
The realms, where Heaven, ere Time's great empire fall,
Shall bid new Edens dress this dreary ball;
He frown'd; the world grew dark; the mountains shook,
And nature shudder'd as the spirit spoke.
"What wasted years," with angry voice he cries,
"I wage vain wars with yonder hated skies?
Still, as I walk th'unmeasur'd round of things,
From deepest ill what good perpetual springs;   (20)
What order shines, where blest confusion lay,
And from the night of death, what splendid day?
How near me seem'd, ere Bethlehem's wonder rose,[1]
The final victory o'er my struggling foes;
All nations won to ignorance, and sin,
Without the Gentile, and the Jew within?
How near, when cross'd, he met th'accursed doom,
Or lay, extinguish'd in the mortal tomb?
Yet then, even whilst I felt my pinions rise
Above the arches of a thousand skies,   (30)
Even then, deep plung'd beneath the lowest hell,
As erst when hurl'd from heaven, my kingdom fell,

1. State of infidelity at the birth of ———.

And oh, by what foul means![2] An angel I,
A god, the rival of yon haughty sky!
They the last sweepings of the clay-born kind,
The dunghill's offspring, and the reptile's mind.
Yet their creating voice, with startling sound,
From death and darkness wak'd the world's wide round;
Before it crumbled, mid my groans and tears,
The Pagan fabric of a thousand years; (40)
The spells, the rites, the pomp, the victims fled,
The fanes all desert, and the lares dead.
In vain fierce persecution hedg'd their way;
In vain dread pow'r's huge weight incumbent lay;
As sand-built domes dissolve before the stream,
As visions fleet upon th' awakening beam,
The structure fled; while hell was rack'd to save,
And all my heaven-bright glories sought the grave.
Amaz'd, awhile, I saw the ruin spread,
My hopes, my efforts, with my kingdom, dead. (50)
But soon I bade the floods of vengeance roll,[3]
Soon rous'd anew my mightiness of soul,
With arts my own, th' opposer's power withstood,
And reign'd once more the universal God;
Mine, by all-poisoning wealth, his sons I made,
And Satan preach'd, while proud Messiah fled.
Surpriz'd, enrag'd, to see his wiles outdone,
His power all vanquish'd, and his kingdom gone,
From the stern North, he hail'd my darling host,[4]
A whelming ocean, spread to every coast; (60)
My Goths, my Huns, the cultur'd world o'er-ran,
And darkness buried all the pride of man.
On dozing realms he pour'd his vengeance dread,
On putrid bishops, and on priests half dead,

2. Injuries done to infidelity, by Peter, Paul, and others.
3. Progress of infidelity after the death of Constantine the Great.
4. Infidels injured unwittingly by their friends, the northern barbarians.

Blotted, at one great stroke, the work he drew,
And saw his gospel bid mankind adieu.
The happy hour I seiz'd;[5] the world my own:
Full in his church I fix'd my glorious throne;
Thrice crown'd, I sat a God, and more than God;
Bade all earth's nations shiver at my nod; (70)
Dispens'd to men the code of Satan's laws,
And made my priests the columns of my cause.
In their bless'd hands the gospel I conceal'd,
And new-found doctrines, in its stead, reveal'd;
Of gloomy visions drew a fearful round,
Names of dire look, and words of killing sound,
Where, meaning lost, terrific doctrines lay,
Maz'd the dim soul, and frighten'd truth away;
Where noise for truth, for virtue pomp was given,
Myself the God promulg'd, and hell the heaven. (80)
To this bless'd scheme I forc'd the struggling mind;
Faith sunk beneath me; sense her light resign'd;
Before, rebellious conscience clank'd the chain;
The rack, the wheel, unbosom'd all their pain;
The dungeon yawn'd; uprose the faggot pyre,
And, fierce with vengeance, twin'd the livid fire.
These woes I form'd on earth; beyond the tomb,
Of dreams, I built the purgatorial doom;
Hurl'd round all realms the interdictive peal;
Shut kings from heaven, and nations scourg'd to hell; (90)
All crimes forgave; those crimes indulg'd again;
Disclos'd the right divine to every sin;
To certain ecstasies the faithful led;
Damn'd Doubt, when living; double damn'd, when dead;
O'er bold Inquiry bade all horrors roll,
And to its native nothing shrunk the soul.
Thus, round the Gothic wild, my kingdom lay,
A night, soon clouded o'er a winter's day.

5. New progress of infidelity, under the papal hierarchy.

But oh, by what fell fate,[6] to be entomb'd
Are bright ambition's brightest glories doom'd?   (100)
While now my rival every hope forsook,
His arts, his counsels, and his sceptre broke,
This vast machine, so wondrous, so refin'd,
First, fairest offspring even of Satan's mind,
This building, o'er all buildings proudly great,
Than Heaven more noble, and more fix'd than fate,
This glorious empire fell; the world grew pale,
And the skies trembled, at the dreadful tale.
In vain my arm, in vain my sword, I bar'd;
In vain my angels o'er example dar'd;   (110)
My priests, high-fed on all the spoils of man,
Outran belief and even my hopes outran;
Hell hop'd, and toil'd in vain: Thro' all her coast,
A general sigh declar'd her kingdom lost.
    Blush, Satan, blush, thou sovereign of mankind,
When, what thy reptile foes, thou call'st to mind.
New fishermen, mechanic worms, anew
The unfolded gospel from my kingdom drew.
From earth's wide realms, beneath the deluge bare,
As suns reviving bade the spring appear,   (120)
So, at their startling voice, from shore to shore,
A moral spring my winter cover'd o'er,
The mind new sprang; rebudding virtue grew;
And trembling nations rose from death anew.
From them roll'd on, to bless this earth's cold clime,
A brighter season, and more vernal prime,
Where, long by wintry suns denied to rise,
Fair Right and Freedom open'd on the skies,
Virtue, and Truth, and Joy, in nobler bloom,
Call'd earth and heaven to taste the sweet perfume,   (130)
Pleas'd, to the scene increasing millions ran,
And threaten'd Satan with the loss of man.

6. Injuries done to infidelity by Luther, Calvin, and others.

These ills to ward, I train'd my arts anew;[7]
O'er truth's fair form the webs of sophism drew;
Virtue new chill'd, in growing beauties gay,
Wither'd her bloom, and puff'd her sweets away.
Against her friends I arm'd new bands of foes;
First, highest, all-subduing Fashion rose.
From courts to cottages, her sovereign sway,
With force resistless, bade the world obey. (140)
She molded faith, and science, with a nod;
Now there was not, and now there was, a God.
'Let black be white,' she said, and white it seem'd,
'Hume a philosopher,' and straight he dream'd
Most philosophically. At her call,
Opinions, doctrines, learn'd to rise, and fall;
Before her, bent the universal knee,[8]
And own'd her sovereign, to the praise of me.
With her, brave Ridicule,[9] 'twixt ill and good,
Falsehood and truth, satanic umpire stood. (150)
He, Hogarth like, with hues and features new,
The form of providence, persuasive drew:
Round its fair face bade hell's black colors rise,
Its limbs distorted, blear'd its heaven-bright eyes.
At the maim'd image gaz'd, and grinn'd aloud—

7. Progress of infidelity, under the auspicious influence of Charles II. and his contemporaries.

8. Phil. ii. 10, 11.

9. The doctrine that ridicule is a test of truth cannot, even on the scheme of infidels, justify their application of it. Wherever any object, or if you please, proposition, when seen clearly and certainly in all its nature, parts, and relations, is evidently absurd, and ridiculous, it may be an objection against its reality, or truth. But a man, in his natural and proper appearance, may be a beautiful object; and a proposition, in its real nature, and necessary consequences, may contain a truth important and noble, altho' when a sign-post painter shall have drawn one with a pair of horns and a tail, and an infidel annexed his own dreams as appendages to the other, all the fraternity of blockheads will laugh at both. Anon.

'Yon frightful hag's no semblance of a god.'
  Mean time my friends,[10] the veterans of my cause,
Rack'd every nerve, and gain'd all hell's applause,
Thro' realms of cheat and doubt, and darkness, ran,
New-made creation, uncreated man,   (160)
Taught, and retaught, asserted and denied,
As pamper'd pleasure, or as bolster'd pride.
Now, groping man in death's dim darkness trod,

10. See the host of infidel writers, during the last age.

Such advantages does Infidelity enjoy over Revelation, that both sides of moral questions will equally support that, and weaken this. Thus one infidel will overthrow Revelation by proving that there is not one honest man living; another will as successfully attack it by asserting, and the assertions of Infidels are always to be taken for proofs, that there are honest men of all religions and opinions. One sees intuitively that God never did, nor can, reveal his pleasure to mankind. Another finds the Koran and Shahstan in the list of Revelations. Plato's devotion of himself to a courtesan, and Socrates' to Alcibiades, were the effusions of honest, virtuous hearts; but Paul's dedication of his life to the REDEEMER was a reverie of enthusiasm. God also, though dishonored by adoration, presented to him in the character of a holy, sin-hating God, and incapable of being pleased, when invoked in the name of Jesus Christ, is yet glorified, when honest votaries address him in the elevated character of an ox, an onion, or a snake, and is highly delighted with invocations, when offered in the pleasing and prevailing name of the devil.

  Happy, happy, happy cause!
  None but the wise,
  None but the wise,
  Have such sharp eyes,
  Or tell such lies.   Morgan*.

The Devil's Feast, or the power of Falsehood. An ode, by the very same Laureate, who wrote another, on the death of David Hume, Esq. in which, out of compassion to our Lord Jesus Christ, he forbears to tell how effectually said Hume has overthrown him.
  *(Morgan) An unhappy man, who went to bed one night, and dreamed he was a great man, and a moral philosopher, which so turned his brain with surprise, that he never knew himself in the glass afterwards; but thought he was a moral philosopher, to the day of his death.   SCRIBLERUS.

Now, all things kenn'd, with eyelids of a god.
Now, miracles, not God himself could spell;
Now, every monk could grunt them from his cell.
Priests now were dullest, last, of mortal things;
Now outflew Satan's self, on cunning's wings.
No system here, of truth, to man is given;
There my own doctrines speak the voice of heaven;   (170)
While God, with smiling eyes, alike surveys
The pagan mysteries, and the Christian praise.
While here on earth no virtuous man was found,
There saints, like pismires, swarm'd the molehill round;
Like maggots, crawl'd Caffraria's entrail'd forts;
Or mushroom'd o'er Europa's putrid courts;
To deist clubs familiar dar'd retire,
Or howl'd, and powaw'd, round the Indian fire,
Such feats my sons achiev'd, such honors won;
The shores, the blocking, of th' infernal throne!   (180)
And tho' yon haughty world their worth deny,
Their names shall glitter in the nether sky.
    But ah, their wisdom, wit, and toils were vain,
A balm first soothing, then increasing pain.
Thro' nature's fields while cloud-borne Bacon ran,[11]
Doubtful his mind, an angel, or a man;
While high-soul'd Newton, wing'd by Heaven abroad,
Explain'd alike the works, and word, of God;
While patient Locke illum'd with newborn ray,
The path of reason, and the laws of sway;   (190)
While Berkeley, bursting like the morning sun,
Look'd round, all parching, from his lofty throne,
In all events, and in all beings shew'd
The present, living, acting, speaking God,
Or cast resistless beams the gospel o'er,
Union supreme of wisdom, love, and power!

11. Names of a few silly men, whose minds were too small to comprehend the nature
and evidences of Infidelity.   COLLINS.

Pain'd, shrivell'd, gasping, from the forceful ray
How crept my mite philosophers away?
In vain my Methodist, brave Herbert, cried,
And whin'd, and wrote, pretended, pray'd, and lied,[12]   (200)
In vain my Shaftesbury, to his master true,
Dread humble bee![13] o'er burrs and thistles flew;
Encupp'd, and ravish'd with the fussful noise,
To praise the wondrous flowers, he rais'd his voice.
Of nature, beauty, dream'd and humm'd amain,
And sung himself, and buzz'd at truth, in vain.
Ah Bolingbroke, how well thy tatter'd robe,
Poor, Bedlam king of learning's little globe!
Amus'd thy fancy? He, with glory fir'd,
Myself in miniature! to heaven aspir'd.   (210)
For fame, his heaven, thro' falsehood's realms he ran,
And wish'd, and watch'd, and toil'd, and hop'd, in vain,
Misread, miswrote, misquoted, misapplied,
Yet fail'd of fame, and miss'd the skies, beside.
In views, in pride, in fate, conjoin'd with me,
Even Satan's self shall drop a tear for thee.
   My leaders these; yet Satan boasts his subs,
His Tolands, Tindals, Collinses, and Chubbs,
Morgans and Woolstons, names of lighter worth,
That stand, on falsehood's list, for &c.   (220)
That sworn to me, to vice and folly given,
At truth and virtue growl'd, and bark'd at heaven.
Not men, 'tis true, yet manlings oft they won,
Against their God help'd blockheads oft to fun,
Help'd fops to folly, and help'd rakes to sin,

12. See Lord Herbert's Cock-Lane-Ghost Tale of thunder's answer to prayer.

SCRIBLERUS.

13. The characteristics of which insect are, busily to bustle about with a great shew of stateliness and mock majesty, with a noisy, solemn hum, that sounds much, and means nothing, to be forever poring over flowers, but never to gather, or yield, any honey.   Linnaeus—properties of humble bees.

And marr'd all sway, by mocking sway divine.[14]
My list of authors too they help'd to count,
As ciphers eke the decimal amount.
As writers too, they proffer'd useful aid,
Believ'd unseen, and reverenc'd tho' unread.   (230)
Against their foe no proof my sons desire,
No reasoning canvas and no sense require.
Enough, the Bible is by wits arraign'd,
Genteel men doubt it, smart men say it's feign'd,
Onward my powder'd beaux and boobies throng,
As puppies float the kennel's stream along.
But their defects to varnish, and, in spite
Of pride and dignity, resolv'd to write,
I seiz'd the work myself. Straight, in a cloud
Of night involv'd, to Scotia's realms I rode.   (240)
There, in the cobwebs of a college room,
I found my best Amanuensis, Hume,
And bosom'd in his breast. On dreams afloat,
The youth soar'd high, and, as I prompted, wrote.
Sublimest nonsense there I taught mankind,
Pure, genuine dross, from gold seven times refin'd.
From realm to realm the strains exalted rung,
And thus the sage, and thus his teacher, sung.
All things roll on, by fix'd, eternal laws;
Yet no effect depends upon a cause: (250)
Hence every law was made by Chance divine,
Parent most fit of order, and design!
Earth was not made, but happen'd: Yet, on earth,
All beings happen, by most stated birth;
Each thing miraculous; yet strange to tell,

14. The same principles, which support or destroy Christianity, alike support or destroy political order and government. So manifest is this, that Lord Bolingbroke, when contending against those whom he esteems enemies of the British government, treats them unwittingly, I presume, as enemies also to Christianity, and loads them, for their combined folly and perverseness, with many epithets of supreme contempt.

Not God himself can shew a miracle.
   Mean time, lest these great things, the vulgar mind,
With learning vast, and deep research, should blind,
Lest dull to read, and duller still when known,
My favorite scheme should mould, and sleep, alone;   (260)
To France I posted,[15] on the wings of air,
And fir'd the labors of the gay Voltaire.
He, light and gay, o'er learning's surface flew,
And prov'd all things, at option, false or true.
The gospel's truths he saw were airy dreams,
The shades of nonsense, and the whims of whims.
Before his face no Jew could tell what past;
Or know the right from left, the first from last;
Conjecture where his native Salem stood,
Or find, if Jordan had a bank, or flood.   (270)
The Greeks, and Romans, never truth descried;
But always (when they proved the gospel) lied.
He, he alone, the blest retreat had smelt,
The Well,[16] where 'long with frogs, the goddess dwelt;
In China dug, at Chihohamti's[17] call,
And curb'd with bricks, the refuse of his wall.
There, mid a realm of cheat, a world of lies,
Where alter'd nature wears one great disguise,
Where shrunk, misshapen bodies mock the eye,
And shrivell'd souls the power of thought deny,   (280)
Mid idiot Mandarins, and baby kings,
And dwarf philosophers, in leading-strings,

---

   15. Satan seems guilty of an anachronism here, Voltaire being the eldest writer of
the two.   SCRIBLERUS.
   16. It appears, by the testimony of all the ancient historians, that truth originally
lived in a well; but Voltaire was the first geographer, who discovered where it was
dug—LORD KAMES' sketches of the weakness of man; article Voltaire.
   17. The Emperor, who burnt all the ancient records of his country, and built the
great wall to defend it from the Tartars. Quere—In which instance did he do his countrymen most good; if the books he burnt were like these written by them afterwards?

Mid senseless votaries of less senseless Fo,[18]
Wretches who nothing even seem'd to know,
Bonzes, with souls more naked than their skin,
All brute without, and more than brute within,
From Europe's rougher sons the goddess shrunk,
Tripp'd in her iron shoes, and sail'd her junk.
Nice, pretty, wondrous stories there she told,
Of empires, forty thousand ages old, (290)
Of Tohi, born with rainbows round his nose,
Lao's long day—Ginseng,[19] alchymic dose—
Stories, at which all Behmen's dreams awake,
Start into truth, and sense and virtue speak;
To which, all, lisping children e'er began
With, 'At a time,' and 'Once there was a man,'
Is reason, truth, and fact; and sanction'd clear
With heaven's own voice, or proof of eye and ear.
He too reveal'd,[20] that candor bade mankind
Believe my haughty rival weak, and blind; (300)
That all things wrong a ruling God denied;
Or a satanic imp that God implied;
An imp, perchance of power and skill possessed
But not with justice, truth, or goodness blessed.
Doctrines divine! would men their force receive,
And live to Satan's glory, as believe.
  Nor these alone: from every class of man,

18. Fo, principal idol of the Chinese.

19. A plant, to which the Chinese ascribe all virtues of food and medicine, and proved by European scrutiny to be just as remote from them, as the date of the Chinese empire from 40,000 years. In the same manner, all Chinese extraordinaries, except a few mechanical ones, when examined, descend to plain dock and plantain. Yet, when swallowed by Voltaire, they will help to expel gripes of conscience, as a decoction of Ginseng will those of the flatulent cholic, full as well as warm water.

GARTH's alphabetical prophesies, article Ginseng.

20. See Voltaire's Candide, the great purpose of which is to prove, that whatever is, is *not* right.

I gain'd new aids to build the darling plan,
But chief his favorite class, his priests, I won,
To undermine his cause, and prop my own.   (310)
Here Jesuitic art its frauds combin'd
To draw ten thousand cobwebs o'er the mind,
In poison'd toils the flutterer to enclose,
And fix, with venom'd fangs, eternal woes.
On sceptic dross they stamp'd Heaven's image bright,
And nam'd their will-a-wisp, immortal light,
Thro' moors, and fens, the sightless wanderer led,
'Till down he plung'd, engulph'd among the dead.
To life, Socinus[21] here his millions drew,
In ways, the art of Heaven conceal'd from view,   (320)
Undeified the world's almighty trust,
And lower'd eternity's great fire[22] to dust.
He taught, O first of men! the Son of God,
Who hung the globe, and stretch'd the heavens abroad,
Spoke into life the sun's supernal fire,
And mov'd to harmony the flaming choir,
Who in his hand immensity enfolds,
And angels, worlds, and suns, and heavens, upholds,
Is—what? a worm, on far creation's limb,
A minim, in intelligence extreme.   (330)
O wondrous gospel, where such doctrines rise!
Discoveries wondrous of most wondrous eyes!
From him, a darling race descended fair,
Even to this day my first and chiefest care,

21. Great men, if closely examined, will generally be found strongly to resemble each other. Thus Milton, Homer and Ossian were blind. Thus this great man exceedingly resembled Milton. There were, however, one or two trifling circumstances of difference. Milton, for instance, was stone-blind in his bodily eyes, but had clear and intuitive moral optics. In Socinus, the case was exactly reversed. Milton also rose in his moral conceptions, with no unhappy imitation of the scriptural sublimity: Socinus, on the contrary, anticlimaxed the scriptural system down to nothing.   SCRIBLERUS.
22. Isai. ix. 6.

When pertest Priestley[23] calls mankind, to see
His own corruptions of Christianity.
     Mean time, less open friends my cause sustain'd,
More smoothly tempted and more slily gain'd;
Taught easier ways to climb the bright abode;
Less pure made virtue, and less perfect God;   (340)
Less guilty vice, the atonement less divine,
And pav'd, with peace and joy, the way to sin.
While thus by art and perseverance won,
Again, the old world seem'd almost my own.
     In this wild waste, where Albion's lights revive,
New dangers threaten, and new evils live.[24]
Here a dread race, my sturdiest foes design'd,
Patient of toil, of firm and vigorous mind,
Pinion'd with bold research to truth's far coast,
By storms undaunted, nor in oceans lost,   (350)
With dire invasion, error's realms assail,
And all my hardy friends before them fail.
     But my chief bane, my apostolic foe,
In life, in labors, source of every woe,
From scenes obscure, did Heaven his E****** call,
That moral Newton, and that second Paul.
He, in clear view, saw sacred systems roll,
Of reasoning worlds, around their central soul;
Saw love attractive every system bind,
The parent linking to each filial mind;   (360)
The end of Heaven's high works resistless shew'd,
Creating glory, and created good;
And, in one little life, the gospel more
Disclos'd, than all earth's myriads kenn'd before.

23. A celebrated philosopher of the present day, who has carried chemical composition to higher perfection than any other man living; for he has advanced so far, as to
form a whole system of divinity cut of fixed air.   SCRIBLERUS.
     24. Opposition to infidelity by disciples of Peter, Paul, &c. in this country.

Beneath his standard, lo! what number rise,
To dare for truth, and combat for the skies!
Arm'd at all points, they try the battling field,
With reason's sword and faith's etherial shield.
To ward this fate all irreligion can,
Whate'er sustains, or flatters sinning man; (370)
Whate'er can conscience of her thorns disarm,
Or calm, at death's approach, the dread alarm;
Whate'er, like truth, with error cheats mankind;
Whate'er, like virtue, taints with vice the mind;
I preached, I wrote, I argued, pray'd, and lied,
What could my friends, or even myself, beside?
But tho' with glad successes often crown'd,
Unceasing fears my troubled path surround.
While with each toil my friends the cause sustain,
Their toils, their efforts, and their arts are vain. (380)
    Even plodding L****** did but little good,
Who taught, the soul of man was made of mud:[25]
Cold mud was virtue; warmer mud was sin;
And thoughts the angle-worms, that crawl'd within:
Nor taught alone; but wise, to precept join'd
A fair example, in his creeping mind.
In vain thro' realms of nonsense A**** ran,[26]
The great Clodhopping Oracle of man.[27]
Yet faithful were his toils: What could he more?
In Satan's cause he bustled, bruised, and swore; (390)

---

25. See a late American treatise entitled *A Philosophical Essay on Matter*, in which this great doctrine is fully proved.

26. Otherwise called *Oracles of Reason*.

27. New name elegantly given to man in Oracles of Reason.   Anon.
The annotator above mistakes, in calling this epithet a new name. I could easily shew, by a series of learned deductions, that Clodhopper was the very original name of mankind, when they wore tails, as Lord Monboddo has most ingeniously proved they did, at their first creation.   SCRIBLERUS.

And what the due reward,[28] from me shall know,
For gentlemen of equal worth below.
    To vengeance then, my soul, to vengeance rise,
Assert thy glory and assault the skies.
What tho' dull seers have sung, in dreams sublime,
Thy ruin floats along the verge of time,
Tho' without hands the stone from mountains riven,[29]
Alarms my throne, and hastes the ire of Heaven;
Tho bliss' dread heralds earth's far limits round,[30]
Pardon, and peace, and joy, ere long shall sound;   (400)
How beauteous are their feet! all regions cry
And one great, natal song salute the sky:
Still, should I sink, a glorious fate I'll find,
And sink amid the ruins of mankind.
    But what new onset shall I now begin,
To plunge the New World in the gulph of sin?
With sweet declension, down perdition's steep,
How, in one host, her cheated millions sweep?
I hail the glorious project, first, and best,
That ever Satan's bright invention blest;   (410)
That on this world my kingdom first began,[31]
And lost my rival paradise, and man.
Twice fifteen suns are past, since C*******'s mind,
Thro' doctrines deep, from common sense refin'd,
I led, a nice, mysterious work to frame,
With love of system, and with lust of fame.
Fair in his hand the pleasing wonder grew,
Wrought with deep art, and stor'd with treasures new:
There the sweet sophism led the soul astray;

28. In A——n's journal, the writer observes, he presumes he shall be treated, in the future world, as well as other gentlemen of equal merit are treated: A sentiment, in which all his countrymen will join him.   SCRIBLERUS.

29. Dan. ii. 44–45.

30. Isai. lii. 7.

31. Genesis iii, 4. *And the serpent said unto the woman—Ye shall not surely die.' &c.*

There round to heaven soft bent the crooked way: (420)
Saints, he confess'd, the shortest route pursue;
But, scarce behind, my children follow too.
Even Satan's self ere long shall thither hie;
On cap, huzza!³² and thro' the door go I!
Now palsied age has dimm'd his mental sight,
I'll rouse the sage his master's laws to fight,
The injuries, long he render'd, to repair,
And wipe from Heaven's fair book his faith and prayer.
To wound the eternal cause with deepest harms,
A cheated gospel proves the surest arms: (430)
Those arms, no hand can, like a preacher's wield;
False friends may stab, when foes must fly the field.
     This M***** proves, in whom my utmost skill
Peer'd out no means of mischief, but the will.
He, in hard days, when ribbons gave no bread,
And Spitalfield's brave sons from Tyburn fled,
Scampering from bailiffs, wisely dropp'd the shuttle,
To preach down truth, and common sense to throttle.
With cunning, oft in scrapes and bustles tried,
Tongue at-your-service, in all stories plied,   (440)
The dirtiest ridicule of things most holy,
And dirtier flattery of sin and folly,
A mimickry, at which buffoons would blush,
Religion cent-per-cented, at a rush,
Boldness, that dares to make the Bible lie,
And brass, that would a foundery supply,
Mid gather'd rogues, and blockheads, oft he stood,
And rous'd to fun the genuine brotherhood;
Scripture, and argument, oblig'd to yield,
Made learning, sense, and virtue, quit the field,   (450)
While fainting decency sunk down to see
The desk of God a puppet-show for me."

32. Magical incantation used formerly by the witches at Salem, when they went
thro' key holes.

This said, invested with the robes of day,
To C*******'s dome he winged his gladsome way,
And spread delightful to his wilder'd sense,
The pride of system, and the increase of pence.
Forth from his cobwebs straight the work he drew,
In mould still precious, and in dust still new.
This darling pet to usher to mankind,
High blown to ecstasy, the sage design'd;   (460)
And conn'd, with grand-parental love, the day,
When thro' the world the heir should make its way.
    The laughing spirit seized the lucky hour,
And round Columbia bade the trumpet[33] roar,
And thus thro' all her regions rang the song—
"To Pandemonia's[34] plains, ye mortals, throng!
Here shall you, raptur'd, find there is no hell;
A priest shall teach it, and the gospel tell;
The pleasing truth, so long from earth conceal'd,
To bless desponding guilt, is now reveal'd."   (470)
Thus rang the thrilling voice the new world round;
Each villain started at the pleasing sound,
Hugg'd his old crimes, new mischiefs 'gan devise,
And turn'd his nose up to the threat'ning skies.
    The perjur'd wretch, who met no honest eye,
But felt his own retreat, his spirit die,
Clear'd up his wither'd front, and true he cried,
"I've sometimes been forsworn, and sometimes lied;
But all's a farce; as proves this doctrine new,

33. Otherwise called Salvation unto all men. A treatise, published as a harbinger to the great one, having this motto on the title page——

    I leave you here a little book,
    For you to look upon,
    That you may learn to curse and swear,
    When I am dead and gone.

SCRIBLERUS.

34. Otherwise called the field of mischief.   SCRIBLERUS.

For God must help the perjur'd, as the true." (480)
    Up Florio sprang; and with indignant woes,
As thus he cried, his startled bosom rose——
"I am the first of men in ways of evil,
The truest, thriftiest servant of the devil,
Born, educated, glory to engross,
And shine confess'd, the Devil's Man of Ross.
Here's three to one, I beat him e'en in pride;
Two whores already in my chariot ride:
Shall then this wretch?—forbid it Florio, heaven!
Shall sin's bright laurels to this priest be given? (490)
No, still on Satan's roll shall shine my praise,
As erst on C——'s lists of yeas and nays."
    Half pleas'd, the honest tar out bolted—"whew"!
"Good doctrine, Jack," "Aye, too good to be true."
P**** scowling heard, and growl'd—"The day's our own!
I'll now tell two lies, where I told but one."
W****** more hard than flint, in sin grown old,
Clinch'd close his claws, and gripp'd his bags of gold.
"In vain," he cried, "their woes let orphans tell;
In vain let widows weep; there is no hell. (500)
Six, six per cent, each month must now be given,
For pious usury now's the road to heaven."
All who, tho' fair without, yet black within,
Glued to their lips the choice liqueur of sin,
Whose conscience, oft rebuff'd, with snaky power,
Empoison'd still the gay and gleeful hour,
Check'd the loose wish, the past enjoyment stung,
And oft the alarm of retribution rung,
Thrill'd at each nerve, to find their fears were vain,
And swung triumphant caps at future pain. (510)
    And now the morn arose; when o'er the plain
Gather'd, from every side, a numerous train;
To quell those fears, that rankled still within,
And gain new strength, and confidence, to sin.
There the half putrid Epicure was seen,

His cheeks of port, and lips of turtle green,
Who hop'd a long eternity was given,
To spread good tables, in some eating heaven.
The letcher there his lurid visage shew'd,
The imp of darkness, and the foe of good; (520)
Who fled his lovely wife's most pure embrace,
To sate on hags, and breed a mongrel race;
A high-fed horse, for others' wives who neigh'd;
A cur, who prowl'd around each quiet bed;
A snake, far spreading his empoison'd breath,
And charming innocence to guilt, and death.
Here stood Hypocrisy, in sober brown,
His sabbath face all sorrow'd with a frown.
A dismal tale he told of dismal times,
And this sad world, brimful of saddest crimes, (530)
Furrow'd his cheeks with tears for others' sin,
But clos'd his eyelids on the hell within.
There smil'd the Smooth Divine, unus'd to wound
The sinner's heart, with hell's alarming sound.
No terrors on his gentle tongue attend;
No grating truths the nicest ear offend.
That strange new-birth, that methodistic grace,
Nor in his heart, nor sermons, found a place.
Plato's fine tales he clumsily retold,
Trite, fireside, moral seesaws, dull as old; (540)
His Christ, and Bible, plac'd at good remove,
Guilt hell-deserving, and forgiving love.
"'Twas best," he said, "mankind should cease to sin";
Good fame requir'd it; so did peace within:
Their honors, well he knew, would ne'er be driven;
But hop'd they still would please to go to heaven.
Each week, he paid his visitation dues;
Coax'd, jested, laugh'd; rehears'd the private news;
Smok'd with each goody, thought her cheese excell'd;
Her pipe he lighted, and her baby held. (550)
Or plac'd in some great town, with lacquer'd shoes,

Trim wig, and trimmer gown, and glistening hose,
He bow'd, talk'd politics, learn'd manners mild;
Most meekly questioned, and most smoothly smil'd;
At rich men's jests laugh'd loud; their stories prais'd;
Their wives' new patterns gaz'd, and gaz'd, and gaz'd;
Most daintily on pamper'd turkeys din'd;
Nor shrunk with fasting, nor with study pin'd:
Yet from their churches saw his brethren driven,
Who thunder'd truth, and spoke the voice of heaven,   (560)
Chill'd trembling guilt, in Satan's headlong path,
Charm'd the feet back, and rous'd the ear of death.
"Let fools," he cried, "starve on, while prudent I
Snug in my nest shall live, and snug shall die."
      There stood the infidel of modern breed,
Blest vegetation of infernal seed,
Alike no Deist, and no Christian, he;
But from all principle, all virtue, free.
To him all things the same, as good or evil;
Jehova, Jove, the Lama, or the Devil;   (570)
Mohammed's braying, or Isaiah's lays;
The Indian powaws, or the Christian's praise.
With him all *natural* desires are good;
His thirst for stews, the Mohawk's thirst for blood:[35]
Made, not to know, or love, the all-beauteous mind;
Or wing thro' heaven his path to bliss refin'd:
But his dear self, choice Dagon! to adore;
To dress, to game, to swear, to drink, to whore;
To race his steeds; or cheat, when others run;
Pit tortur'd cocks, and swear 'tis glorious fun: (580)
His soul not cloath'd with attributes divine;
But a nice watch-spring to that grand machine,
That work more nice than Rittenhouse can plan,
The body; man's chiefest part; himself, the man;

35. Both justified, as all other crimes are, on the great scale that they are natural.
                                        SCRIBLERUS.

Man, that illustrious brute of noblest shape,
A swine unbristled, and an untail'd ape:
To couple, eat, and die—his glorious doom—
The oyster's church-yard, and the capon's tomb.
    There ****** grinn'd, his conscience sear'd anew,
And scarcely wish'd the doctrine false or true;   (590)
Scarce smil'd, himself secure from God to know,
So poor the triumph o'er so weak a foe.
In the deep midnight of his guilty mind,
Where not one solitary virtue shin'd,
Hardly, at times, his struggling conscience wrought
A few, strange intervals of lucid thought,
Holding her clear and dreadful mirror nigher,
Where villain glow'd, in characters of fire.
Those few the tale dispers'd: His soul no more
Shall, once a year, the Beelzebub run o'er;   (600)
No more shall J——n's ghost her infant show,
Saw his hard nerves, and point the hell below;
Fix'd in cold death, no more his eyeballs stare,
Nor change to upright thorns his bristly hair.
    There Demas smil'd, who once the Christian name
Gravely assum'd, and wore with sober fame.
Meek, modest, decent, in life's lowly vale,
Pleas'd he walk'd on; nor now had grac'd this tale;
But, borne beyond the Atlantic ferry, he
Saw wondrous things, his schoolmates did not see.   (610)
Great houses, and great men, in coaches carried;
Great ladies, great lords' wives, tho' never married;
Fine horses, and fine pictures, and fine plays,
And all the finest things of modern days.
Chameleon like, he lost his former hue,
And, mid such great men, grew a great man too;
Enter'd the round of silly, vain parade;
His hair he powder'd, and his bow he made.
"Shall powder'd heads," he cried, "be sent to hell?
Shall men in vain in such fine houses dwell?"   (620)

There Euclio—Ah my Muse, let deepest shame
Blush on thy cheek, at that unhappy name!
Oh write it not, my hand! the name appears
Already written: Wash it out, my tears!
Still, Oh all pitying Savior! let thy love,
Stronger than death, all heights, and heavens above,
That on the accursed tree, in woes severe,
The thief's dire guilt extinguish'd with a tear,
Yearn o'er that mind, that, with temptations dire,
Rank appetites, and passions fraught with fire,   (630)
By each new call without, each thought within,
Is forc'd to folly, and is whirl'd to sin;
In conscience spite, tho' arm'd with hissing fears,
Strong pangs of soul, and all his country's tears,
Is charm'd to madness by the old serpent's breath,
And hurried swiftly down the steep of death.
Burst, burst, thou charm! wake, trembler, wake again,
Nor let thy parent's dying prayers be vain!
    The hour arriv'd, th'infernal trumpet blew;
Black from its mouth a cloud sulphureous flew;   (640)
The caverns groan'd; the startled throng gave way,
And forth the chariot rush'd to gloomy day.
On every side, expressive emblems rose,
The man, the scene, the purpose to disclose.
Here wrinkled Dotage, like a fondled boy,
Titter'd, and smirk'd its momentary joy:
His crumbs there Avarice gripp'd, with lengthen'd nails,
And weigh'd clipp'd halfpence in unequal scales.
Trim Vanity her praises laugh'd aloud,
And snuff'd for incense from the gaping crowd.   (650)
While Age an eye of anguish cast around,
His crown of glory prostrate on the ground.
There C****** sat, aloud his voice declar'd,
"Hell is no more, or no more to be fear'd.
What tho' the Heavens, in words of flaming fire,
Disclose the vengeance of eternal ire,

Bid anguish o'er the unrepenting soul,
In waves succeeding waves, forever roll;
The strongest terms, each language knows, employ
To teach us endless woe, and endless joy: (660)
'Tis all a specious irony, design'd
A harmless trifling with the human kind:
Or, not to charge the sacred books with lies,
A wile most needful of the ingenious skies,
On this bad earth their kingdom to maintain,
And curb the rebel, man: but all in vain.
First Origen, then Tillotson, then I
Learn'd their profoundest cunning to descry,
And shew'd this truth, tho' nicely cover'd o'er,
That hell's broad path leads round to heaven's door.   (670)
See *kai*'s and *epi*'s build the glorious scheme![36]
And *gar*'s and *pro*'s unfold their proof supreme!
But such nice proof, as none but those can know,
Who oft have read the sacred volume thro',
And read in Greek: but chiefly those, who all
The epistles oft have search'd of cunning Paul.
He, he alone, the mystery seem'd to know,
And none but wizard eyes can peep him thro'.
Then here, at second hand, receive from me
What in the sacred books you'll never see.   (680)
For tho' the page reveal'd[37] our cause sustains,
When search'd with cunning, and when gloss'd with pains,

36. How much alike are great men, still say I? The Doctor has found a whole system of divinity, in three or four Greek adverbs, and prepositions; as Lord Coke had before discovered, that there is much curious and cunning kind of learning, in an &c.

SCRIBLERUS.

37. Witness Matthew vii. 13–14. *Straight is the gate, and narrow the way, that leadeth to destruction, and NO BODY THERE IS, who goes in thereat:*

Because wide is the gate, and broad is the way, that leadeth unto life, and ALL THEY BE, who find it. Murray's new version of the Bible, very proper to be kept by thieves, whore-mongers, idolaters, and all liars; with others, who mean to go to heaven, via hell.

Yet our first aids from human passions rise,
Blest friends to error, and blest props to lies!
And chief, that ruling principle within,
The love of sweet security in sin:
Beneath whose power all pleasing falsehoods, blind
And steal, with soft conviction, on the mind.
No good more luscious than their truth she knows,
And hence their evidence will ne'er oppose. (690)
Aided by this, she mounts th' Eternal Throne,
And makes the universe around her own,
Decides the rights of Godhead with her nod,
And wields for Him dominion's mighty rod.
Whate'er He ought, or ought not, she descries,
Beholds all infinite relations rise,
Th' immense of time and space surveys serene,
And tells whate'er the Bible ought to mean;
Whate'er she wishes, sees Him bound to do,
Else is His hand unjust, His word untrue. (700)
    Then would you lay your own, or others' fears,
Search your own bosoms, or appeal to theirs.
Know, what those bosoms wish, Heaven must reveal;
And sure no bosom ever wish'd a hell.
But, lest sustain'd by underpinning frail,
Our hopes and wits, our proofs and doctrines fail,
Admit a hell; but from its terrors take
Whate'er commands the guilty heart to quake.
Again the purgatorial whim revive,
And bid the soul by stripes and penance live. (710)
And know, with search most deep, and wits most keen,
I've learn'd, that hell is but a school for sin;
Which yields, to heaven, the soul from guilt refin'd,
And, tho' it mars the devils, mends mankind.
And thus the matter stands. When God makes man,
He makes him *here* religious, if he can;
If he cannot, he bids him farther go,
And try to be religious, down below;

But as his failure is his fault, ordains
His soul to suffer dire repentance' pains,   (720)
Repentance, fearful doom of sinner vile!
The law's whole curse, and nature's highest ill!
If there the wretch repent, the work is done;
If not, he plunges to a lower zone,
A lower still, and still a lower, tries,
'Till with such sinking tir'd, he longs to rise;
And finding there the fashion to repent,
He joins the throng, and straight to heaven is sent.
Heaven now his own he claims; nor can the sky
Preserve its honor, and his claim deny.   (730)
Thus stands the fact; and if the proof should fail,
Let Heaven, next time, some better proof reveal.
I've done my part; I've given you here the pith;
The rest, the bark and sap, I leave to S****."
   Thus spoke the sage: a shout, from all the throng,
Roll'd up to heaven, and roar'd the plains along;
Conscience, a moment, ceas'd her stings to rear,
And joy excessive whelm'd each rising fear.
But soon reflection's glass again she rear'd,
Spread out fell sin; and all her horrors bar'd;   (740)
There anguish, guilt, remorse, her dreadful train,
Tremendous harbingers of endless pain,
Froze the sad breast, amaz'd the withering eye,
And forc'd the soul to doubt the luscious lie.
   Yet soon sophistic wishes, fond and vain,
The scheme review'd, and lov'd, and hop'd again;
Soon, one by one, the flames of hell withdrew;
Less painful conscience, sin less dang'rous grew;
Less priz'd the day, to man for trial given,
Less fear'd Jehovah, and less valued heaven.   (750)
   No longer now by conscience' calls unmann'd,
To sin, the wretch put forth a bolder hand;
More freely cheated, lied, defam'd, and swore;
Nor wish'd the night to riot, drink, or whore;

Look'd up, and hiss'd his God; his parent stung,
And sold his friend, and country, for a song.
The new-fledg'd infidel of modern brood
Climb'd the next fence, clapp'd both his wings, and crow'd;
Confess'd the doctrines were as just, as new,
And doubted if the Bible were not true.   (760)
The decent Christian threw his mask aside,
And smil'd, to see the path of heaven so wide,
To church, the half of each fair Sunday, went,
The rest, in visits, sleep, or dining, spent;
To vice and error nobly liberal grew;
Spoke kindly of all doctrines, but the true;
All men, but saints, he hop'd to heaven might rise,
And thought all roads, but virtue, reach'd the skies.
    There Truth and Virtue stood, and sigh'd to find
New gates of falsehood open'd on mankind;   (770)
New paths to ruin strew'd with flowers divine,
And other aids, and motives, gain'd to sin.
    From a dim cloud, the spirit eyed the scene,
Now proud with triumph, and now vex'd with spleen,
Mark'd all the throng, beheld them all his own,
And to his cause NO FRIEND OF VIRTUE won:
Surpriz'd, enrag'd, he wing'd his sooty flight;
And hid beneath the pall of endless night.

APPENDIX B *Textual Notes to*
The Triumph of Infidelity

NOTE ON THE TEXT

The Triumph of Infidelity appeared in 1788 in two separate editions, which were designated as A and B in Jacob Blanck, comp., *Bibliography of American Literature,* II (New Haven, Conn., 1957). Jack Stillinger has persuasively argued that the A text constitutes the original edition, and B a cheaper edition derived from a corrected copy of A ("Dwight's *Triumph of Infidelity:* Text and Interpretation," *Studies in Bibliography,* XV [1962], 259–266). The text printed below follows Stillinger's recommendation that a modern text should be drawn primarily from A but should incorporate those variants in B that can reasonably be attributed to Dwight's revision. Edition B was followed in cases of substantial revisions, such as changing entire words or capitalizing entire words, and in the use of apostrophes for elision when it follows a pattern elsewhere used in A. Obvious errors in spelling and punctuation have been corrected, following B or departing from both A and B in cases where both are in error. Inconsistencies in capitalization have also been conformed to the pattern otherwise used in A. Quotation marks have been added to all separate speeches, following the pattern used some of the time in both editions, and all footnote markers have been changed from symbols (such as asterisks) to numbers.

VARIANTS

Dedication: VOLTAIRE] A Voltaire   action,] B action   celebrates]
    B celebrates,   Christianity] A christianity
1 ERE] B 'ERE
9 Heaven's] A heaven's   B heav'ns
13 Heaven] AB heav'n
17 "What] AB What   years,"] AB years,
23 ere] B 'ere
25 sin,] B sin;
26 Gentile,] B Gentile;
27 th'] B the

28 lay,] B lay
31 plung'd] AB plunged
32 heaven] AB heav'n
35 sweepings] B sweeping
41 rites] B rights
44 pow'r's] A power's   B pow'rs
48 heaven] B heav'n
56 preach'd] A preached
57 enrag'd,] B enrag'd
64 bishops] B Bishops   priests] B Priests
71 Satan's] A Satan'
74 new-found] B new found
77 Where,] B Where
79 given] B giv'n
81 scheme] B scheme,
83 Before,] A Before
84 unbosom'd] A unbosomed   B unbosom d
90 heaven] B heav'n
99 entomb'd] B entomb'd,
100 ambition's] B Ambition's
101 forsook,] B forsook
108 trembled,] B trembled
110 dar'd;] A dared,
113 coast,] B coast.
115 mankind,] B mankind.
123 grew;] A grew,
128 Right] B Right,
129 Joy,] A joy,
132 man.] B man,
133 ward,] A ward
133n infidelity,] B infidelity
134 truth's] A truths
141 faith,] B faith   science,] B science
144 philosopher,] A philosopher
147 her,] B her
147n ii.] A ii,
149n infidels,] A infidels   or] B or,   nature,] B
    nature   altho'] B although,   sign-post] B sign post
152 providence,] B providence
157 Mean time] B (no new paragraph)

157n that] B that,   infidel] A Infidel   Infidels] B
   infidels   Socrates'] A Socrate's   Alcibiades,] B
   Alcibiades   REDEEMER] A [Redeemer B REDEEMER,   holy,]
   A holy   him] A him,   snake,] B snake;   Morgan*.] A
   Morgan.   B Morgan+.   ode,] B ode   man,] B man
159 cheat] B cheat,
160 New-made] B new made
167 last,] B last
168 outflew] B out flew
174 molehill] B mole hill
179 honors] B honours
180 shores] B shoars
182 sky.] B sky,
183 ah,] A ah   wit,] B wit
185 cloud-borne] B cloud borne
185n COLLINS.] A COLLINS
188 works,] B works
189 newborn] B new-born
190 sway;] B sway:
192 round,] A round   parching,] A parching
195 beams] A beams,
196 love,] B love
197 gasping,] B gasping
200 pray'd,] B pray'd
200n Lord Herbert's] A Lord Cherburg's   SCRIBLERUS.] AB
   SCRIBLERUS
206 truth,] B truth
209 He,] B He
212 hop'd,] B hop'd
220 stand,] B stand
223 'tis] B tis
226n them] B them,
229 too,] A too   proffer'd] A profer'd   aid,] A aid
230 tho'] A though
234 it's] B its
255 yet] B yet,
259 known,] B known.
264 things,] A things
273 alone,] B alone
274 frogs,] B frogs

274n appears,] B appears   geographer,] B geographer   LORD
    KAMES'] A LORD KAIMS'   B Lord Kaims's
275n Quere] B Quaere   books] A books,   burnt] A burnt,)
278 wears] B were
281 Mandarins,] B Mandarins   kings,] B kings
282 leading-strings] B leading strings
290 old,] B old
291 nose,] B nose,—
292n plant,] B plant   Yet,] B Yet
296 *At a time*,] A At a time   and] A or   *Once there was a man*,] A
    Once there was a man
297 sanction'd] A sanctioned   clear] B clear,
299n Voltaire's] A Voltair's
302 implied;] A implied
303 perchance] A per chance
308 plan,] A plan
311 combin'd] B combin'd,
312 mind,] A mind.
313 poison'd] AB poisoned
315 Heaven's] A heaven s
319 To] B (begins new paragraph)
319n were,] A was   B were   however,] A however   stone-blind]
    B stone blind   bodily] A bodly   SCRIBLERUS.] AB
    SCRIBLERUS
322n Isai.] B Isaiah
328 heavens,] B heavens
329 worm,] B worm
330 intelligence] B intelligence'
335n other] B (omitted)   SCRIBLERUS.] AB SCRIBLERUS
336 Christianity] A christianity
346 threaten,] A threaten
354 labors] A labours
355 obscure,] B obscure   Heaven] AB heaven   E******]
    A *******   B E——
358 soul;] B soul,
365 standard,] A standard;   lo!] A lo
366 dare] B care
367 field,] B field.
369 fate] B fate,
370 sustains,] B sustains

372 death's] B death s
373 Whate'er,] A Whate'er
377 tho'] B though
381 L******] A *******   B L——
382 taught,] B taught
382n treatise] B treatise,   *A Philosophical Essay on Matter,*] A A
    Philosophical Essay on Matter
384 angle-worms] B angle worms
387 In] B (new paragraph begins)   A****] A *****   B ——
387n *Oracles of Reason*] A Oracles of Reason
388 great] B great,   Oracle] A oracle
388n mistakes,] B mistakes
390 Satan's] A Satans
391n journal,] A Journal   treated,] A treated;   world,] A world
398 Heaven] AB heaven
399 round,] A round
405 new] A blest
407 declension,] B declension
409 first,] B first
411n *&c.*] B (omitted)
413 C*******] B C——
415 nice,] B nice
420 way:] B way;
427 repair,] A repair
428 Heaven's] AB heaven's
430 arms:] B arms;
437 bailiffs] B Bailiffs   dropp'd] B dropt
447 rogues,] B rogues   blockheads,] B blockheads
452 me."] AB me
462 world] B world,
464n unto] A to   one,] A one   curse] A lie
465 thus] B thus,
466 "To] AB To
470 reveal'd."] AB reveal'd
471 voice] B voice,   round;] B round,
474 threat'ning] A threatening
478 "I've] AB I've   forsworn] A forsworne
480 true."] AB true
487 e'en] A even
492 nays."] AB nays

494 Jack,] AB Jack
495 "The] AB The
496 one."] AB one.
499 "In] AB In   vain,"] AB vain,   "their] AB their
500 weep;] B weep,
501 cent,] B cent.
502 heaven."] AB heaven
503 tho'] B though
508 rung] B hung
516 of] A with
518 heaven] B heav'n
519 letcher] A leacher
523 others'] AB others
526 guilt,] B guilt   death.] A death,
530 world,] A world
532 within.] A within.]
534 sinner's] A sinners
536 truths] B truths,
540 fireside] B fire side   seesaws,] A seesaws   B see saws
541 Christ,] B Christ   Bible] AB bible
543 "'Twas] AB 'Twas   best,"] AB best,   "mankind] AB
    mankind   sin";] A sin;   B sin.
545 honors,] A honours,   B honors
549 Smok'd] AB smoak'd
555 men's] AB mens   loud;] A loud
556 gaz'd, (second instance)] B gaz'd
557 turkeys] A turkies
558 pin'd:] B pin'd;
559 driven] B driv'n
560 heaven] B heav'n
562 the] B tde
564 die."] A die
567 Deist] B deist   Christian] B christian
570 Devil;] B Devil
572 Christian's] B christian's
574 stews,] A stews;
574n scale] A principle
575 all-beauteous] A all beauteous
576 refin'd:] B refin'd.
579 cheat,] B cheat

580 tortur'd] B tortured
584 man;] B man:
589 ******] B ——
597 mirror] AB mirrour
603 Fix'd] A Fixd   eyeballs] B eye balls
605 Christian] B christian
609 Atlantic] B atlantic
610 see.] A see,
612 ladies] A Ladies   lords'] A Lord's   B lords
618 powder'd,] B powder'd
619 "Shall] AB Shall   heads,"] AB heads,   "be] AB be
620 dwell?"] AB dwell?
629 that,] B that
630 fire,] B fire.
639 th'] B 'th'
645 Dotage] AB dotage
647 Avarice] AB avarice   gripp'd] AB grip'd
648 halfpence] A half pence
649 Vanity] AB vanity
650 crowd] B croud
653 C*******] B C——
654 "Hell] AB Hell
670 heaven's] A heavens
671n SCRIBLERUS] B (omitted)
673 proof,] B proof
674 thro'] B through
675 Greek:] B Greek;   those,] B those
677 know,] B know.
679 me] B me,
680 see.] B see,
681 For] B For,   tho'] B though
681n *Straight*] AB *strait*   *way,* (first instance)] B way   *NO BODY*
   THERE IS] A *no body there is*   *ALL THEY BE*] A *all they be*
684 lies!] A lies:
686 sin:] B sin;
687 blind] A blind,
689 knows,] A knows.
691 Throne] B throne
694 Him] AB him
695 He] AB he

698 Bible] AB bible
699 Him] AB him
700 His (first instance)] AB his   His (second instance)] AB his
701 others'] AB others
703 wish,] A wish
713 yields,] B yields
725 lower,] (second instance) B lower
726 'Till] B 'Till,   rise;] B rise,
727 repent,] B repent.
728 straight] AB strait
729 claims;] B claims,
730 his] A its
732 Heaven,] B Heaven
734 S****."] A *****.   B S——.
737 Conscience,] B Conscience
748 dang'rous] A dangerous
755 hiss'd] B hist
756 country,] B country
758 Climb'd] B Clim'd
760 Bible] AB bible
761 Christian] AB christian
763 Sunday] A sunday
767 hop'd] B hop'd,
768 skies.] A skies,
769 There] B (no new paragraph)
775 own,] A own
776 NO FRIEND OF VIRTUE] A no friend of virtue
777 flight;] B flight,

Explanatory Notes to
The Triumph of Infidelity

Dedication. *VOLTAIRE:* François-Marie Arouet (1694–1778), French philosophe whose outspoken opposition to Christianity made him the great symbol of infidelity for Dwight's generation. By dedicating the poem to Voltaire, Dwight immediately draws a connection between Charles Chauncy's Universalist treatise and more obvious forms of infidelity. *chief end . . . him forever:* allusion to the Shorter Catechism in the *New England Primer,* "What is the chief end of man? Man's chief end is to glorify God and enjoy Him forever." *The subject . . . old enemies:* The subject of the poem, Dwight tells Voltaire, is Chauncy's most recent tactic in the war against true Christianity, his ingenious misinterpretation of Scripture in *Salvation for All Men* (1782) and *The Mystery Hid* (1784).

Epigraph. *Audies, & veniet . . . sub imos:* allusion to a line from Virgil's *Aeneid* (4.387) in which Dido, grief stricken because of Aeneas's decision to leave her, predicts his downfall and states, "Audiam, et veniet manes haec fama sub imos" (I will hear of this news in the lowest depths of the underworld). Dwight changes *audiam* (I will hear) to *audies* (you will hear), altering the sentence so that the joke is on Voltaire: You will hear this news (of Charles Chauncy's publication of *Salvation for All Men*) from the lowest depths of hell.

The Triumph of Infidelity: The word "triumph," here, is meant, not in the modern sense of "victory," but refers to the Roman *triumph,* a ritual parade given for an *imperator* after a great victory. Satan's procession through the American streets with Chauncy parallels this parade in a particularly ironic way. According to Roman practice, the *imperator* was accompanied in his chariot by a slave who says, "Remember that you are mortal." Similarly, Satan's victory parade ultimately reveals his own mortality.

3. *What time:* at the time at which.

5. *gloomy car:* Satan's chariot. *his path around:* one of numerous examples of inversion, read as around his path.

7. *bloody spires:* the spiral tails of the dragons from l. 6.

8. *Tartarean:* pertaining to Tartarus, the infernal region of the underworld in Greek and Roman mythology, often used to describe the Christian hell. Compare

John Milton's *Paradise Lost,* bk. 2, l. 69: "Mixt with Tartarean sulphur, and strange fire."

9. *image:* create the image of, duplicate.

12. *realms of freedom, peace, and virtue:* America.

13–14. *ere Time's . . . dreary ball:* Before the end of the world (that is, during the millennial period), new Edens will emerge in America.

17–22. *What wasted . . . splendid day:* Satan's complaint is the result of viewing the virtue and order of America in a region that was once defined by "confusion" and "ill"; he thus feels that his continuing struggle against God has been wasted. Dwight's Satan emerges here as an ongoing allusion to Milton's in *Paradise Lost,* willfully misinterpreting his role in an imagined war against God.

19. *th'unmeasur'd round of things:* the heavens.

23. *Bethlehem's wonder:* Christ. In ll. 23–26, Satan recalls that, before the birth of Christ, his own victory over heaven seemed certain.

23 n. ———: Christ.

27. *cross'd:* crucified.

30. *arches:* arcs, that is, the arc of the horizon. *a thousand skies:* meant to suggest Satan's imagined control over the entire world, that is, rising in the sky above Europe, Asia, America, etc.

31. *the lowest hell:* the lowest depths of hell, alluding to *sub imos manes* in the epigraph.

33. *And oh, by what foul means!:* Compare *Paradise Lost:* "Oh foul descent! that I who erst contended / With gods to sit the highest, am now constrained / Into a beast, and mixed with bestial slime" (bk. 9, ll. 163–165).

35–36. *They the . . . reptile's mind:* Satan describes the early Christians with particular disdain because of their generally low social status ("clay-born kind" referring to all of humanity). *dunghill's offspring:* insects, according to the ancient theory that insects spontaneously generate from dung.

39. *Before:* in front of.

40. *fabric:* structure, as in a building.

42. *fanes:* pagan temples. *lares:* pagan household gods. This description of the empty pagan temples, as well as the other events related in this section of *The Triumph of Infidelity,* follows Jonathan Edwards's *History of the Work of Redemption.* Edwards cites Pliny, for instance, who witnessed the flourishing of early Christianity and remarked that "the temples and sacrifices are generally desolate and forsaken" (Edwards, *A History of the Work of Redemption: Containing the Outlines of a Body of Divinity, in a Method Entirely New* [1774; reprint, Boston, 1782], 203).

43–44. *In vain fierce . . . incumbent lay:* Satan describes the ineffective practice of Roman persecution of Christians. (See Edwards, *History of the Work of Redemption,* 202–203: "Thus a great part of the first 300 years after Christ was spent in violent and cruel persecutions of the Church by Roman powers. . . . But still, in spite all that they could do, the kingdom of Christ wonderfully prevailed.")

45. *domes:* buildings.

47. *rack'd:* stretched, strained.

51 n. *Constantine the Great:* Constantine I (280–337), Roman emperor who established Christianity as the religion of the later empire.

53. *With arts . . . withstood:* With my own arts, I withstood the opposer's (Christ's) power.

55. *Mine, by . . . I made:* By means of all-poisoning wealth, I made his (Christ's) sons my own.

57–62. *Surpriz'd . . . of man:* Satan (as in *Paradise Lost*) projects his own limitations and demonic motives onto Christ, imagining him as surprised and enraged at Satan's corruption of the early church (which is impossible for an omniscient God), and even vengeful, using Satan's own army of Germanic tribes to sack Rome. Note that the goddess Dulness tells a similar story of the effect of the Germanic conquests on learning in Alexander Pope's *Dunciad:* "How little, mark! that portion of the ball, / Where, faint at best, the beams of Science fall: / Soon as they dawn, from Hyperborean skies / Embody'd dark, what clouds of Vandals rise! / . . . / . . . / The North by myriads pours her mighty sons, / Great nurse of Goths, of Alans, and of Huns! / See Alaric's stern port! the martial frame / Of Genseric! and Atilla's dread name! / See the bold Ostragoths on Latium fall; / See the fierce Visigoths on Spain and Gaul!" (bk. 3, ll. 83–94). Note that Dwight's Satan also alludes here to the famous final line of *The Dunciad:* "And Universal Darkness buries all" (bk. 4, l. 656).

63–64. *dozing . . . half dead:* experiencing a period of moral or spiritual slumber.

64. *putrid:* corrupted.

65–66. *Blotted, at . . . mankind adieu:* Satan believes that Christ, by destroying the corrupt church, unwittingly hurt his own cause, the true church.

68–69. *Full in . . . than God:* Satan describes himself as occupying the office of pope, consistent with the Protestant belief that the anti-Christ in the book of Revelation represents the papal succession.

69. *Thrice crown'd:* The papal mitre or tiara is composed of three crowns, one on top of another. *a God, and more than God:* As viceregent of Christ on earth, the pope was proclaimed "God on earth," and, insofar as he also held the power of a temporal prince, his power transcended that of even the highest religious office.

70. *Bade all . . . my nod:* the power of the pope to determine the future of nations by bestowing favor or censure upon monarchs.

73. *In their . . . conceal'd:* A major grievance against the Catholic Church concerned the use of the Latin Vulgate Bible, preventing most Christians from understanding Scripture.

74. *And new-found . . . reveal'd:* new doctrines introduced into Christianity by the Catholic Church, such as purgatory.

75. *Of gloomy . . . fearful round:* the medieval practice of painting images of sinners being cast into hell around the interior circumference of a cathedral.

76. *Names of . . . killing sound:* the pope's power of excommunication and anathema, amounting to words that effectively "kill" or damn individuals.

79–80. *Where noise . . . the heaven:* Where noise was given in place of truth, pomp in place of virtue, myself (Satan) in place of the promulgated (biblically declared) God, and hell in place of the promulgated heaven.

81. *I forc'd the struggling mind:* the power of the Inquisition to force people into professing Catholicism against their conscience.

82. *sense her light resign'd:* In the face of forced professions of faith, the faculties of the senses (which would recognize, for example, the impossibility of the doctrine of transubstantiation) are denied.

83–84. *the chain, the rack, the wheel:* methods of torture employed during the Inquisition.

85. *faggot pyre:* fire used to burn heretics.

86. *twin'd:* coiled.

89. *interdictive peal:* the power of the church to withhold sacraments or Christian burial from persons, districts, or entire nations.

91. *All crimes . . . indulg'd again:* The pope possessed the power to forgive any crimes he chose, and to "indulge" them again through the sale of indulgences, whereby one would pay a fee for the remission of purgatorial punishment.

92. *the right divine to every sin:* any of the special dispensations granted by the pope to specific people.

94. *Damn'd Doubt . . . when dead:* The church made it a sin to doubt or seriously question its doctrines. "Double-damn'd" refers to the practice of exhuming the bodies of people who were posthumously declared heretics either for ritual excommunication or burning.

95. *O'er bold . . . horrors roll:* the punishment of scientists and philosophers (such as Galileo) for making discoveries that opposed official doctrine.

96. *And to . . . the soul:* As a result of the corruptions mentioned in the lines above, the soul, which in the eighteenth century referred also to the intellectual faculties, shrank to the minimal capabilities one possesses at birth ("native nothing").

99–100. *But oh . . . glories doom'd:* But oh, by what fell (cruel) fate are my bright ambition's brightest glories doomed to be entombed?

101. *While now . . . forsook:* While now my rival (Christ) forsook every hope.

103. *vast machine:* complex system of Catholic theology.

104. *First, fairest . . . Satan's mind.* Compare James Miller's description of "True Politeness" in *Of Politeness; an Epistle to the Right Honourable William Stanhope, Lord Harrington* (1788): "That fairest offspring of the social mind" (l. 11).

109. *In vain . . . I bar'd:* In Germany, for instance, Catholic armies were formed to wage war against those princes who converted to Protestantism.

110. *o'er example dar'd:* ventured beyond their own example.

113. *Thro' all her coast:* throughout hell's entire expanse.

116–117. *reptile foes, new fishermen, mechanic worms:* Like the early Christians, whom Satan above calls the "last sweepings of the clay-born kind" and the "dung-hill's offspring" (ll. 35–36), the Protestant reformers are seen as issuing primarily from the lower classes. "New fishermen" also alludes to Christ's calling the fishermen, Simon and Andrew, as his apostles (Mark 1:17).

118. *unfolded gospel:* the Protestant ideal of having returned the gospel to the hands of the common people by translating it into the vernacular.

119–122. *From earth's . . . cover'd o'er:* As reviving suns bade the spring appear from earth's wide realms, left bare beneath the deluge, so at the startling voice of the reformers, a moral spring covered over my winter from shore to shore.

125–126. *From them . . . vernal prime:* From them (reformers), a brighter season and more vernal prime (spring) rolled on, to bless this earth's cold clime.

133 n. *Charles II:* king of Great Britain from the restoration of the throne (1660) to 1685. Dwight characterizes his reign as the period in which infidel philosophy first became fashionable.

134–136. *O'er truth's . . . sweets away:* "I" from l. 133 is the implied subject of each clause in this sentence (for example, I drew the webs of sophism over truth's fair form).

135. *Virtue new . . . beauties gay:* I chilled new virtue, which was still gay in its growing beauties. Satan is continuing his metaphor from ll. 128–130, describing virtue as a flower.

138. *Fashion:* Here Fashion is an allegorical figure representing not merely novelty but the more fundamental tendency of human nature to be drawn to fleeting pleasures in direct opposition to reason and virtue. Specifically, Satan is describing the fashionable skepticism of Christianity assumed in much of seventeenth- and eighteenth-century thought.

142. *Now there . . . a God:* an example of the power of fashion to draw people, at one moment, to atheism and, at another, back to the belief in God.

143. *Let black . . . it seem'd:* Compare Pope's *Rape of the Lock*, in which the heroine takes on a similarly godlike air during a game of ombre: "*Let Spades be Trumps!* she said, and Trumps they were" (bk. 3, l. 46).

144. *Hume:* David Hume (1711–1776), Scottish philosopher and historian whose

---

skepticism caused him to be grouped with Voltaire and the philosophes as a leader of infidelity. The reference to his dreaming is meant to ridicule the radical assertions in his *Treatise of Human Nature* (1739), discussed in detail in ll. 241–256.

147–148. *Before her . . . praise of me:* The universal knee bent before her (Fashion) and acknowledged her sovereign, which amounted to the praise of me (Satan).

147 n. *Phil. ii. 10, 11:* Dwight cites his allusion to a passage from Paul's *Letter to the Philippians:* "That at the name of Jesus every knee should bow." Ironically, this passage had been used by Universalists as proof of the final reconciliation of God and all mankind.

149–150. *With her . . . umpire stood:* With her (Fashion), brave Ridicule acted as Satanic umpire, deciding between good and ill, truth and falsehood. This idea of using ridicule as a test of truth (cf. Dwight's footnote to l. 149) is proposed by Anthony Ashley Cooper, third earl of Shaftesbury (1671–1713) in *Characteristics of Men, Manners, Opinions, Times* (1711). His point is that one can use ridicule to test ideas: if the idea can be shown to be ridiculous, it will be exposed as false, but truth will always stand up against any attempt to ridicule it.

151–152. *He, Hogarth . . . drew:* Like William Hogarth (1697–1764), an English painter who satirized contemporary morals in his work, he (Ridicule) persuasively drew the form of Providence (God) with new hues and features.

153–156. *Round its . . . a god:* Satan refers to the practice (explained in the note to l. 147) of depicting the God of Calvinism as unworthy of being called benevolent because he condemns so many sinners to hell. Dwight's point is that, before such infidels make this observation, they first distort the true image of God and thus end up describing a mere caricature.

157 n. *Alcibiades:* Athenian aristocrat, general, and politician who, in his youth, was a friend of Socrates. *Morgan:* Thomas Morgan (d. 1743), Welsh deist, author of *The Moral Philosopher* (1738). Compare Dwight's description of him to Pope's in *The Dunciad*, bk. 2, l. 414 n: "A writer against Religion . . . having stolen his Morality from Tindal, and his Philosophy from Spinoza, he calls himself, by the courtesy of England, a *Moral Philosopher.*" SCRIBLERUS: imaginary annotator of several of the poem's footnotes, a version of the pedantic scholar and annotator Martinus Scriblerus from Pope's *Peri Bathous* and *The Dunciad.*

160. *New-made . . . man:* The subject of this line is Satan's "friends" from l. 157, who, by means of various theories, have revised the notion of Creation by de-emphasizing God's role, often to the point of suggesting that man is not created at all.

162. *As pamper'd . . . pride:* For Dwight, the weakness of infidel philosophy is that its many forms (deism, atheism, skepticism, Latitudinarianism) are mutually contradictory, yet they both appeal to the human tendency to avoid acknowledging one's own sinfulness.

163–164. *Now . . . Now:* in one case and in another case.

165–166. *Now, miracles . . . his cell:* In numerous deist tracts, the truth of Christianity is denied by disproving the miracles of Christ and the apostles, yet other versions of infidelity imply that the miracles professed by non-Christian mystics are true.

167–168. *Priests now . . . cunning's wings:* In their efforts to attack Christianity, infidels will sometimes describe priests as dullards and other times as cunning and as evil schemers.

169–170. *No system . . . of heaven:* In one case, man is given no system of truth; in another, my own (Satan's) doctrines are the representation of God-given truth.

171–172. *While God . . . praise:* In a world of contradictory theories such as those of the previous lines, God is seen as drawing no distinctions between Christianity and pagan ritual.

173–174. *While here . . . molehill round:* While in one case, no virtuous man can be found on earth, in other cases saints swarm the earth (molehill) like ants (pismires). The former belief, popularized by Thomas Hobbes (1588–1679), asserts that human motivation is defined by mere self-interest; the latter is the Shaftesburian-Pelagian notion of universal human benevolence.

175–178. *Like maggots . . . Indian fire:* According to the modern Pelagian conception of human nature, the infidels of Caffraria, the corrupt courtiers of Europe, deists, and native Americans are all equally virtuous. *Caffraria:* name used to describe certain territories in southern Africa, deriving from the Arabic *kafir,* meaning "infidel."

178. *Or howl'd . . . Indian fire:* the Rousseauean notion of the noble savage, which describes the native American as living in an ideal state of nature.

180. *shores, the blocking:* means of support, as at the bottom of a structure.

181. *yon haughty . . . deny:* Satan interprets the general lack of popularity of the infidel doctrines as merely an act of spite.

182. *nether sky:* the lower sky, that is, the sky in hell.

184. *A balm . . . increasing pain:* The works of infidel philosophers first soothe the pain of human existence but, because they prove to be false, eventually increase that pain.

185–189. *Bacon, Newton, Locke:* Dwight's praise of these figures is significant, for, although their advancement of empiricism and the New Science allowed Voltaire and the philosophes to claim them as their intellectual precursors, Dwight emphasizes that their work is wholly harmonious with Christianity. Compare Settle's similar attack of the three in *The Dunciad,* bk. 3, ll. 215–216: "'Tis yours, a Bacon or a Locke to blame, / a Newton's genius, or a Milton's flame."

185. *Thro' nature's . . . Bacon ran:* While cloud-borne Bacon ran through nature's fields. Francis Bacon (1561–1626), English statesman and philosopher of science,

whose works such as *The Advancement of Learning* (1605), *Novum Organum* (1620), and *The New Atlantis* (1626) established him as the founder of the scientific method.

185 n. *Collins:* Anthony Collins (1676–1729), English deist, author of numerous tracts including *A Discourse of Free-Thinking* (1713), and among the first to introduce the historical criticism of the Bible. Collins here criticizes Bacon, Isaac Newton, and John Locke for being small-minded in their adherence to Christianity.

186. *Doubtful his . . . man:* "Doubtful" should be read, not in the modern sense, but in the eighteenth-century sense of doubt as inquiry (see also l. 94). Satan is most likely alluding to Bacon's suggestion, in *The Advancement of Learning,* that knowledge, more than any other human achievement, is worthy of being described as an apotheosis, for the benefits of military or political achievements are limited by the age or the nation they serve, but "the other is indeed like the benefits of heaven, which are permanent and universal." Thus, he writes, in ancient times, political figures were honored with the titles of demigods, and artists and inventors were "consecrated among the gods themselves" (Francis Bacon, *The Works of Francis Bacon,* 10 vols. [London, 1826], I, 47).

187–188. *While high-soul'd . . . God:* Sir Isaac Newton (1642–1727), English mathematician and physicist whose mechanical model of nature revolutionized the understanding of the universe. Newton, a Christian apologist who also wrote works of scriptural interpretation, signifies, for Dwight, the compatibility of religion and science.

189–190. *While patient . . . of sway:* John Locke (1632–1704), English philosopher and political theorist, is described as patient for his refusing to rely on the systems of previous metaphysicians and limiting his assertions to those that could be empirically proved. He is credited for illuminating the path of reason in *An Essay concerning Human Understanding* (1690) and the laws of sway, or political power, in *Two Treatises of Government* (1690).

191–195. *While Berkeley . . . gospel o'er:* Satan includes in his list of great philosophers George Berkeley (1685–1753), bishop of Cloyne, whose *Principles of Human Knowledge* (1710) introduced the theory of idealism, a radical version of Locke's argument that all knowledge is gained through the senses. Because knowledge is limited to perception, he reasons, one cannot assume the existence of material reality. Instead, he proposes that all being is perceived through a direct communication from the mind of God, thus emphasizing God's active role in the workings of the universe.

192. *all parching:* drying all things.

198. *mite:* tiny.

199. *my Methodist, brave Herbert:* Edward Herbert, first Baron Herbert of Cherbury (1583–1648), considered the first to systematize the principles of deism. Satan refers to him as his "Methodist" (referring to the common association of the Meth-

odists with excessive religious enthusiasm) because, according to Dwight's source, Herbert's system included beliefs other deists would have rejected as superstitions. Dwight is alluding to a story recorded by John Leland in which Herbert is said to have been unsure about whether to publish his deist work *De Veritate* (1624) and thus prayed for a sign from God, which he received in the form of a thunder clap (see John Leland, *A View of the Principal Deistical Writers That Have Appeared in England in the Last and Present Century* . . . , 5th ed., 2 vols. [London, 1766], I, 26–27). Dwight refers to this story in his footnote to l. 200 ("Cock-Lane-Ghost Tale of thunder's answer to prayer").

201–206. *In vain . . . truth, in vain:* Shaftesbury (see note to ll. 149–150) is described as a humble bee or bumblebee (that is, that his philosophical writings amount to a great deal of buzzing, but no real truth) in part because his philosophical work, *Characteristics of Men, Manners, Opinions, Times* (1711) deals with numerous subjects in an elegant style but presents no comprehensive argument. The description of his rapturous praise of nature and beauty is an allusion to a similarly satirical portrait of Shaftesbury's *Moralists, a Philosophical Rhapsody* (1709) in a footnote to *The Dunciad:* Here Pope (or Warburton) quotes directly the "prayer" to Nature of Shaftesbury's speaker Theocles and puts it in verse form no doubt to emphasize its "visionary" quality: "O glorious *Nature*! / Supremely fair, and sovereignly good! / All-loving, and all-lovely! all divine! / Wise substitute of Providence! *impower'd / Creatress*! or *impow'ring Deity*! / *Supreme Creator*! / Thee, I invoke, and thee alone adore!" (bk. 4, l. 488 n).

202 n. *Linnaeus:* Carolus Linnaeus (1707–1778), Swedish naturalist who introduced the standard nomenclature for biological classification.

207. *Bolingbroke:* Henry St. John, Viscount Bolingbroke (1678–1751), English statesman identified with the opposition Tory party. Long recognized as a major political figure, his reputation later in the century suffered as a result of the posthumous publication of his deistic and skeptical writings. *how well thy tatter'd robe:* how much thy robe was tattered.

208. *Poor, Bedlam king:* Bolingbroke's posthumously published writing had long been criticized for his harsh ridicule of those with whom he disagreed. Satan takes this notion to its logical conclusion, describing him as the classic paranoiac who imagines himself as a king (hence the tattered robe in l. 207).

209–210. *He, with . . . aspir'd:* Fired with glory, he aspired to heaven, therefore representing Satan in miniature.

214. *Yet fail'd . . . beside:* Because Bolingbroke was finally unmasked as an infidel, he was unsuccessful in his quest for fame, and also unfit for heaven.

217. *subs:* subordinates, lesser infidels.

218–219. *Toland, Tindal, Chubb, Woolston:* John Toland (1670–1722), Matthew Tindal (1657?–1733), Thomas Chubb (1679–1746), Thomas Woolston (1670–1731),

English deists. Compare *The Dunciad*, bk. 2, ll. 399–400: "Toland and Tindal, prompt at priests to jeer, / Yet silent bow'd to Christ's No kingdom here."

220. *That stand . . . for &c.:* The abbreviation "&c." should be read as "and so forth." These writers, Satan jokes, aren't significant enough to be individually named on a list of famous infidels, making their names interchangeable with the words "and so forth."

223. *Not men . . . they won:* These writers are only clever enough to win "man-lings," or lesser men, to the cause of infidelity.

224. *fun:* meant throughout *The Triumph of Infidelity* in the sense of "foolish pleasure."

228. *As ciphers . . . amount:* Satan's joke is that these lesser infidels are themselves insignificant, but they increase the number of his philosophers just as adding zeroes (ciphers) multiplies by ten the value of a number.

230. *Believ'd unseen . . . unread:* Because infidelity had become fashionable, such writers were often praised, though their works were seldom read.

232. *canvas:* weigh the pros and cons.

233. *arraign'd:* answered, refuted.

235. *powder'd beaux:* genteel and well-dressed gentlemen who are most prone to fashionable infidelity. *boobies:* fools.

236. *As puppies . . . along:* Eighteenth-century roads were equipped with gutters at the side, called kennels, in which waste was washed away by rain. When the rain fell hard, puppies were pulled along by the stream of the kennel. This image is a commonplace in Augustan poetry, seen in Swift's "Description of a City Shower," for instance: "Now from all parts the swelling kennels flow, / And bear their trophies with them as they go: / . . . Drown'd puppies, stinking sprats, all drench'd in mud, / Dead cats and turnip-tops come tumbling down the flood" (ll. 53–63). It is also an allusion to *The Dunciad*, as the same image had been used by Pope to describe a similar group of dunces: "Next plung'd a feeble, but a desp'rate pack, / With each a sickly brother at his back: / Sons of a Day! Just buoyant on the flood, / Then number'd with the puppies in the mud" (bk. 2, ll. 305–308).

240. *involv'd:* enveloped. *Scotia:* Scotland, birthplace of Hume (see note to l. 144).

243. *dreams:* overly speculative or metaphysical ideas.

244. *The youth:* Hume began work on his philosophic system at the age of fifteen.

246. *Pure, genuine . . . refin'd:* Satan reverses the metaphor commonly used in the eighteenth century to describe the method of purifying truth from superstition and sophistry, that is, purifying gold from dross or impurities.

249-250. *All things . . . upon a cause·* Hume is criticized for relying on the mechanics of the Newtonian universe but subverting it in his well-known denial of certainty in questions of cause and effect.

251. *Chance divine:* Dwight misinterprets Hume's skepticism of reasoning causes from effects as a denial of any causes, suggesting that everything occurs by chance.

255-256. *Each thing . . . miracle:* According to Hume's skepticism about determining the cause of a specific event, every event might be considered a miracle; yet Hume also argued against the possibility of Christian miracles. The larger point is that infidel philosophers will argue against Christianity even if that argument contradicts another of their assertions.

259. *Lest dull . . . known:* Satan fears that Hume's obscure *Treatise* will be too tedious for general readers; in fact, this work went largely unread for many years.

263-264. *He, light . . . true:* Voltaire's writing (see note to "Dedication") is described, not as truly learned or logically consistent, but merely witty. *o'er learning's surface flew:* Compare *The Dunciad,* bk. 4, ll. 241-242: "Like buoys, that never sink into the flood, / On Learning's surface we but lie and nod."

267. *Before his . . . past:* Voltaire's criticism of Old Testament Jewish history.

269. *Salem:* biblical city usually identified as Jerusalem.

271-272. *The Greeks . . . lied:* Dwight accuses Voltaire of arguing any point that denies Christianity; thus, classical writers are always attacked when their testimony supports the gospel.

273. *He, he . . . smelt:* In the midst of unmasking Christianity as mere superstition, Voltaire is implicitly claiming his own monopoly on absolute truth.

274-276. *The Well . . . his wall:* Voltaire's admiration for Chinese philosophy, as seen, for instance, in *The Philosophical Dictionary* (1764), is the primary subject of Dwight's satire. Voltaire has found the fabled well of truth in China and built the curb of this well with bricks from the Great Wall.

274. *the goddess:* truth.

274n. LORD KAMES' . . . *of man:* Henry Home, Lord Kames (1696-1782), wrote *Sketches on the History of Man* (1774), but this allusion is to Voltaire's famous distaste for Kames, which began when the latter used one of Voltaire's poems in his *Elements of Criticism* (1762) as an example of a failed epic. Voltaire responded harshly in a review of Kames's *Elements* and was said to have held the grudge for years.

275. *Chihohamti:* Shih Huang-ti, Chinese emperor who oversaw the building of the Great Wall and who is fabled to have ordered the destruction of all books other than those of architecture or medicine (see Dwight's note to l. 275). An allusion to *The Dunciad,* in which Dulness reveals to Cibber the history of dulness: "Far eastward cast thine eye, from whence the Sun / And orient Science their bright course

begun: / Here god-like Monarch all that pride confounds, / He, whose long wall the wand'ring Tartar bounds; / Heav'ns! what a pile! whole ages perish there, / And one bright blaze turns Learning into air" (bk. 3, ll. 73-78).

278-279. *alter'd nature, shrunk, misshapen bodies:* most likely a reference to the practice of binding women's feet to keep them tiny (according to the common notion of beauty).

281. *Mandarins:* Chinese government officials. *baby kings:* referring to K'ang Hsi, who ascended the throne in 1661 at the age of seven.

282. *leading-strings:* harnesses by which parents would keep children from straying.

283. *Fo:* Western derivative of the Chinese name for Buddha.

285. *Bonzes:* Buddhist monks.

290. *empires, forty . . . old:* According to Chinese historiography, their empire had existed for forty thousand years.

291. *Tohi:* misprint for Fohi (Fu Hsi), the mythic first emperor of China, called the "Son of Heaven," fabled to have been born without a father. Dwight follows the misprint from one of his sources on Chinese culture; see Louis Le Compte, *Memoirs and Observations . . . Made in a Late Journey through the Empire of China . . .* , 3d ed., corr. (London, 1699), 119.

292. *Lao's long day:* Lao is Lao-Tsu, founder of Taoism, one of the principal religions of China. Dwight refers elsewhere to the long day, a Chinese myth about a particular day that "was as long as ten"; see Theodore Dwight, Jr., *President Dwight's Decisions of Questions Discussed by the Senior Class in Yale College, in 1813 and 1814* (New York, 1833), 154.

292 n. *dock and plantain:* herbs sometimes used as medicines. *gripes:* intestinal pains associated with flatulence. GARTH'*s alphabetical prophesies:* Sir Samuel Garth (1661-1719), English poet and physician, whose poem *The Dispensary* (1699), a satire against those who opposed the establishment of a medical dispensary for the poor, includes numerous comic prophesies.

293-297. *Stories, at . . . and fact:* Stories that make the dreams of Behmen seem to constitute truth, sense, and virtue and that make children's stories, such as those beginning with "once there was a man," appear as reason, truth, and fact. *Behmen:* Jacob Boehme (1575-1624), German mystic whose theological system made his name synonymous with enthusiastic speculation.

299-300. *He too . . . and blind:* In his later writing, such as *Candide* (1759), Voltaire is particularly skeptical of optimistic assumptions that natural and moral evil are consistent with a beneficent and all-powerful God.

299 n. *whatever is . . . right:* In *Candide,* Voltaire satirizes the philosophy of the character Pangloss, who insists that "this is the best of all possible worlds." The phrase alludes to Pope's *Essay on Man,* bk. 1, l. 294: "Whatever is, is right."

---

302. *a satanic . . . implied:* (Voltaire revealed) in the place of a benevolent God, a Satanic imp.

305-306. *would men . . . as believe:* If only men would receive the force of these doctrines, and live according to Satan's glory, as easily as they believe them.

311. *Jesuitic art:* artifices introduced to Roman Catholic doctrine by the Society of Jesus (such as probabilism and laxism, explained below in the note to l. 315).

313-314. *In poison'd . . . eternal woes:* (Jesuitic art combined its frauds) to enclose the flutterer in poisoned toils and to fix eternal woes with (its) venomed fangs.

315. *On sceptic . . . bright:* This line refers to probabilism and laxism, casuistic theories in which an individual may break a law if there is a probability or possibility that the law can morally be broken. Thus "sceptic dross" is any doubt that can, for one's purposes, be regarded as truth (stamping heaven's image on it).

316-318. *And nam'd . . . the dead:* According to probabilism and laxism, one might believe to be the "light" or truth of God what is in fact merely a "will-a-wisp," or *ignis fatuus,* a phosphorescent light that seems to hover over moors or marshy ground, deceiving those walking at night. Such practices deceptively lead a person toward moral laxity, and, finally, eternal death. Compare *Paradise Lost,* bk. 9, ll. 634-642: ". . . as when a wand'ring fire, / Compact of unctuous vapor, which the night / Condenses, and the cold environs round, / Kindled through agitation to a flame, / . . . / Misleads th' amazed night-wanderer from his way / To bogs and mires, and oft through pond or pool, / There swallowed up and lost, from succor far."

319. *Socinus:* Faustus Socinus (1539-1604), Italian religious reformer who taught that Christ was, not the son of God, but a mere mortal whose teachings alone are the essence of Christianity.

319-320. *To life . . . from view:* Continuing the metaphor of art and drawing (from ll. 311-312), Satan explains that Socinus drew his followers as if already possessing Christian salvation ("To life") while simultaneously denying Christ's role as savior, concealing the art of heaven that makes this salvation possible.

321. *the world's almighty trust:* that which has been entrusted to Christ for the benefit of all people (that is, dying for their sins).

322 n. *Isai. ix. 6:* "For unto us a child is born, unto us a son is given: and the government will be on his shoulder."

324. *Who hung the globe:* As one person of the Trinity, Christ is part of God and thus also the creator.

329. *on far creation's limb:* far on the limb of the tree of Creation, that is, born late in history, not preexisting all things, as in Trinitarian Christianity.

330. *minim:* insignificant thing.

333. *a darling race descended:* Socinus died in 1604, but forms of Socinianism lived on in Arminianism and Unitarianism.

---

335. *Priestley:* Joseph Priestley (1733–1804), British scientist and nonconformist theologian famous for chemical experiments such as the separation of pure oxygen from common air. His comprehensive philosophy-theology blended Unitarianism, materialism, millenarianism, and political radicalism.

335 n. *system of divinity cut of fixed air:* Priestley was one of the discoverers of oxygen, then called fixed air. The point is that Priestley has allowed his chemical studies to dominate his theological inquiry, specifically because his materialism determines his belief that Christ, by virtue of his material existence, is a mere man.

336. *His own . . . Christianity:* The description of Priestley's doctrines as corruptions alludes to Priestley's *History of the Corruptions of Christianity* (1782), in which he argued that the religion of the early Christians had been a form of Unitarianism.

337. *less open friends:* liberal or Latitudinarian ministers, whose contribution to Satan's cause are more difficult to detect but whose emphasis on the moral aspect of religion is understood as a watering down of Christianity.

339. *Taught easier . . . abode:* taught that eternal happiness was easier to achieve than Calvinism maintains.

340–341. *Less pure . . . divine:* Made virtue less pure, God less perfect, vice less guilty, and the atonement less divine. (By emphasizing the role of human morality rather than the dependence on God's grace for salvation, liberal Protestants diminish the divinity of Christ's atonement.)

345. *this wild waste:* America. *Albion:* England.

347. *a dread race, my sturdiest foes:* American Puritans, whom Satan regards, of course, as his enemies.

349–351. *Pinion'd with . . . realms assail:* The Puritans' journey toward religious and moral truth is described using the image of their immigration to New England.

353. *bane:* curse.

355. *E******:* Jonathan Edwards (1703–1758), American religious leader and theologian and Dwight's grandfather, best known for inspiring the religious revivals that set the stage for the Great Awakening and considered the colonial period's greatest philosophical and theological mind.

356. *moral Newton:* In the lines that follow, Satan suggests that Edwards is to moral science what Newton had been to physical science: both did not merely create systems but described, in empirical fashion, the works of God. *second Paul:* Like the apostle Paul, Edwards brought new converts to Christianity during the Great Awakening.

357–359. *He, in clear . . . system bind:* Edwards's theological system is compared to Newton's description of the solar system, in which human consciousness revolves around God's love, seen as possessing a gravitational force comparable to the sun's.

365. *standard:* emblem or flag, as in battle.

369-375. *To ward . . and lied:* To ward off this fate (threatened by Edwards and his followers), I preached, I wrote, I argued, prayed and lied all that irreligion can (preach, etc.): whatever sustains sinning man, whatever can disarm one's conscience of her thorns, or calm the dread alarm felt at death's approach, whatever cheats mankind with error that seems to be truth, and whatever taints the mind with vice that seems to be virtue.

376. *What could . . . beside:* What else could my friends, or even myself beside, do?

377-378. *But tho' . . . . surround:* But though often crowned with glad successes, unceasing fears surround my troubled path.

381. *L******:* Isaac Ledyard (1754-1803), American materialist whose work, *An Essay on Matter* (1784), follows the general principles of La Mettrie's *Man a Machine* (1748).

382. *the soul . . . mud:* Materialism argues that human consciousness is, not a soul, but merely one of the workings of the material body.

385-386. *Nor taught . . . mind:* Satan jokes that Ledyard not only argued that the soul is made of mud but exemplified this fact by his own stupidity.

387. *A****:* Ethan Allen (1738-1789), American patriot and Revolutionary soldier who led the Green Mountain Boys, a regiment of Vermont settlers originally raised to defend lands granted to them by New Hampshire against claims to those lands by New York. Allen, who was also a professed deist, offered his own theological system in *Reason, the Only Oracle of Man* (1784). *thro' realms of nonsense:* Compare John Dryden, *MacFlecknoe:* "Through all the Realms of Non-Sense, absolute" (l. 6).

387n. *Oracles of Reason:* alternate title of Allen's book.

388. *Clodhopping:* At one point in *Reason, the Only Oracle of Man,* Allen refers to mankind as "clodhoppers," a word meaning clumsy and rustic. Dwight uses it to ridicule Allen's backwoods upbringing.

388n. *Lord Monboddo:* James Burnet, Lord Monboddo (1714-1799), presented an early version of the theory of human evolution in his *Origin and Progress of Language* (1773-1792). Monboddo argued that human beings originally had tails and that they evolved from the orangutan.

395-396. *What tho' . . . of time:* Although dull seers (the prophets) have, in sublime dreams, sung that thy ruin floats along the threshold of time. Satan is reminding himself that his own demise is predicted in Scripture.

397n. *Dan. ii. 44-45:* "Forasmuch as thou sayest that the stone was cut out of the mountain without hands . . . the Great God hath made known to the king what shall pass hereafter."

399-400. *Tho' bliss' . . . sound:* Though dreaded heralds of bliss shall proclaim, throughout the limits of the earth, pardon, peace, and joy.

399n. *Isai. lii. 7:* "How beautiful upon the mountains are the feet of him that bringeth good tidings, that publisheth peace; that bringeth good tidings of good, that publisheth salvation."

402. *natal song:* song of Christ's figurative rebirth or return at the end of time.

403–404. *Still, should . . . mankind:* If I should fall as predicted in Scripture, I'll still find a glorious fate by bringing mankind down with me. Another indication of Satan's willful blindness, for he accepts that his own fate is fixed by God but forgets that it would follow that the fate of mankind is similarly fixed.

407–408. *With sweet . . . sweep?:* How shall I sweep her (the New World's) millions down the steep hill of perdition all at once (in one host)?

409. *the glorious . . . best:* the first temptation of Adam and Eve in Eden. In the Bible, Satan (the serpent) deceives them into believing they will achieve immortality, even by disobeying God. Satan suggests below that in the case of Chauncy's Universalism, he will be employing the same tactic (see ll. 413–416).

411. *That on this . . . began:* As a result of their sins, Adam and Eve were cast from Eden, into the world of natural and moral evil, which Satan claims as his kingdom.

411 n. *Ye shall . . . die. &c.:* The "&c." alludes to the rest of this biblical verse, in which Satan promises Eve precisely what Dwight insists Universalism is promising all people: "that in the day ye eat thereof, then your eyes shall be opened, and ye shall be as gods."

412. *lost my . . . man:* Satan suggests that when God ("my rival") punished Adam and Eve and cast them out of Eden (paradise), he lost paradise (his plans for man in paradise were foiled) and lost mankind to Satan's power.

413. *C*******:* Charles Chauncy, which Dwight spelled "Chauncey" (corresponding to the number of asterisks in the name).

413–416. *Twice fifteen . . . of fame:* Thirty years have passed since I led Chauncy's mind, with love of system and lust for fame, through deep doctrines, refined from common sense, to frame a nice, mysterious work. Satan recalls that Chauncy had written the manuscript that would become *The Mystery Hid* in the 1750s, roughly thirty years earlier.

414. *from common sense refin'd:* Dwight employs the same inversion of the Enlightenment metaphor of the purification of truth (as in l. 246).

416. *love of system:* love of excessive metaphysical speculation.

420. *to heaven . . . crooked way:* In Chauncy's version of Universalism, sinners go to hell for a finite period of time, to be purged of their sinfulness before proceeding to heaven.

423. *Even Satan's . . . hie:* Even Satan will hasten there (to heaven) before long. Chauncy's system does not explicitly argue that Satan will ultimately repent and go to heaven, but it does assert that, at the end of time, all things in the universe will be reconciled to God.

---

424. *On cap . . . go I:* Satan jokingly recites this magic incantation that will supposedly get him into heaven, thus admitting the preposterousness of the idea (going back to Chauncy's theological source, Origen) that he too will be saved.

425. *palsied age . . . sight:* At the time he published *The Mystery Hid*, Chauncy was seventy-nine years old. Satan suggests that his participation in the cause of infidelity is due to senility.

426–427. *I'll rouse . . . repair:* Satan admits that, before professing Universalism, Chauncy had rendered numerous injuries to Satan's cause.

430. *A cheated . . . arms:* The best weapon against God is the false interpretation of the Bible, for it harms people in the guise of helping them.

432. *False friends . . . field:* Compare this passage to the Dedication to Voltaire: "The sword and javelin, however keen, may be dreaded and shunned, while the secret and deadly dirk is plunged to the heart of unsuspecting friendship, unhappily trusting the smooth-faced assassin."

433. *M*****:* John Murray (1741–1815), American Universalist, born in Britain, who began his career as a Methodist preacher and converted to Universalism in the 1760s. In 1770, he immigrated to America, where he preached a version of Universalism different in many points from Chauncy's, and in 1774 he settled in Gloucester, Massachusetts. For the Congregationalist clergy, Murray signified a relationship between Universalism and backwoods itinerant religion, causing Chauncy publicly to distance his own doctrine from Murray's.

433–434. *my utmost . . . the will:* Murray possessed only the will to commit mischief, not the intellectual means to succeed. Compare the description of Zimri in Dryden's *Absalom and Achitophel:* "Thus, wicked but in will, of means bereft" (pt. 1, l. 567).

435–438. *He, in hard . . . to throttle:* In hard days, when being a weaver provided no money (ribbons gave no bread), and the sons of Spitalfield (a London weaving community) fled from the Tyburn gallows, Murray, avoiding prosecution for debt, wisely gave up weaving (dropped the shuttle) and began preaching doctrines that defied truth and common sense. Murray did, in fact, work at a textile factory and served time in debtors prison before emigrating to America.

440. *Tongue at-your-service:* one who is paid to tell people whatever they wish to hear.

444. *Religion cent-per-cented:* religion that pays a 100 percent return on one's investment (that is, Universalism promises the certainty of eternal happiness for which one pays the preacher to hear). *at a rush:* in great demand.

446. *brass:* nerve.

448. *genuine brotherhood:* guild members or workers. Satan suggests that Murray's preaching deceives the working classes in particular.

450. *the field:* field of battle.

452. *desk of God:* pulpit.

453. *This said . . . day:* Satan finishes the long speech that began at l. 17. Having begun speaking at dawn, he is now adorned in the morning sunlight.

455–456. *And spread . . . of pence:* Satan, full of delight, spread the pride of system and the (desire for) increase of pence to Chauncy's bewildered senses.

457–458. *Forth from . . . still new:* The manuscript of *The Mystery Hid,* written thirty years earlier, is moldy, dusty, and covered with cobwebs.

459–460. *This darling . . . sage design'd:* The sage (Chauncy), high blown to ecstasy, designed to usher this darling pet (his book) to mankind.

461–462. *And conn'd . . . its way:* Dwight depicts Chauncy as the doting grandfather of his book, eager to show this "heir" to the world.

464. *And round . . . roar:* published the book for all of America.

464 n. *Salvation unto all men:* While Chauncy was still unsure of whether to publish his entire treatise *The Mystery Hid,* he and his fellow pastor at First Church, John Clarke, published a short pamphlet entitled *Salvation for All Men* (1782), which summarizes Chauncy's position; thus, Scriblerus refers to the pamphlet as the "harbinger to the great one."

466. *Pandemonia:* alluding to Pandemonium, the city built by Satan and his demons in *Paradise Lost.* Here it refers to the place where the audience of sinners and rogues forms to hear Chauncy preach.

467. *raptur'd:* enraptured.

475. *perjur'd wretch:* the first of Dwight's allegorical figures, listed in the following lines, each representing a particular vice or sin. This figure is not merely a liar but one who is paid to give false testimony in court.

475–476. *who met . . . own retreat:* The perjurer, ashamed by his sins, is unable to face the eyes of honest people.

481. *Florio:* This name, meaning "flower," is a stock name in Augustan satire for a fop or lover of pleasure. Leonard Chester, the Democratic-Republican editor of the *American Mercury,* attacked Dwight in 1803 in a series of essays entitled "*The Triumph of Infidelity* Resuscitated." There Chester identified Florio as Charles Cotesworth Pinckney, a South Carolina Federalist whom Dwight supported in the early 1800s. Chester is thus suggesting that Dwight now hypocritically supports someone whom he had earlier satirized. Federalists responded by asserting that Florio represents another member of the Pinckney family, the Honorable Charles Pinckney. When the *Triumph of Infidelity* was written, only the latter Pinckney had served in Congress (Continental and Confederation), which is mentioned in l. 492, thus supporting the Federalists' identification. Moreover, Lemuel Hopkins's 1795 poem, *The Democratiad,* quotes l. 488 of the *Triumph of Infidelity* in reference to the latter Pinckney.

486. *the Devil's Man of Ross:* allusion to Pope's encomium of the Man of Ross, an obscure British philanthropist, in the *Epistle to Bathurst* (ll. 249-280). Florio boasts that he is to Satan what the Man of Ross is to God.

487. *Here's three . . . pride:* Florio is so open about his sins that he is willing to wager that his pride exceeds even Satan's.

488. *chariot:* coach.

488-490. *Two whores . . . be given?:* Florio is boasting about the extent of his libertinism, which explains his subsequent outrage that Chauncy might now be Satan's favorite.

491-492. *No, still . . . and nays:* No, praise of me will still shine on Satan's roll, or list of sinners, as my name formerly appeared on Congress's (C——'s) lists of yeas and nays.

493-494. *Half pleas'd . . . true:* An honest sailor (tar) responds to Chauncy's doctrine by saying to a friend, "Good Doctrine, Jack," and his friend answers knowingly, "Aye, too good to be true."

495. *P****:* unidentified.

497. *W******:* identified by Chester as Jeremiah Wadsworth, a Connecticut banker and friend of Dwight, although the number of asterisks used in "W******" does not correspond to the letters in Wadsworth's name. More likely, this is a first-name identification of William Duer of New York, who, in addition to serving as a delegate in the Continental Congress and as assistant to Alexander Hamilton in the Treasury, led several speculation schemes in both land and securities, including the one alluded to in ll. 499-502, involving federal 6-percent stocks (see Robert F. Jones, *"The king of the alley": William Duer: Politician, Entrepreneur, and Speculator, 1768-1799* [Philadelphia, 1992], 118-119, 125-126).

499-502. *"In vain" . . . to heaven:* During the economic crisis of the 1780s, many veterans of the Revolution (as well as widows and children of soldiers killed) were forced to sell the devalued 6-percent federal stocks (what would today be called bonds) to speculators at a fraction of their face value. Dwight suggests that W****** accepts the 6-percent stocks in lieu of hard money as payments for debts but demands an unreasonable number of them ("six, six percent per month") and holds them until the government is able to pay their full value, thus getting rich as widows and orphans deplete their only resources. At the same time, by accepting the stocks, he appears to be providing for the widows and orphans, thus practicing "pious usury," following the biblical injunction to aid widows and orphans in their affliction. Dwight discusses the scheme in the *Travels* as perpetrated by William Duer, Walter Livingston, and Alexander Macomb; the result, he states, was that "multitudes of all classes, among them many widows and orphans, lost the whole of their property" (Dwight, *Travels in New England and New York* [1819], ed. Barbara Miller Solomon, with the assistance of Patricia M. King, 4 vols. [Cambridge, Mass., 1969]), I, 159.

503. *All who . . . within:* those who seemed not to worry over their sins but secretly felt the pangs of conscience.

505–508. *Whose conscience . . . rung:* Whose conscience, although often ignored by the snaky (deceptive) power of rationalization, still impoisoned the gay and gleeful hour, still checked the loose wish, stung the past enjoyment, and often rang the alarm bell of retribution.

515. *half putrid Epicure:* one who is devoted to the pleasure of food and drink, whose abused body is already in the process of corruption.

516. *cheeks of port:* red cheeks, a sign of habitual drunkenness. *lips of turtle green:* lips green from having eaten turtle soup, a delicacy associated with an overly indulgent, luxurious diet.

522. *sate:* satisfy himself. *breed a mongrel race:* produce illegitimate offspring.

523. *high-fed horse:* a horse sent to pasture to impregnate numerous mares.

525. *A snake . . . breath:* Dwight describes the lecher's seduction of other women using the image of Satan's symbolic seduction of Eve while in the form of the serpent.

527. *Hypocrisy:* identified by Chester as either Joseph Lyman or Benjamin Trumbull; more generally, this figure signifies any overly grave Puritan.

532. *But clos'd . . . within:* This line demonstrates that the object of Dwight's satire is not necessarily a specific doctrine; it is any form of religion that does not emphasize self-scrutiny.

533. *the Smooth Divine:* identified by Chester as James Dana. More important, this character embodies the logical conclusion of Chauncy's doctrine and other modern Pelagian forms of religion. Literary sources of this divine are found in the satires of Pope and Edward Young. Compare Pope's *Epistle to Burlington*, describing the "soft Dean" at Timon's mansion, "who never mentions Hell to ears polite"(ll. 149–150), and Young's *Love of Fame, the Universal Passion*, describing the religion of the upper-class lady, who asks in disbelief, "Shall pleasures of a short duration chain / A *lady's* soul in everlasting pain?" (bk. 4, ll. 437–438).

537–538. *That strange . . . a place:* A clergyman whose religion is watered down to merely moral advice for the wealthy avoids preaching the Protestant doctrines of grace and regeneration ("new-birth") for fear of appearing too "methodistic," too much like the religion of the lower classes.

539. *Plato's fine tales:* theological and moral system based on Platonic principles such as the capacity of reason to comprehend absolute values and unchanging realities, introduced into Christianity by, among others, the seventeenth-century Cambridge Platonists.

540. *moral seesaws:* lessons that focus so greatly on both sides of a moral question that they fail to teach the moral laws of Christianity.

544. *Good fame . . . peace within:* The Smooth Divine's emphasis on mere morality is not even for the simple sake of being virtuous, but of having a good reputation and peace of mind.

545–546. *Their honours . . . heaven:* The Smooth Divine knows that his parishioners will continue to desire honor even if it contradicts the essence of Christianity, so he attempts to equate Christian morality with social propriety.

549. *goody:* short for goodwife, a form of address to a woman.

551. *Or plac'd in some great town:* Chester read this line as introducing a different character from the Smooth Divine, one who represented another of Dwight's contemporaries, John Henry Livingston of New York. Yet the line demands to be read "Or when the Smooth Divine is placed in some great town," which directs the satire at a variant of the type rather than a specific individual.

552. *Trim:* neat. *glistening hose:* shiny stockings, suggesting that this divine follows high fashion in wearing silk, which would have been considered too luxurious for a clergyman.

556. *Their wives' . . . gaz'd:* In praising the women's new dresses, he has an opportunity to stare at their figures.

558. *Nor shrunk . . . pin'd:* This clergyman experiences none of the physical effects of his profession, associated with fasting or studying for long hours.

559–562. *Yet from . . . of death:* Yet he saw his brethren (other divines) driven from their churches: those who thundered truth, spoke the voice of heaven, chilled (with fear) trembling guilt, charmed the feet of those who were moving headlong in Satan's path back to the true path, and roused the ears of sinners with the death they face. Clergymen who tell the truth about sin and earnestly attempt to reform their congregations are often dismissed from their posts by parishioners who prefer to listen to smooth divines.

566. *Blest vegetation . . . seed:* that which grows from the seed of hell, that is, a more fully realized form of infidelity.

570. *Jove:* Jupiter, chief deity in Roman mythology. *the Lama:* Dalai Lama, spiritual leader of Tibetan Buddhism.

574. *stews:* brothels.

577. *Dagon:* false idol, named for the god of the Philistines from the first book of Samuel.

581–582. *His soul . . . machine:* The modern infidel or materialist rejects the notion that the soul is created in God's image, asserting that it is to the body what a watchspring is to a timepiece.

583–584. *That work . . . body:* The body, according to the materialist scheme found in, for example, La Mettrie's *Man a Machine*, is imagined as an elaborate machine or timepiece. *Rittenhouse:* David Rittenhouse (1732–1796), American clockmaker and scientist who developed precise scientific instruments.

586. *swine unbristled . . . ape:* Dwight argues that materialism reduces human beings to the level of animals, as in Monboddo's evolutionism (see note to l. 388).

587–588. *To couple . . . tomb:* Dwight jokes that a purely materialist existence, in which to copulate, eat, and die are the only meaningful activities, transforms the modern infidel into merely the final resting place for his food.

589. *******:* unidentified. *sear'd:* dried up, withered.

590. *And scarcely . . . true:* This person is so secure in his infidelity that even Chauncy's promises of universal salvation have no effect on him.

595–596. *Hardly, at . . . lucid thought:* At times, his struggling conscience wrought, with difficulty, a few strange intervals of lucid thought.

597–598. *Holding her . . . of fire:* Conscience, at these rare moments, holds a mirror to his soul, revealing the word "villain" written in fiery letters.

599–600. *Those few . . . run o'er:* Those few (letters) told the tale of his guilt: no longer shall the Beelzebub (demon) run through his soul once a year (that is, no longer will he even benefit from a yearly moment of seeing his demonic self in clear view).

601–602. *No more . . . below:* J——n, an unidentified woman, represents the sinner's memory of seducing a woman who later bore his illegitimate child; this memory, in which J——n's ghost points to his future in hell, will no longer reappear in his conscience.

603–604. *Fix'd in . . . bristly hair:* No longer will his eyeballs, fixed as if in death, stare (at these visions), or change his bristly hair to upright thorns.

605. *Demas:* Named for a companion of Paul, who abandoned the apostle, "having loved this present world" (2 Tim. 4:10), he has been identified as New Haven physician Ebenezer Beardsley (see Leon Howard, *The Connecticut Wits* [Chicago, 1943], 218). Compare the story of Demas's grand tour to that of the youth in *The Dunciad:* "Led by my hand, he saunter'd Europe round, / And gather'd ev'ry Vice on Christian ground; / Saw ev'ry Court, heard ev'ry King declare / His royal Sense, of Op'ras or the Fair; / The Stews and Palace equally explor'd, Intrigu'd with glory, and with spirit whor'd" (bk. 4, ll. 311–316).

608. *nor now . . . tale:* Having been a modest Christian, he would not have been mentioned in this story if not for the events in the following lines.

609–610. *But, borne . . . see:* Demas represents a familiar type in eighteenth-century literature, the virtuous young man who is corrupted by his grand tour of Europe.

612. *Great ladies . . . married:* In the company of European lords, Demas met "great ladies" who turned out to be the lords' concubines.

619-620. *"Shall powder'd . . . houses dwell?:* Having been corrupted by luxury and fashion, Demas can only conclude that such important people must necessarily enjoy eternal happiness.

621. *Euclio:* This figure, his name meaning "famous" in Greek, has been identified as Pierrepont Edwards, son of Jonathan Edwards and Dwight's uncle, a New Haven lawyer whose apathy toward religion and his later support of the Jeffersonian party made him the black sheep of the Edwards family. The poet's more personal tone supports this identification.

621-622. *Ah my . . . unhappy name:* Here the narrator falters, momentarily forgetting the imaginative renderings of Satan and Chauncy to say a prayer for Euclio's soul.

623-624. *Oh write it . . . tears:* direct quote from Pope's *Eloisa to Abelard* (ll. 13-14).

625-632. *let thy love . . . to sin:* Let thy love, that is stronger than death and above all heights and heavens; the love that on the accursed tree (cross) and in the midst of severe woes, extinguished with a tear the thief's dire guilt; (let that love) yearn over that mind that is forced to folly and whirled to sin with dire temptations, rank appetites, and passions fraught with fear. Dwight refers to Christ's forgiveness of the repentant thief who was crucified with him (Luke 23:39-43).

639-640. *th'infernal trumpet blew:* trumpet that announces the Roman *triumph* (see note to title) in which Chauncy and Satan proceed past the crowd of sinners.

643. *expressive emblems rose:* Allegorical figures emerged (described in the following lines).

645. *wrinkled Dotage:* the state of aged feeblemindedness. *fondled:* indulged, spoiled.

647. *lengthen'd nails:* Avarice is depicted with long nails to suggest his lack of concern over personal appearance.

648. *clipp'd halfpence:* half pennies that have had some of their metal shaved off.

649-650. *Trim Vanity . . . gaping crowd:* Vanity is depicted as "snuffing for incense," that is, breathing in the admiration she imagines she is receiving from the crowd.

651: *Age:* allegorical figure representing maturity or wisdom.

655-660. *What tho' . . . endless joy:* Even though the Heavens in words of flaming fire, disclose the vengeance of God's eternal anger, state that anguish will forever roll, in waves succeeding waves, over the unrepentant soul, and employ the strongest terms that each language knows, to teach us of eternal woe and eternal joy.

663-666. *Or, not . . . in vain:* Chauncy suggests in his treatises that the truth of universal salvation has remained a "mystery hid from ages" and is meant to be revealed in the modern era, according to God's plan.

667. *First Origen, then Tillotson:* Origen, third-century philosopher who synthesized Christian doctrine with Neoplatonism, and whom Chauncy cites as an ancient source of his Universalism; John Tillotson, archbishop of Canterbury (1630–1694), English Latitudinarian reputed to believe in universal salvation. Dwight's source for this lineage is Young's *Love of Fame:* "Dear Tillotson! be sure the best of men; / Nor thought he more, than thought great Origen. / Though once upon a time he misbehav'd; / Poor Satan! doubtless, he'll at length be sav'd" (bk. 4, ll. 447–450).

670. *That hell's . . . door:* Chauncy's system argues that sinners go to hell for a finite period before eventually proceeding to heaven.

671–672. *See kai's . . . supreme:* Chauncy explains in the introduction to *The Mystery Hid* that his method of scriptural interpretation consists of comparing words and phrases from the Greek New Testament in those passages that speak of man's future state with the same words and phrases in other passages (in one case, the word *epi* is used to prove universal salvation). Dwight's point is that Chauncy makes too much of these relatively unimportant words.

671n. *Lord Coke:* Sir Edward Coke (1552–1634), English legal scholar known for his subtle use of common law precedent to support a case.

673–675. *But such . . . in Greek:* Chauncy suggests, in *The Mystery Hid,* that only those who read the Bible diligently in Greek can understand his proof of universal salvation.

675–676. *chiefly those . . . cunning Paul:* Chauncy's proof relies mainly on interpretations of Paul's epistles; Dwight suggests that Chauncy overemphasizes this one part of the Bible.

681–683. *For tho' . . . passions rise:* Chauncy admits that, although cunning and diligence can discover Paul's meaning, the best aid to Chauncy's proof is the appeal to human passions.

681n. *Witness Matthew . . . find it:* Dwight reverses the warning of Matt. 7:13–14 ("For wide is the gate, and broad is the way, that leadeth to destruction . . . because straight is the gate, and narrow is the way, which leadeth unto life.") to satirize Chauncy's interpretation of Scripture.

689–690. *No good . . . ne'er oppose:* She (the love of sweet security of sin, l. 686) knows no good more luscious than their truth (the apparent truth of pleasing falsehoods), and, hence, she will never oppose their evidence.

691: *she mounts th' Eternal Throne:* Compare *The Dunciad,* bk. 4, ll. 17–25: "She mounts the Throne: her head a Cloud conceal'd, / In broad Effulgence all below reveal'd. / . . . / Beneath her foot-stool, *Science* groans in Chains, / And *Wit* dreads Exile, Penalties and Pains. / There foam'd rebellious *Logic,* gagg'd and bound, / There, stript, fair *Rhet'ric* languish'd on the ground; / His blunted Arms by *Sophistry* are born."

693–694. *Decides the . . . mighty rod:* The love of sweet security in sin ultimately decides what is proper for God (for example, that it is impossible for a wholly benevolent God to punish anyone for eternity), thus wielding God's scepter, the symbol of his power. Compare Pope, *An Essay on Man,* bk. 1, ll. 121–122: "Snatch from his hand the balance and the rod, / Re-judge his justice, be the GOD of GOD!"

696. *infinite relations:* relationships between infinite things, that is, things that only God can comprehend.

705–708. *But, lest . . . to quake:* But, unless our proofs and doctrines, our hopes and wits, fail because they are sustained by frail underpinnings, then we will admit a hell, but take from its terrors whatever commands the guilty heart to quake. Chauncy's system admits the existence of hell but denies that it is eternal.

709. *the purgatorial whim revive:* One critique of Chauncy's notion of a temporary hell is that it recalls the Catholic purgatory, thus contradicting the efforts of the Protestant reformers.

710. *And bid . . . live:* The argument that sinners are purged of their sinfulness in hell implies that the regenerate soul lives eternally, not because of God's grace, but as a result of being punished.

712. *hell is . . . sin:* Chauncy's system makes hell a part of one's moral education.

724–726. *If not . . . to rise:* Chauncy's system does not demarcate levels of hell, but Dwight suggests that its assumed process of salvation amounts to much the same thing.

729–730. *nor can . . . claim deny:* God cannot, according to Chauncy's logic, deny the newly purged sinner admittance to heaven without compromising his honor (legitimate claim to benevolence).

734. *The rest . . . S****:* William Pitt Smith (1764–1795) wrote a treatise entitled *The Universalist* (1787), in which he praises Chauncy as his intellectual precursor.

739–740. *But soon . . . bar'd:* But soon she (Conscience) reared her glass (raised her mirror), revealed cruel sin, and bared her horrors.

748–750. *Less painful . . . valued heaven:* Conscience grew less painful, sin grew less dangerous, the day given to man for trial became less prized, Jehovah less feared, and heaven less valued.

754. *Nor wish'd . . . whore:* Convinced of his final happiness, the wretch who used to sin only secretly, at night, will now sin openly, during the day.

756. *And sold . . . song:* The political implications of infidelity are here revealed: the sinner who no longer fears God will be more likely to "sell his country," and thus compromise the future of the Republic. Compare Pope, *Epilogue to the Satires,* bk. 1, ll. 157–158: "See thronging Millions to the Pagod run, / And offer Country, Parent, Wife, or Son!"

757–758. *The new-fledg'd . . . and crow'd:* The materialist philosophy of the "infidel of modern breed" (from ll. 565–588) finally transforms him into an animal.

759–760. *Confess'd the . . . not true:* The modern infidel would otherwise never have admitted the truth of Scripture, but, after hearing Chauncy, he wonders whether it might be true.

761. *The decent Christian:* "Decent" is here meant in the sense of well bred, referring to those Christians whose faith is chiefly a matter of pretense, and who would likely be among those flattered by the Smooth Divine from ll. 533–564. Now that Chauncy has revealed the ease of attaining heaven, the decent Christian no longer feels the need to keep the appearance of piety.

767. *saints:* regenerate Christians.

774–776. *Now proud . . . VIRTUE won:* At first, Satan is proud with triumph at seeing the throng of sinners, but, a moment later, he is vexed with spleen because he realizes that these sinners are already "his own" (those who were always destined for a life of sin). Thus, he has not won any new souls from among the friends of virtue.

INDEX

68, 132–133, 145–146, 156; *The Conquest of Canaan*, 2, 22; *The Nature, and Danger, of Infidel Philosophy*, 9, 18, 58, 119, 130, 151, 157, 172; *The True Means of Establishing Public Happiness*, 9, 135–137; "An Extract from 'The Retrospect,'" 9, 142–147, 149–151, 155, 172–173, 176; "On the Duties Connected with a Professional Life," 17; "America; or, A Poem on the Settlement of the British Colonies," 42; "Columbia," 42; *A Sermon, Preached at Northampton*, 43–44; "An Essay on the Judgment of History concerning America," 44–45; "The Folly of Trusting Our Own Hearts," 90; *The Duty of Americans, at the Present Crisis*, 132, 151, 157; *A Discourse, in Two Parts, Delivered August 20, 1812*, 132; *A Discourse, in Two Parts, Delivered July 23, 1812*, 132; *Virtuous Rulers a National Blessing*, 136, 138; "Address of the Genius of Columbia, to the Members of the Continental Convention," 137; "Address to the Ministers of the Gospel of Every Denomination in the United States," 137; *A Discourse on Some Events of the Last Century*, 151, 154–155, 159; "Morpheus," 155–157; *The Charitable Blessed*, 157; *The Dignity and Excellence of the Gospel*, 157; *The Harvest Past*, 157; "Lectures on the Evidences of Divine Revelation," 157; "On the Manner in Which the Scriptures Are to Be Understood," 157; "Observations on the Present State of Religion in the World," 159. See also *Triumph of Infidelity, The*

Eckley, Joseph: *Divine Glory Brought to View, in the Condemnation of the Ungodly*, 28, 82–83

Edwards, Jonathan, 7, 61, 85, 93–94, 110, 113–114, 162, 232–233; theology of, 21, 93. Works: *The Great Christian Doctrine of Original Sin Defended*, 12, 113; *Religious Affections*, 90; *Freedom of the Will*, 113; *The Nature of True Virtue*, 114; *A History of the Work of Redemption*, 128, 220

Edwards, Jonathan (the younger): *The Salvation of All Men Strictly Examined*, 29

Edwards, Pierrepont, 241

Eliot, John, 27, 65

Emerson, Ralph Waldo, 171

Emmons, Nathaniel: *A Discourse, concerning the Process of the General Judgment*, 28–29

Empiricism, 105–106, 112, 169; and religion, 113–115

Enlightenment, 24, 56–57, 85, 107–111, 117–119, 128–130, 144, 154, 156; and Pelagianism, 8–9; political implications of, 18; competing view of, in *The Triumph of Infidelity*, 110–112

Evarts, Jeremiah, 158–159; "Review of American Unitarianism," 159

Fairfield County Bible Society, 157

Fashion, 48–50

Federalist, The, 137

Federalists, 1, 19, 22, 110, 141, 153, 156, 160, 162

Foucault, Michel: *The Order of Things*, 10–11, 122

Fourierism, 172

Franklin, Benjamin, 9, 131